Machat Shel Yad

מחט
של י״ד
על התורה

Bereishis
ספר בראשית

RABBI YITZCHOK D. FRANKEL

Rav, Agudath Israel of the Five Towns
Cedarhurst, NY

ISBN: 978-965-73704-3

Printing and publishing by:
Nehorah Publications
נהורא מכון להוצאה לאור
1-888-546-0298
nehorah@gmail.com

Distribution by:
Lambda Publishers, Inc.
3709 13th Avenue
Brooklyn, NY 11218 U.S.A.
Tel: 718-972-5449 Fax: 718-972-6307

Urim Publications
P.O.Box 52287
Jerusalem 91521 Israel
Tel: 02-679-7633 Fax: 02-679-7634
www.UrimPublications.com

הספר הזה מוקדש
לכבוד הורינו היקרים שליט"א

הרב שניאור יחזקאל ב"ר אברהם ראובן
מרים בת ר' אברהם חיים יהודה הכהן
פרענקל

ר' חיים זאב ב"ר משה יעקב
חיה שרה בת ר' שמואל
באמשטיין

לזכרון בהיכל ה'

Dedicated in memory of

ר' בנימין ב"ר שמואל האן

מוקיר תורת ה' ולומדיה
ומתחמם כנגד אורן
חבל על דאבדין ולא משתכחין
תנצב"ה

By his Chidren
Mechel & Brenda Frankel
&Family

Table of Contents

פרשת תולדות

פרשת ויצא

פרשת וישלח

פרשת וישב

בס"ד

TALMUDICAL YESHIVA OF PHILADELPHIA

6063 Drexel Road
Philadelphia, Pennsylvania 19131
215 - 477 - 1000

Rabbi Elya Svei
Rabbi Shmuel Kamenetsky
Roshei Yeshiva

בס"ד י"ד מ"ח תשס"ו

לכבוד ידידי הנכבד החשוב מרביץ תורה לרבים
ר' יצחק דוד פרענקל שליט"א

אתכבד פה הפעם לברכה מעומקא דלבא ושפע
ברכות לרגל התחלת עת מוכן לגליון לאור ולכבוד
ברים נחמדים ורעיונות ישרים מאתו לגל. שמחתי פנים
יקרים מאתו לב לפתח יפתח פרחי לב מא דברי
הנעימים.

יתן השי"ת שיזכה להשלים בכל התורה כי ידיו
לו ויגדל הדעת לחכמה

ויתברך מכל מילי דמיטב וברכה והרבה נחת מכל חברי המשפחה

בידידות

שמואל קמנצקי

בס"ד יב סיון תשס"ז

למע"כ ידידי הנכבד הרה"ג מרביץ תורה לרבים
ר' יצחק דוד פרענקל שליט"א

אחדשה"ט בכל הכבוד וברכה מרובה כמשפט.
שמחתי לראות המחט של יד שכ' מוכן להוציא לאור בקרוב, דברים נחמדים ורעיונות ישרים משמחי לב, מוציא פנינים יקרים
משמחי לב, ובטח יהנו דורשי טוב מכל דבריו הנעימים.
יתן השי"ת שיזכה להשלים בכל התורה כי ידיו רב לו ויתרבה הדעת והחכמה.
יתברך כב' בכל מילי דמיטב והרבה נחת מכל חברי המשפחה.

בידידות
שמואל קמנצקי

RABBI MOSHE FEINSTEIN זצ"ל
Founder

RABBI REUVEN FEINSTEIN
Rosh HaYeshiva

RABBI GERSHON WEISS
Menahel-Ruchni

ישיבה ד'סטעטן איילנד
yeshiva of staten island
The Andrew N. & Rose Miller Yeshiva
1870 Drumgoole Rd. E. / Staten Island, N.Y. 10309
(718) 356-4323

RABBI YISRAEL H. EIDELMAN
Executive Vice-President

[handwritten letter in Hebrew]

RESIDENT DIVISION OF

EXECUTIVE OFFICES: 145 EAST BROADWAY / NYC 10002 / (212) 964-2830

הנה שלח אלי ידידי בן ידידי הרה"ג ר' יצחק פרענקל נ"י, אחד מחשובי תלמידי ישיבתינו, קטעים שדרש לבני קהילתו בבית מדרשו "אגודת ישראל" מדי שבת בשבתו, דברים לעורר המחשבה ולהתלהב הלב, לקרב מחשבות ולבבות בני קהילתו לעבודת ה.

ועכשיו רצה להדפיסם על סדר הפרשיות בספר להשפיע על יתר אחינו בני ישראל. ובודאי דבר טוב הוא עושה להשתדל להודיע תורתו בשער בת רבים, ובפרט שעיקר כוונתו לבאר פרשיות התורה באופן שיהיה ברור ופשוט על פי דעות והשקפות שקיבל מרבותיו, ודבר נחון הוא בזמנינו.

יהי רצון שיהיה עבודתו לנחת רוח ליוצרו, ויזכה שעל ידו יתקדש שם שמים, וימשיך להשפיע על קהילתו ועל שאר אחינו בני ישראל, מתוך בריאות הנפש והגוף בשלו' ושלוה יחד עם כל משפחתו עד ביאת גואל צדק בב"א.

ראובן פיינשטיין
כ"ה תמוז תשס"ז

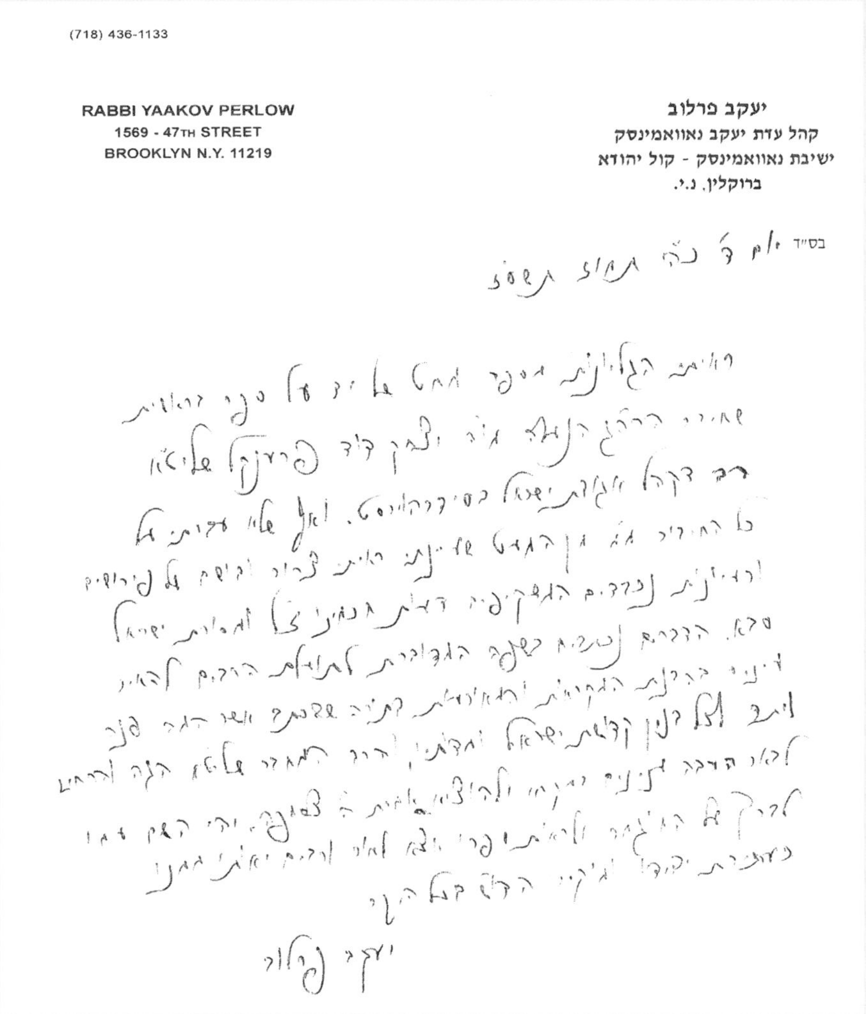

(718) 436-1133

RABBI YAAKOV PERLOW
1569 - 47TH STREET
BROOKLYN N.Y. 11219

יעקב פרלוב
קהל עדת יעקב נאוואמינסק
ישיבת נאוואמינסק - קול יהודא
ברוקלין, נ.י.

בס"ד יום ד' כה תמוז תשס"ז

[handwritten letter]

יעקב פערלאוו

יום ד' כ"ה תמוז תשס"ז

ראיתי הגליונות מספר מחמ של יד על ספר בראשית שחיבר הרה"ג הנעלה מו"ה יצחק דוד פרענקל שליט"א רב דקהל אגודת ישראל בסידרהוירסט.

ואף שלא עברתי על כל החיבור, מ"מ מן המעט שעיינתי ראיתי צרור ובושם על פירושים ורעיונות נכבדים המשקיפים דעות חכמינו ז"ל ומסורת ישראל סבא. הדברים נכתבים בשפה המדוברת לתועלת הרבים, להאיר עינים בהבנת המקראות והמאורעות בתורה שבכתב, אשר המה מה פנה ויתד לכל בנין קדושת ישראל ומדותיו, והרב המחבר שליט"א הגה והרחיב לבאר ענינים במקרא ולהוציא אמרת ה' הצרופה.

יהי ה' עמו לברך על המוגמר, ולראות ספרו יוצא לאור ורבים יאותו ממנו.

כעתירת ידידו ומוקירו הדו"ש בכל היקר
יעקב פרלוב

RABBI ARYEH MALKIEL KOTLER
BETH MEDRASH GOVOHA
LAKEWOOD, N.J. 08701

ארי' מלכיאל קוטלר
בית מדרש גבוה
לייקוואוד, נ. דז.

רחל אב תשס"ז

בסימן טבא בהקדמה לפי' על התורה פרח שהדרושים הם כלבושים להתורה

והנה נהניתי מאד מעברי על הגליונות של הספר החשוב עה"ת

מחט של יד' מידידי היקר החה"ש ר' יצחק דוד פרענקל שליט"א

מחשובי הרבנים המרביצים תורה ויראת שמים לעדתם, והנה הספר

הנ"ל הה מלא עם דרושים יפים ויסודות נאמנים ומוסרים לימודים

מהפרשיות ובפרט שמועתא לאור על ספר בראשית שכתב הרמב"ן שהם

מקרי האבות שהם כעין יצירה לבנים, ומחדש חידושים נעימים ויפים.

לבנים ואחה"ח חידושי' קי"ש ...

ולזה אף שיבורכו מעיינותיו יתקבלו קפחיו בבי מדרשא עוד יזכה לאסף

כהנה נותר. ... על שאר פרשיות התורה ולהוציא עוד חיבורים

יקרים להגדיל תורה ולהאדירה

הכו"ח לכבוד התורה ולהוקירה

אריה מלכיאל קוטלר

באאמו"ר הגר"ש זצ"ל

ר"ח אב תשס"ז

באבן עזרא בהקדמה לפי' על התורה כתב שההדרושים הם כלבושים להתורה. והנה נהניתי מאוד בעברי על הגליונות של הספר החשוב עה"ת "מחט של יד" מידידי היקר הרה"ג ר' יצחק דוד פרענקל שליט"א מחשובי הרבנים המרביצים תורה ויראת שמים לעדתם.

הנה הספר הנ"ל ה"ה מלא עם דרושים יפים ויסודות נאמנים ומוסרים לימודים מהפרשיות, ובפרט שמועתיא לאור על ספר בראשית שכתב הרמב"ן שהם מקרי האבות שהם כעין יצירה לבנים, ומחדש חידושים נעימים ונחמדים נאמרים בטוב טעם ודעת, ובודאי יהנו המעיינים ויהיה לתועלת.

וע"כ יה"ר שיפוצו מעיינותיו, יתקבלו דבריו בבי מדרשא, עוד יזכה להוסיף כהנה וכהנה על כל שאר פרשיות התורה ולהוציא עוד חיבורים יקרים להגדיל תורה ולהאדירה.

אריה מלכיאל קוטלר
באאמו"ר הגר"ש זצ"ל

הקדמה

The Gemara tells us in *Shabbos* 87a that Moshe Rabbeinu made three decisions on his own, to which Hashem later agreed. The first was when they came to Mount Sinai. Hashem told Moshe Rabbeinu to designate three days to prepare for *Matan Torah*, but Moshe decided on his own to add a fourth day of preparation. The Gemara asks what was Moshe's justification, and answers that he found an allusion in Scripture to the added day.

Moshe Rabbeinu's second decision was to separate from his wife, since the Shechinah would regularly speak to him without prior warning and he needed to be ready at all times. We know that Hashem agreed to Moshe's decision because He told the rest of Klal Yisrael to return to their homes after Matan Torah, saying: "שובו לכם לאהליכם." However, to Moshe He said: "ואתה פה עמוד עמדי". Hashem was saying: "Everyone else can return to their tents and their families; but as for you, stay with Me!"

Moshe's third decision was to break the luchos habris. As with his other decisions, the Gemara asks where Moshe derived this idea from, and here, too, the Gemara explains his source from the Torah.

What is this Gemara saying? It starts out claiming that Moshe Rabbeinu made three decisions on his own. Then it proceeds to explain exactly how Moshe expounded the relevant pesukim to come to the conclusions he did. So we ask: Did Moshe make these decisions on his own, or not?[1]

---

[1] עיין תוספות שם ד"ה ומה ישראל כו'.

Let's say Reuven claims that he "decided on his own" to fulfill a certain mitzvah. We ask him: "What moved you to take such a step?" to which he replies: "The Gemara clearly derives the obligation of this mitzvah from a Torah pasuk." The man's answer makes no sense. If the Gemara derived it from a pasuk, it must have employed the י"ג מידות שהתורה נדרשת בהם – the thirteen hermeneutical principles of Scriptural exposition. This means that the Torah is instructing us what to do! Thus, Reuven did not make an independent decision but faithfully obeyed the Divine instructions.

If so, how, are we to understand the Gemara's statement that Moshe Rabbeinu decided to do these things on his own?

The answer lies in the uniqueness of Moshe Rabbeinu's prophecy. It was qualitatively different from that of all other prophets, as Hashem spoke "mitoch gerono shel Moshe." When Moshe opened his mouth to speak, it was Hashem's voice that came out. Thus, Moshe was the conduit of Hashem's word to the world, in the most direct possible manner, known as Aspeklaria Hame'irah. This unique way of receiving Hashem's word and transmitting it to Am Yisrael is called Toras Moshe. The Rambam explains in Hilchos Yesodei HaTorah, ch. 8, that this level of prophecy was exclusive to Moshe Rabbeinu so that all should know and realize that the Torah, both Written and Oral, was given to the world only once. It is not a repeatable experience.

It turns out that anything that Moshe taught us, he heard directly, in the clearest fashion, from *Hakadosh Boruch Hu*. The truth of any Torah idea that we would expound over the course of the generations is ultimately derived from the fact that Hashem taught it to Moshe Rabbeinu at Mount Sinai. Rashi says this in the beginning of Parashas Behar when he states that every detail of the Torah was taught to Moshe at Mount Sinai. This implies, as brought in Vayikra Rabba 22:1, that any true *chiddush* ever to be said was already transmitted to Moshe Rabbeinu:

ואפי' מה שתלמיד ותיק עתיד לומר לפני רבו כלן נאמרו למשה בסיני.

Hashem transmitted the Torah to Moshe in a manner more comprehensive than anyone could imagine. Yet, there was one facet of Torah that Moshe could not possess. Moshe lacked a basic and fundamental aspect of *kinyan Torah* that every other *talmid chacham* of the future would have. As the Gemara says in *Kiddushin* 32b:

הדר אמר רבא אין תורה דיליה היא דכתיב ובתורתו יהגה יומם ולילה.

When a *talmid chacham* says a true *chiddush,* it is called *toraso,* "his Torah." The *talmid chacham* has what is known as a *kinyan Torah*. But Moshe Rabbeinu did not possess that attribute. Though he received the Torah directly from Hashem, and obviously acquired it on that highest of levels, he did not have the *kinyan Torah* of the type of *drashos Chazal*. He did not have *chiddushim* derived from a *pasuk,* through a *hekeish* or a *kal vachomer*. And for good reason: That type of Torah learning would have contradicted the very purpose of Moshe Rabbeinu's mission in conveying the Torah!

Moshe Rabbeinu's transmission could not be through making *drashos*. It had to be one hundred percent direct. Hence, Hashem gave Moshe Rabbeinu three places where he could derive the mitzvah through Scriptural interpretation, as *Chazal* did. "Moshe Rabbeinu made three decisions on his own." Relative to the direct way that Moshe knew everything else in the Torah, these three were considered his own decisions.

And this was essential for Moshe Rabbeinu. In these three places Hashem gave him the opportunity to create *toraso,* his own true Torah *chiddushim*. This was through making his own *drashos* according to the accepted principles of Torah interpretation. Moshe used a *hekeish* to derive the extra day of preparation for *Matan Torah*. He expounded a *kal vachomer* to learn that he should separate from his wife. He smashed the *luchos habris* based on another *kal vachomer*.

And *Hakadosh Boruch Hu* agreed to his *drashos*! Of course, those *drashos* were Hashem's intention from the outset. Yet they were not expressly taught to Moshe, which afforded him the opportunity to achieve this unique form of *kinyan Torah*.

Chazal tell us (*Avos* 6:6):

גדולה תורה יותר מן הכהונה ומן המלכות, שהמלכות נקנית בשלשים מעלות, והכהנה בעשרים וארבע, והתורה נקנית בארבעים ושמונה דברים.

Torah is greater than the kehunah and greater than the malchus. This is because one needs thirty qualities to make a kinyan on malchus, i.e., to be a king. And for a kinyan on the kehunah, one needs twenty-four qualities. But a kinyan on Torah requires forty-eight ways, and this is what Moshe Rabbeinu was able to accomplish in these three instances.

But as we saw above from the Midrash, Hashem transmitted to Moshe all aspects of Torah, including any true chiddushim or interpretations ever to be made in later generations. This leads us to a serious problem. If every valuable comment, insight or interpretation has already been expounded and derived from the relevant pesukim of the Torah, how can anyone in a later generation achieve a kinyan in Torah? Whatever he says was already known.

The Gemara says in Chullin 7a: מקום הניחו לו אבותיו להתגדר (להתגדל - רש"י) בו. Our forefathers left us a place [in Torah] to make our own. Some sources say that the Gemara is not to be understood exclusively as "hinichu lo avosav," but rather "hinichu lo min hashamayim." This means that Hashem set up a situation in which every Jewish neshamah has the opportunity to make his own kinyan Torah – to expound and acquire some aspect of Torah knowledge that is exclusively his.

Throughout the generations, Hashem has given us Torah Sages who are like lofty mountains in their stature. Each generation is blessed with the most suitable leaders and scholars required by that generation. Nevertheless, even the smallest and most insignificant Jew, even in our late generation, is left the possibility of achieving his own kinyan Torah, however small that may be. Thus, I believe that Hakadosh Boruch Hu has allowed even a katan shebaketanim such as myself to find the small area in Torah that belongs to me.

Furthermore, Hashem has graced me with the opportunity to bring some of those Torah ideas to publication and in this way share them with the wider Torah learning public. That is why I have chosen to call this work by the name of מחט של י"ד, which means literally "a sewing needle." י"ד are the initials of my name, Yitzchok Dovid and a needle is the smallest of utensils that retains the Halachic status and value of a kli. It is the smallest of utensils that, should it become tamei, still may be purified in a mikveh (Mishnah Mikva'os 7:7). And the Rambam rules (Hilchos To'ein VeNit'an 3:5) that a needle, even if it lacks the minimum value of a perutah, is nevertheless considered a kli as regards shavu'os – oaths. A needle also possesses other attributes. Although it is small, it is still quite sharp and piercing and it is able to connect two disparate pieces of cloth into harmony.

Hakadosh Boruch Hu has granted me the opportunity to learn with the distinguished members of the Long Beach and Cedarhurst, New York, communities along with hundreds of talmidim in different high schools over several decades. During this time, He has enabled me to teach, listen to their questions, be inspired by their desire to learn and resolve for them some of the difficulties they faced in understanding Chumash and Peirush Rashi. On occasion, I confronted certain modern-day attempts to chas veshalom impugn the words of Chazal, Rishonim and Acharonim. When such occasions arose, Hashem assisted me in supporting and defending the words of our holy Torah in some small way.

Although I know that I am not worthy on my own to be considered amongst the explicators of Torah, perhaps it is in the z'chus of the giants that I was given the tremendous divine providence and good fortune to have studied under and to have basked in their holy aura. First and foremost

רשכבה"ג מרן הרב משה פיינשטיין זצוק"ל

along with

חתנה דבי מלכא וצדיק דורנו הרה"ג הרב אליהו משה שיסגל זצוק"ל

ויבלחטו"א

מרן הרה"ג הרב דוד פיינשטיין שליט"א

ומרן הרה"ג הרב ראובן פיינשטיין שליט"א.

It is my fervent hope that even as a pin amongst *chachamim* taller then towering Himalayan Mountains, yet within the universe of the righteous *chachamim* who preceded me, I have contributed in some small measure to illuminate Torah knowledge in the world.

Acknowledgements:

יתגדל הבורא ויתהלל החונן לאדם דעת, הפעם אודה את־ה' הודו לו ברכו
שמו כי הביאתני עד־הלם פתחת שקי ותאזרני שמחה. ברוך שם כבודו
לעולם וימלא כבודו את־כל־הארץ אמן ואמן:

This project could not have even begun without the cheerful advice and counsel of Rabbi Aryeh Mezei. Reb Aryeh always gladly and willingly gave of his valuable time. He would deferentially give guidance and encouragement. No matter how often I dropped in on him, each and every time he would receive me with a smile and a good word. Words are not a sufficient thank you.

Mrs. Ruth Unger and Mrs. Shoshana Walker for their patient and expertly transcribing of my audio files.

Mr. Shmuel Globus for his most valuable editorial work. The character and quality of this work was tremendously enhanced by his expert translations, editorial skills, along with his proficiency and mastery over the written word.

Mrs. Hadassah Goldsmith a most talented copy editor whose discerning eye and desire for perfection is nothing but extraordinary.

Rabbi Yisrael Chesir who reviewed the entire manuscript and added many invaluable, astute and insightful comments. The quality of this work has been elevated by his thoughtful and erudite additions.

Rabbi Yakov Ehrenreich, my first and only *chavrusa* in chumash and Rashi for more than thirty-five years.

My oldest sons: Rabbis Moshe Ya'akov, Avraham Eliyahu and Shimon Meir, who reviewed the manuscript. It was their intensive scrutiny, constructive criticisms, analyses and suggestions that weeded out many unintended errors.

Mrs. Zippy Thumim for her artistic eye and expertise in graphic arts. It is her talents that draped my work in an appealing mantle of beauty worthy of the Torah.

Rabbi Dovid L. Blasbalg and Rabbi Yisroel Goldberg of Nehorah Publishing for their professional regard to every detail of the process that brought this work to fruition. Second best was never good enough.

My profound appreciation to all those that continuously encouraged me to bring my *chidushim* to print. I am forever grateful.

בראשית

BEREISHIS

1 Marking the Spot

וַיַּצְמַח ה' אֱלֹקִים מִן הָאֲדָמָה כָּל עֵץ נֶחְמָד לְמַרְאֶה... וְנָהָר יֹצֵא מֵעֵדֶן
לְהַשְׁקוֹת אֶת הַגָּן וּמִשָּׁם יִפָּרֵד וְהָיָה לְאַרְבָּעָה רָאשִׁים:

G-d made grow out of the ground every tree that is pleas-
ant to look at... A river flowed out of Eden to water the
garden. From there it divided and became four major rivers.
(Bereishis 2:9–10)

When the Torah describes Gan Eden, it first mentions the trees that are grown there. After that it proceeds to give us a rather detailed map – as if we ought to be able to figure out the exact location of Gan Eden. We are told the names of the rivers whose source is Gan Eden: Pishon, Gichon, Chidekel (Tigris) and Pras (Euphrates).

However, once we start to investigate, things become puzzling. It is understandable that the Chidekel and Pras rivers are near each other since we know they are situated in Iraq. But Rashi defines Pishon as the Nilos or Nile River, which is in North Africa. One would be hard pressed to explain how the Nile flows from the same water source as the Tigris and the Euphrates.

So if it is impossible to figure out where Gan Eden is, what was the point of giving us detailed instructions as to its location?

We can provide an answer once we compare this enigma at the beginning of the Torah with a similar challenge found at the end of the Torah in *Parshas Vezos HaBrachah*. Just as we find that the Torah provides a well-marked map for the location of Gan Eden, yet we fail to find it, so it is regarding the *kever*, burial place, of *Moshe Rabbeinu*. The *kever* is on Mount Nevo and the Torah is very clear as to the exact location where Moshe is buried. Nevertheless, the Torah testifies: "No man knows the place of his *kever*."

ויקבר אותו בגיא בארץ מואב מול בית פעור ולא ידע איש את קברתו עד היום הזה:

(דברים ל"ד:ו')

And He buried him in the valley in the land of Moab opposite Bais Peor. No man knows the place that he was buried, up to this day. (Devarim 34:6)

And the Gemara comments on this:

א"ר ברכיה: סימן בתוך סימן, ואפ"ה ולא ידע איש את קבורתו. וכבר שלחה מלכות הרשעה אצל גסטרא של בית פעור: הראנו היכן משה קבור? עמדו למעלה נדמה להם למטה, למטה — נדמה להם למעלה, נחלקו לשתי כיתות, אותן שעומדים למעלה נדמה להן למטה למטה, למטה — נדמה להן למעלה: (סוטה י"ג ע"ב בסופה)

Rabbi Berachya said: [The Torah provides us with] a sign within a sign. Yet, "no man knows the place that he was buried"! And the wicked kingdom (Rome) once sent [emissaries] to Bais Peor [and demanded]: Show us where Moshe is buried. They stood at the top, and it (the grave) appeared to be below. [When they stood down] below, it appeared to be above. They divided into two groups. For those that stood above, it appeared to them to be below. For those below, it appeared to them to be above. (Sotah 13b)

Here we find *Chazal* tell an actual story of people trying to find the *kever* of *Moshe Rabbeinu*. They saw it on top of the mountain—but when they got to the top, it appeared as if it was at the bottom of the mountain. Wherever they went it was somewhere else. There is a striking parallel with the Torah's instructions of the location of Gan Eden. The Torah gives us a well-defined map telling us where Gan Eden is, but we cannot locate it. Similarly, the Torah clearly tells us the exact place where *Moshe Rabbeinu* is buried on Mount Nevo, but still, "no man knows his burial place."

So what is the Torah trying to tell us with these two inscrutable map references that are inscribed at the beginning and end of the Torah?

We are being taught something fundamental and significant: We only know what we are supposed to know. What we see is only what we are supposed to see. We might be supplied exact directions how to arrive at a certain place and be told exactly what to find there – yet never find the place nor see what is there! We will see it *only* when Hashem opens our eyes.

Thus, even if the Torah gives us clear and definitive directions on how to find something, it will not help. Until Hashem wants us to know or see it, it will not be known or seen.

This rule can be perceived throughout history. Many things existed in the early days of human history that we now have no connection with at all, to the point that we have no understanding of the actions, motivations and activities of the Ancients. We cannot comprehend what inspired them to act in ways that they did because they were able to see and know things that we cannot.

Correspondingly, we have been able to find and see things that the Ancients could not have fathomed. We seemingly have wisdom in certain areas that did not exist then, and that is because the Ancients were not supposed to see those things. We make technological advances and astonishing discoveries on a continuous basis. Yet, despite their intelligence and brilliance, the Ancients did not have any inkling of modern knowledge. How could this be? It is all due to the above. We know only what Hashem wants us to know and see only what He wants us to see. We have the abilities to find and access only that which Hashem allows us to.

That is the beginning and end of the whole Torah.

Telling the Nations

בְּרֵאשִׁית בָּרָא אֱלֹקִים אֵת הַשָּׁמַיִם וְאֵת הָאָרֶץ:

In the beginning, G-d created the heavens and the earth.
(Bereishis 1:1)

O n the above verse Rashi explains that the Torah starts with the account of the Creation, in accord with the following verse:

ומה טעם פתח בבראשית משום (תהלים קי"א) כח מעשיו הגיד לעמו לתת להם נחלת גוים שאם יאמרו אומות העולם לישראל ליסטים אתם שכבשתם ארצות שבעה גוים הם אומרים להם כל הארץ של הקב"ה היא היא הוא בראה ונתנה לאשר ישר בעיניו ברצונו נתנה להם וברצונו נטלה מהם ונתנה לנו: (רש"י בראשית א:א)

He declared to His people the strength of His works [i.e., the Creation], in order to give them the heritage of the nations. (Tehillim 111:6) For if the nations will say to the people of Israel: "You are thieves, because you conquered the lands of the seven [Canaanite] nations," Israel may reply: "All the earth belongs to Hashem. He created it and gave it to whom He wanted. When He willed it, He gave it to them. And when He willed it, He took it from them and gave it to us." (Rashi, Bereishis 1:1, based on Yalkut Shemos)

It is hard to understand what Rashi is saying here. How does the fact that we know that Hashem created the world and gave us the Torah and *Eretz Yisrael* help us deal with the non-Jewish nations? How does our reply to them help us? They will say that we are robbers, that we took the land from someone else, and we will respond that it is Hashem's land. He created it; He can give it to anyone He wants. That's wonderful for us. However, the nations of the world do not believe in the truth of the Torah! They do not believe in the revelation of the Torah to *K'lal Yisrael* at Mount Sinai. In fact, some even deny Hashem's very existence. So what is the point of declaring "*the strength of His works*"? How does it help us with the non-Jews?

There is an additional problem with the fact that the Torah declares *Eretz Yisrael* to belong undisputedly to *K'lal Yisrael*. This reality seems to be at odds with modern day fact because the three places that were bought outright by our Jewish ancestors are the most hotly contested by the non-Jews: Jerusalem, the *Me'aras HaMachpelah* (Cave of the Patriarchs) in Hebron and Shechem (also known as Nablus). *Chazal* say that we purchased them with money in order to show that they clearly are ours. Thus, *Dovid HaMelech* bought Jerusalem from Aravna the Jebusite; *Avraham Avinu* bought *Me'aras HaMachpelah* from Ephron the Hittite; *Yaakov Avinu* bought Shechem from its inhabitants.

These very same areas are the ones in most contention with the Arabs today. The descendants of Yishmael seem to feel that those very areas that we bought and paid for in cash are those that they have the greater claim to. This is strange and runs against our expectations, both because of the *Chazal* just quoted and because it is in opposition to Yishmael's more general claim, demanding from us the entire *Eretz Yisrael*. It also runs counter to the very beginning of the Torah, where Hashem starts with the Creation in order to show that *Eretz Yisrael* really belongs to us!

As in the section above, *Marking the Spot*, we can connect the end of the Torah to the beginning of the Torah. For in *Parshas Vezos HaBrachah* the verse states:

ה' וכו'. וזרח משעיר למו הופיע מהר פארן וכו'. (דברים ל"ג:ב')

Hashem...and shone forth to them from Seir, appeared from Mount Paran... (Devarim 33:2)

Hashem went to the nations of the world and offered them the Torah but each one of them declared that they had no need for it. Here, too, Hashem's message falls on deaf ears.

The Gemara in *Avodah Zarah* explains that Hashem first went to the descendants of Eisav living in Seir to offer them the Torah – and they refused it. Then the verse states that "He (Hashem) appeared from Mount Paran." (ibid.) This means that Hashem went to the descendants of Yishmael to offer them the Torah – and they refused it. The *Targum Yerushalmi* describes the discussion that ensued at the time:

ואמר ה' מן סיני אתגלי למתן אורייתא לעמיה דבית ישראל ודנח ביקריה על טורא
דשעיר למתן אורייתא לבנוי דעשו וכיון דאשכחו כתיב בגווה לא תהוון קטולין לא
קבילו יתה הופע ביקריה על טורא דגבלא למתן אורייתא לבנוי דישמעאל וכיון די
אשכחו כתיב בגוה לא תהוון גנבין לא קבילו יתה וחזר ואתגלי על טורא דסיני וכו'.
ויהב אורייתא לעמיה: (תרגום ירושלמי דברים ל"ג:ב)

Hashem revealed Himself from Sinai to give the Torah to His
people, the House of Israel. And He shone with His Honor on
Mount Seir to give the Torah to the descendants of Eisav. But
when they found that [the command] "do not be murderers"
was written in it, they did not accept it. He then appeared in
His Honor on Mount Gaval to give the Torah to the descen-
dants of Yishmael. But when they found that [the command]
"do not be thieves" was written in it, they did not accept it. And
He then returned and revealed Himself on Mount Sinai... and
gave the Torah to His people. (Targum Yerushalmi, Devarim 33:2)

The descendants of Eisav, about whom it says "you shall live by your
sword" (*Bereishis* 27:40), would not accept the Torah due to the prohibition
on murder. The descendants of Yishmael, about whom it says *"his hand will*
be in everything, and everyone's hand will be against him" (*Bereishis* 16:12),
could not and would not accept the Torah due to the prohibition against theft.
Their claim was that theft was actually an essential part of their nature.

This speaks to the issue at hand. There are two kinds of thieves. One feels
a need for the object in question and believes he is forced to steal in order to
obtain it. He may be poverty-stricken and come to the conclusion that he must
steal, although the Torah states that one may not steal. He thus transgresses
leta'avon, for a need or desire.

Then there is a different type of thief. He has a need to steal because it is
part of his essence, his nature, his personality. This is the pathological thief.
For this kind of person, the greater the challenge, the greater is his need to
show that he can "beat the system" and rob. His overall drive creates a situation whereby if he has easy access to an item, then he has no desire for it. If he
can have it in a permissible fashion, he has no need for it.

Such a pathological trait that is manifested in an individual would imply a
type of malfunctioning, a deviation from the norm, from a medical or psycho-

logical perspective. However, that is not the case here when discussing Yishmael. *"His hand will be in everything"* is a character trait prophesied by the angel to Hagar; it is indicative of the most basic and inherent qualities of an entire people. This predilection is part of the spiritual makeup of the angelic representative of Yishmael.

Therefore, Hashem did not start the Torah with *Bereishis,* declaring that *"Eretz Yisrael* belongs to *K'lal Yisrael,"* for the physical eyes and ears of the nations. Rather, the declaration was made for their spiritual counterparts, their angelic powers in heaven.[1] To most of the nations, this message was "heard" and has remained accepted as a fact. Many nations over the millennia have desired to subjugate, conquer and plunder *Eretz Yisrael* and even drive us out of it, but no nation has ever denied our G-d-given connection to it – except for Yishmael.

It is precisely because the Torah so clearly declared our ownership of the Land that this situation arose.

Yishmael has a strong desire for that which does not belong to him. From all the lands of the world that he could have, he wants the relatively small sliver of *Eretz Yisrael* the most. Yes, we bought Jerusalem, Hebron and Shechem, and paid cash for them. That is why it is most desirous to Yishmael. He has a thirst, an irrational craving, to steal that which does not belong to him. He has an indefensible eagerness to take what clearly belongs to someone else.

Therefore, the Torah's affirmation has actually set up the situation for the End of Days, reflected clearly in our time, so that we should have this confrontation with Yishmael. It could only transpire because the Torah is introduced with *"in the beginning, G-d created the heavens and the earth."*

---

1. כעין זה מצאתי בב"ב דף ק' ע"א ברשב"ם בד"ה כדי שיהא נוח וכו'.

3 Precious Dust

וַיִּיצֶר ה' אֱלֹקִים אֶת הָאָדָם עָפָר מִן הָאֲדָמָה...

G-d formed man out of the dust from the earth... (Bereishis 2:7)

Rashi comments on the above verse:

עפר מן האדמה. נטל עפרו ממקום שנאמר בו "מִזְבַּח אֲדָמָה תַּעֲשֶׂה לִּי" (שמות כ':כ"א),
הלואי תהא לו אדמה כפרה ויוכל לעמוד: (רש"י בראשית ב':ז')

"Dust from the earth" – He (Hashem) took his (Adam's) dust from the place about which it is said, "Make an earthen altar for Me." (Shemos 20:21) [Hashem then said:] "If only that [this] earth would be an atonement for him, so that he may endure." (Rashi, Bereishis 2:7, based on Bereishis Rabba 14)

This Rashi can be understood in two ways. It could mean that the altar will be an atonement for Adam. Alternatively, when Adam is created from this special, unique earth, he will somehow become less "earthly" and thus more receptive to atonement.

The *Maharal* comments on this Rashi:

המזבח הוא באמצע מקום ישוב הארץ, ואותה האדמה היא בין הקצוות לגמרי, וכל
דבר שהוא באמצע הוא בשיווי, ואינו נוטה אל אחד הקצוות, והוא המובחר,וכו'. ורוצה
לומר שחומר האדם אינו כחומר שאר הנבראים, רק חומרו ממוצע מזוג בשווי לגמרי,
אינו נוטה אל אחד מן הקצוות. וכו'.

The altar [in the Temple] was at the center of the inhabited land, and the earth [used for it] was equidistant from the extremities. For anything situated in the middle is balanced, not tilting to either extreme. This is the ideal... Thus, the substance making up the human form is distinct from that of the rest of Creation. Only human matter is completely temperate and balanced, not inclining to one side or the other...

וכל זה כדי שיהא לו כפרה, שאם יקרא לו חטא יהא נקל שיוסר החטא, כי החטא הוא בעבור שהוא נוטה אל אחד הקצוות, וכו'.

And all this was intended to bring him atonement. That if he should sin, the sin will be removed easily. For the sin came because he inclined to one of the two extremities...

וזהו שאמרו רז"ל (ב"ר יד:ח) כי ברא את האדם מן המזבח כדי שיהיה לו כפרה, פירוש הסרת הזוהמא. ודבר נפלא הוא מאד מאד איך גורם זה שבראו ממקום המזבח שיהיה לו כפרה, ועיין עוד: (גור אריה שם)

This is the meaning of the Chazal: "He made the man from the altar in order that he should achieve atonement" (Bereishis Rabba 14:8). This means that he will achieve atonement by removal of the impurity. And this is indeed a very wonderful matter – how atonement follows by being created from the place of the altar... (Gur Aryeh, ad loc.)

I would like to add the following perspective. *Chazal* are telling us that, ultimately, just as the altar has the ability to atone, so does the body itself. The body can atone for the soul in the same way as the altar can. The body, taken from the site of the altar, atones in many different ways for Adam's transgressions. Eventually, Adam dies – in this way the body becomes the atonement for his sin. Ultimately, the body needs to decompose, and it is these afflictions that become atonement for Adam. This is true even while one is still alive, as we find in *Chazal*:

אמר רבא אמר רב סחורה אמר רב הונא: כל שהקדוש ברוך הוא חפץ בו — מדכאו ביסורין, וכו'. ואם קבלם מה שכרו — (ישעיהו נ"ג) יראה זרע יאריך ימים ולא עוד אלא שתלמודו מתקיים בידו, שנאמר: (ישעיהו נ"ג) וחפץ ה' בידו יצלח: (ברכות ה' ע"א)

Rava said in the name of Rav Sechorah in the name of Rav Huna: Anyone that Hashem has affection for, He crushes him with afflictions... And if the person accepts them, what is his reward? "[And Hashem wanted to crush him... if his soul makes restitution] he shall see children, prolong his days..." (Yeshaya 53:10) Not only that, but his learning will endure, as the verse concludes: "And G-d's desire shall prosper in his hand." (Brachos 5a)

We see that suffering and afflictions during a person's lifetime have an effect similar to that of death and that which occurs afterwards. It was for this reason, to provide opportunities for atonement, that the body of Adam came from the same source as the altar.

4   Only the Best

In *Parshas Terumah* the Torah describes how the *Mishkan* is to be built from gold and silver and other kinds of precious metals. From the actual structure of the *Mishkan* we see that the majority visible to the eye was made from gold. The silver of the *machatzis hashekel* donations was used to make the *adanim,* which were on the ground at the base of the *Mishkan*. These *adanim* were the sockets into which were inserted the pegs of the boards that formed the *Mishkan*'s walls. The rest of the *Mishkan* and its vessels that constituted the Holy and Holy of Holies was either made of pure gold or gold-plated. (Outside, in the open air courtyard, we also find silver and copper being used.)

Chazal say regarding the *Mishkan*:

אין עניות במקום עשירות: (שבת ק"ב ע"ב)

There should be no poverty in a place of wealth. (Shabbos 102b)

In other words, if you have the best, you use the best. However, there is something strange about this. Does it imply that gold is objectively more beautiful and finer than silver? This would make sense if we were dealing with a subjective economic environment where the laws of supply and demand determine a commodity's value, such that the commodity's objective and intrinsic value or beauty is not the issue but rather its market value. Gold is scarcer than silver and thus commands a higher price. These subjective, human circumstances make it such a precious metal.

However, this cannot explain why gold was used for the *Mishkan* in the *Midbar,* because such circumstances did not exist there. There were no human elements involved. The building of the *Mishkan* was contracted by Hashem Himself, in a wilderness environment where money was not an issue and where gold and silver were meaningless aside from their use in the building of the *Mishkan*. Therefore we must ask: Why did gold hold greater significance than silver? Are we to assume that gold is intrinsically more beautiful and finer than silver?

It is hard to defend such an assumption. If one were asked to choose between yellow gold and white gold, in most situations white gold would be considered more desirous. If one were to choose between gold and platinum, the preference would usually be platinum since it is rarer. Note that both platinum and white gold look quite similar to silver. It would seem that if we were to rate the desirability of these metals from an impartial perspective divorced from all economic considerations, we would say that silver, white gold and platinum all look nicer to the human eye than does yellow gold. If that is true, why was gold preferred in the *Mishkan*?

The same concept applies to the relative value of precious stones. When some sort of currency is needed for purchase or barter purposes, then the scarcer a rock is, the more it is worth. But why do these stones have greater significance for the *Eifod* and the *Choshen*? In the *Midbar,* where *K'lal Yisrael* ate manna and their clothing never wore out but grew with them, where their housing and all other needs were provided for and where there were no commodity markets, no stores and nothing to buy, why did these stones' relative preference as currency determine their value? Why were they superior to pieces of colored glass?

It would appear that the answer is to be found in our *Parsha*. Here we find that when the Torah tells us where the *Eitz HaDa'as,* the Tree of Knowledge, is planted, it says: *"And Hashem, G-d, planted a garden in Eden."* (*Bereishis* 2:8) Following, it tells us, *"And a river goes out from Eden to water the Garden."* (ibid., 2:10) The Torah goes on to tell us how this river splits into four, the first of which is Pishon, which Rashi identifies as the Nile. The Torah reports that *"It is the one that surrounds all the land of Chavilah."* (ibid., v. 11) The Torah then states,*"There is the gold."* This appears to be superfluous information. Why does the Torah have to tell us that the land of Chavilah is where gold is to be found? Then we are told: *"And the gold of that land is good."* (ibid., v. 12) Furthermore, *"There is the crystal and the onyx stone"* — precious stones. (ibid.)

What is the meaning of all this? It is telling us that when Hashem created the world, He did not create just the raw materials of the world. He created concepts, ideas and thoughts. He created the principles by which the world would exist, including the principles of economics. Today, economists are busy researching and doing studies to determine how economies began, how they began in the ancient world and how they developed and continue to develop. We see in our *Parsha* that the development of civilized economies and the initiation of precious items as items of currency are not human creations.

On the contrary, if we think about it, we will realize that it is downright irrational for an intelligent and developed human being to consider a piece of colored rock to be of immense significance. Children may enjoy playing with pretty stones, but why should adults? Yet, wherever we look in the world, precious metals and stones are a matter of great significance. Human beings value them inherently, intuitively. From time immemorial they have been used as currency in economies of all civilizations.

This is because Hashem made it so when He created the world. It did not just arise by itself as some universal convention of human civilization. That is why the verses of our *Parsha* detail these matters of gold and precious stones. It is to teach us that when Hashem created the world at the very beginning, He also created the predispositions and innate attitudes that form the basis of the commodities that promote economic development all over the world. He created gold with an innate spiritual value to it. Gold possesses a quality that goes beyond its shiny appearance and relative scarcity. Hashem created silver, too, with inherent spiritual value, and so with all the precious stones.

They are not just colored rocks. They have imbued into them some sort of sanctity that Hashem created. For what purpose? For the needs of the *Mishkan*. Gold was created to be the primary component of the *Mishkan*. After that silver, and after that copper. Precious stones were created for placement in the *Eifod* and *Choshen*. They were not used for the *Mishkan* because they were precious; they were precious because they were used for the *Mishkan*. All these materials possess special significance and importance from the beginning of Creation, as decreed by the Creator.

5 Clothing

וַיִּהְיוּ שְׁנֵיהֶם עֲרוּמִּים הָאָדָם וְאִשְׁתּוֹ וְלֹא יִתְבֹּשָׁשׁוּ:

וְהַנָּחָשׁ הָיָה עָרוּם מִכֹּל חַיַּת הַשָּׂדֶה אֲשֶׁר עָשָׂה ה' אֱלֹקִים וְכוּ'.

The man and his wife were both naked, but they were not ashamed.

The serpent was the most cunning of all the wild beasts that G-d had made... (Bereishis 2:25, 3:1)

⌒

והנחש היה ערום. מה ענין זה לכאן, היה לו לסמוך "ויעש לאדם ולאשתו כתנות עור וילבישם" (לקמן פסוק כ"א), אלא ללמדך מאיזו עצה קפץ הנחש עליהם וכו'. (רש"י שם ג:א')

"The serpent was the most cunning." What is this passage doing here? The Torah should have placed "G-d made for Adam and his wife garments of skin" (v. 3:21) immediately after [the verse stating that the man and his wife were both naked]. Rather, it was to tell you with what plan the serpent assailed them... (Rashi, Bereishis 3:1)

According to Rashi, the only reason that the Torah told the story of Adam, Chavah and the *Nachash* in the order it did was to inform us why the "cunning serpent" tried to get Adam to eat from the Tree of Knowledge. It was directly related to the lack of embarrassment that existed at that time — "*but they were not ashamed.*" Otherwise, it would appear that the two topics are totally unrelated. It emerges that the reason they were given garments (v. 3:21) had nothing to do with the topic it follows, that of the *Eitz HaDa'as* (v. 3:1-20), because the topic of garments was artificially delayed, so to speak. Rashi repeats this thought later, after what he describes as "an interruption and digression" has concluded:

ויקרא האדם. חזר הכתוב לענינו הראשון "ויקרא האדם שמות" (לעיל ב:כ), ולא הפסיק אלא ללמדך שעל ידי קריאת שמות שמתה נזדוגה לו חוה, כמו שכתוב "ולאדם לא מצא עזר כנגדו" לפיכך "ויפל תרדמה", ועל ידי שכתב "ויהיו שניהם ערומים" סמך לו פרשת הנחש, וכו'. (רש"י בראשית ג:כ')

"And the man called..." The Torah now reverts to its previous subject, "The man gave names." (v. 2:20) It only interrupted the narrative to inform us [of the following]: Through the giving of names, Chavah became his mate, as it writes (ibid.): "But for Adam there was not found a help mate for him." Therefore (ibid., v. 21), "He (Hashem) caused him (Adam) to fall into a deep sleep" [and then He made Chavah]. And since it states "they were both naked" (ibid., v. 25), it therefore follows on with the passage dealing with the Nachash... (Rashi, Bereishis 3:20)

In other words, we should not think that Hashem gave Adam and Chavah clothing because they had discovered that they were naked after they ate from the Tree of Knowledge. Rashi is telling us that they were already attired at that point! Rather, the story is like this: Adam and Chavah had clothing to wear even before they ate from the Tree of Knowledge, and even the naming of Chavah preceded the incident of the sin. (See *Mizrachi* and *Gur Aryeh*.)

In the normal course of events, the serpent would not have seen Chavah unclothed. This occurred only because no sense of modesty existed, or needed to exist, between Adam and Chavah. In reality, they had clothing at that time.

In order to properly understand why they needed clothing *before* they sinned, we need to know that clothing serves two purposes. One is a purely physical need. Clothing covers nakedness and supplies warmth to protect from the cold. However, equally significant is the other role that clothing plays: It provides *kevod ha'adam*, human dignity. This role is illustrated by a king who has special, regal clothing for his honor, not just to cover his body. It is to further the *kevod malchus*, the honor of sovereignty. The same applies here. Hashem gave clothing to Adam and Chavah irrespective of the subsequent events with the *Nachash*.

We find a similar declaration concerning the clothing of the *Kohen*. Even though there were many components to the Priestly Garments that had deeper meaning and significance, nevertheless, the Torah introduces them by saying that they serve to honor the wearer:

ועשית בגדי־קדש לאהרן אחיך לכבוד ולתפארת: (שמות כ"ח:ב')

Make sacred garments that are dignified and beautiful for your brother Aharon. (Shemos 28:2)

In light of this, even in the End of Days after the *yetzer hara* will cease to exist, it will be ridiculous to assume that there will be any radical change in our habits of dress.

However, now we encounter a problem:

ותפקחנה עיני שניהם וידעו כי עירמם הם ויתפרו עלה תאנה ויעשו להם חגרת:

(בראשית ג':ז')

The eyes of both of them were opened and they realized that they were naked. They sewed together fig leaves and made themselves loincloths. (Bereishis 3:7)

If Adam and Chavah already had clothing, why does the Torah say that "they realized that they were naked?" Rashi seems to preempt this problem by explaining the following:

ותפקחנה וגומר. לענין החכמה דבר הכתוב, ולא לענין ראיה ממש, וסוף המקרא מוכיח: וידעו כי עירמים הם. אף הסומא יודע כשהוא ערום, אלא מהו "וידעו כי עירמים הם", מצוה אחת היתה בידם ונתערטלו הימנה (ב"ר יט:ו) : (רש"י שם)

"Their eyes were opened..." The Torah speaks here of under-standing, not of sight. The end of the verse proves this, for it states "and they knew that they were naked." Now, surely even a blind person knows when he is naked. So what does it mean that "they knew that they were naked?" It means that they had only one mitzvah to fulfill, and [now became aware that] they had stripped themselves of it. (Rashi, ibid., based on Bereishis Rabba 19:6)

The realization was an intellectual one, and the nakedness was the loss of the mitzvah. It is now quite clear why Rashi chose to ignore the simple expla-nation of the verse and offer an unusual elucidation instead. Since they had clothing from the beginning, this verse cannot be taken at face value.

This leaves us with the following gnawing problems: If it is true that they were clothed until now, what was the purpose of the fig leaves? What were they trying to accomplish? Similarly problematic is the fact that Rashi brings the following at the end of this entire segment:

כתנות עור. יש דברי אגדה אומרים, חלקים כצפורן היו מדבקים על עורן. ויש אומרים, דבר הבא מן העור כגון צמר הארנבים שהוא רך וחם, ועשה להם כתנות ממנו: (רש"י שם:כ"א)

"[And Hashem made for Adam and his wife] garments of skin [and clothed them]." There are Agaddos that say that they (the garments of skin) were as smooth as fingernails, cleaving to their skin. Others say that it was material that comes from skin, soft and warm like the fur of a hare. From this He made garments for them. (Rashi, ibid., v. 21)

Natural clothing, "soft and warm," would fit in with the above approach we have taken so far. But why does Rashi mention the opinion that the clothing was a type of covering *attached* to the bodies of Adam and Chavah? This would seem to contradict the entire approach that Rashi has taken until now. It would ostensibly mean that they were not clothed at all. Rather, their exposed bodies had a hardened nail-like protective quality, but this would leave them naked, nonetheless!

With the explanation of the *Be'er Besadeh*, our two questions will answer each other.

ונלע"ד לקיים דברי רבינו דכונתו הוא דמעיקרא היו מלבושים בעור צפורן ומכוסין בענן כבודו וכשאכלו מאותו העץ הפשיטם הקב"ה מאותו הלבוש ואח"כ חזר והלבישם מעלה אותו העץ עצמו וכ"ת דאותם חגורות הם מעצמם עשו אותם הרי מפורש בזוה"ק פ' ויקהל ד' ר"ח ב' דהקב"ה עשה אותם וכו'. (באר בשדה בראשית שם)

It seems to me that in order to understand the words of Rashi one must say that he meant the following. At first they were clothed in the skin of a fingernail and covered under the cloud of His glory, but once they ate from the Tree of Knowledge, Hashem removed these special garments. And according to the Zohar (Parshas Vayakhel 208b), it was Hashem who afterwards reclothed them, using leaves from the very tree from which they ate. (Be'er Sadeh, Bereishis, ibid.)

According to Rashi, although they were previously clothed in these special "dignified and beautiful" garments, "covered under the cloud of His glory" and were properly ensconced in utmost sanctity, *ultimately* they were divested of this great honor when they ate from the Tree of Knowledge and required new clothing supplied some time later by "*Hashem who afterwards reclothed them, using leaves from the very tree from which they ate.*" This will now explain, according to this approach, why they referred to themselves as naked if, according to the order of the verses, they were already wearing the *chagoros*. This is because they were not wearing them yet and the verses are not chronological.

What remains unresolved is why it was necessary to make the fig leaf loincloths according to the original approach of Rashi that, even before the episode of the *Eitz HaDa'as*, they were wearing "*material that comes from skin, soft and warm like the fur of a hare?*"

This issue requires further thought. *Tzarich iyun.*

6 Who was the Oldest Person?

The popular notion is that the human with the longest life span was Methuselah, Mesushelach, who lived 969 years. In fact, it is true that amongst those whose ages are actually enumerated in the Torah, Mesushelach's life was the longest. Nevertheless, he was clearly not the person who had the longest life span amongst those mentioned in the early generations of the Creation.

Before we investigate this, let us preface it with the following question: When *Adam HaRishon* was created and he was supposed to live forever, did that mean death would not exist in the world whatsoever?

There are two possible approaches. One is that death would not have existed at all (barring cases of Divine intervention, as we shall see). The other is that death could exist, but only if a person was somehow murdered. People left on their own would normally live forever. If the second approach is correct, it would explain the story of Kayin and Hevel.

The Gemara (*Sanhedrin* 38b) says that Hashem created different things throughout the twelve daylight hours of the first Friday. Rabbi Yochanan bar Chaninah enumerates them. In the first hour, the earth used to create Adam was gathered. In the second hour, it was created into a form. In the third hour, the limbs of the body were formed. In the fourth hour, Adam received his *neshamah*, his soul. In the fifth hour, he stood on his feet. In the sixth hour, he named the animals, and in the seventh hour, Chavah was created.

Then, in the eighth hour of the day, it states: "Two went up to bed and four stepped down" – implying that the children were born in some mysterious "cloning" fashion. Which children is the Gemara referring to? It says that there were two – Adam and Chavah – and then there were four. Simply understood, the Gemara is referring to the birth of Kayin in that occurrence. This is, in fact, how Tosafos (ad loc.) understands this passage, that the four were Adam, Chavah, Kayin and his twin – but not Hevel. He was born later.

Kayin was born together with a sister. This is the meaning of "two went up to bed and four stepped down." It cannot be referring to Kayin and Hevel, says Tosafos, since the Midrash tells us that Hevel was born with *two* sisters. We can assume that at some later hour, Hevel was born.

Since Adam and mankind were to live forever, that there was to be no death, when Hashem decreed that Adam was to die, to whom would this apply? The answer is only to Adam and Chavah who sinned, and to their future children who would be born to them *from then on*. However, since Kayin had already been born, he was not subject to that decree! This should also be true concerning Hevel because Rashi (4:25) informs us that after being expelled from Gan Eden, Adam separated from Chavah for the next one hundred and thirty years, until the birth of Sheis. This being so, Hevel and his two sisters were also born before the sin and its decree of death.

Thus, we see clearly that death could exist before the sin of *Adam HaRishon*, except that it could only be so if a person was slain, as Hevel was.

Continuing with this line of reasoning, we must conclude that Kayin was destined to live forever; i.e., that he would not die of natural causes. So what happened to him? He certainly did not live forever! According to *Midrash Tanchuma* brought by Rashi (*Bereishis* 4:23), Tuval Kayin, his descendant, killed him. This Midrash, again, clearly proves that even someone born before the sin could die, if slain.

On the other hand, if we take the approach that living forever meant just that (and Hevel was born immediately after Adam's sin, before Adam began his penitence), then we can explain the disappearance of Kayin with the *Midrash Rabba* cited by Rashi (ibid., v. 24, s.v. *Shiv'im v'shivah*). According to this account we must conclude that Kayin lived until the *Mabul*, the deluge. This would explain his extraordinary longevity. According to this, Kayin was not killed by Tuval Kayin, rather he died in the *Mabul*. It turns out that Hashem Himself caused Kayin to die; the One who gave him life took it away. However, a human being could not kill him because he was actually destined to live forever, had Hashem not intervened.

Now, according to the second Midrash that Kayin lived until the *Mabul*, he must have lived until the year 1656 from the Creation. This makes him 1,656 years old at the time of his death, much older than Mesushelach. Even according to the first Midrash that he was killed by Tuval Kayin, Mesushelach still was not the person who lived the longest. We will explain:

We find that seven generations of Kayin were born before Sheis was born, and Sheis was born when Adam was one hundred and thirty. According to this, Kayin and all his descendants (who came through the sister that he was "born" with – as *Chazal* say that he married his sister) would also have been destined to live forever. Therefore, the generations that were born from Kayin and his sister/wife were people from before the sin, before the decree of death. They were people who had the ability to live forever.

This is true according to either approach: Whether we say that a man could kill them or not.

Yet, we find one individual who lived longer than Mesushelach according to all views, a person who was able to live even beyond the *Mabul*. That person was Na'amah, the wife of Noach. (See Rashi, ibid., 4:22, s.v. *Na'amah*.)

Na'amah was from the seventh generation of Kayin, born before Adam was one hundred and thirty. Yet, she lived to marry Noach and to actually go into the *Teivah*. If so, she lived over fifteen hundred years before going into the *Teivah*, and then for a time afterwards. What happened to her in the end is not indicated anywhere. We do not find her death mentioned, nor do we find her counted among those who went up to Heaven alive. For all we know, she's still alive with us today! In any event, whichever way we look at it, we must come to the conclusion that Na'amah certainly lived much longer than did Mesushelach.

7 Counting From Day One

The Torah details how long each person lived in the generations that preceded the *Mabul,* as well as for those that followed the *Mabul.* One major outcome of all these dates is that we know we live in the year תשס"ז; it is 5,767 years and counting. Why, though, is it important that we know all this information about the life spans of the first generations of mankind?

A further question revolves around the situation that exists today regarding how we keep track of time. In the early generations, legal documents were written based on the years of the kings. The Gemara's discussion in the beginning of Tractate *Rosh HaShanah* is based on the fact that all documents were dated from the beginning of a king's reign.

Even in the time of *Bayis Sheini,* when there were no longer proper kings, we find that all the legal documents were dated according to what is called *minyan hashtaros,* "the counting of documents." In this way of counting, documents were dated according to the reign of Alexander the Great. Thus, we have a truly unique system of dating called *minyan hashtaros*!

It was not until long after the destruction of *Bayis Sheini* that the present system used by Jews today began to be practiced, that of counting from the Creation of the world.

What significance does our current system of dating have? Obviously, it was not important to count from Creation in the earlier generations. What happened that made it now important to count from Creation? The sages who introduced the present system could have chosen any starting point, any date to count from. They could have chosen to count from *Bayis Rishon,* from *Bayis Sheini* or from any other significant event.

I believe that Heaven's hand directed us to our current dating system so that everyone, wise and ignorant, should know that the world is 5,767 years old. Why? Because the world does not look like it is 5,767 years old! This is the great trial of modern times, of scientific discovery, beginning with the scientific revolution and scientific method that was initiated in the mid 14th to 15th centuries by Galileo and Bacon. That is when the development of modern science as we know it began.

Throughout these last centuries, and all the more so in these latest few generations, science has created its own religion and has begun to veer sharply from knowledge of *HaKadosh Boruch Hu.* For this very reason, I would propose that Hashem wanted us to know clearly and unmistakably how old the world really is. He wanted us to count from Creation for all our significant documents — *Kesubos, Gittin* and promissory notes — as a symbol of our *emunah,* our trust, in the veracity of what the Torah says. If the Torah says that the world was created in six days, and that this took place 5,767 years ago, then we will base all our legal and financial transactions on that fact.

Thus, if someone comes along and claims that the world isn't as old as the Torah says it is, or is older than the Torah says it is, he will be viewed as mouthing obvious *kefirah.* He is denying the facts.

So in order to impress this upon us and make it clear beyond a doubt, to the point that it is basic, public information, the Torah details the years from the day of Creation, and we count from day one. Every schoolchild knows what year it presently is and thereby knows how many years ago the world was created.

This serves to strengthen the Jewish people's belief in what the Torah says, so that if we are confronted by scientific claims to the contrary, we will know who to believe. Indeed, *HaKadosh Boruch Hu* chose this to be a major trial of our times: Will we believe what He says in His Torah, or will we look for some skewed way to reconcile the Torah's account with the prevalent views of the world around us?

8 Explanations that Do Not Explain

In an attempt to resolve the seeming conflict between scientific discoveries and the Torah's account of the beginning of the world, some people want to explain that the six days of Creation were much longer than twenty-four hours each. They believe that this will reconcile the Torah's age of the world with the prevalent scientific views.

There are a number of variations on this approach: Some say that each of the six days was a thousand years, while others say that the days before the creation of the sun, moon and stars (which provide the definition of "days," "months" and "years") were different than the rest of the days. All in all, all these explanations don't really accomplish very much, and they certainly are not in line with what the Torah is actually saying, as I will explain.

As regards the claim that each day was a thousand years, it is quite obvious from what is written in the Torah that this is not the case at all. This simply runs counter to what is stated in the verses. (This will be explained later.) In addition, all you end up with, according to this claim, is that the world is six thousand years older than the standard Torah calculation allows, which does not help much in trying to reconcile the Torah with the age of the universe according to scientific theory — billions of years.

Furthermore, how do these approaches explain the following? Each one of the days has different structures, objects or creatures that were created on it. Day Four, for example, has the creation of the sun, the moon and the stars. Day Five has the fish. Day Six has the animals and the creation of Man. Continuing with Friday, as the Gemara in *Sanhedrin* explains (38b), at each hour of the day something else occurred. One hour Hashem gathered the earth together, at another He created the mass of material that would become Adam and at another He blew life into him. Then Adam named the animals and then Hashem created Chavah and commanded her and Adam not to do the sin. Then three hours before the end of the day they were driven out of Gan Eden.

Friday was one of the six days of Creation. According to the above claim, Friday was one thousand years long. This means that Adam was about seven hundred and fifty years old at the time he was banished from Gan Eden. Even if you consider the one thousand years as starting the night before, whereas Adam was created only in the late morning, he would still be three hundred years old at the end of the day.

This is patently absurd, for the following reason. Adam lived well beyond the period he spent in Gan Eden. He had Sheis when he was one hundred and thirty years old, and *after* he was expelled from Gan Eden! In the end, he lived to nine hundred and thirty. So if the thousand year-count applies to each day, the arithmetic just does not work. We must therefore admit that Day Six was a twenty-four-hour day, because it is counted in the years of Adam, who lived to be nine hundred and thirty, and it was only one day of the nine hundred and thirty years. Clearly, the other days were similarly twenty-four hours long.

Now let us examine the other variation on this claim, that each day had a different length. This also does not coincide with the simple facts. Each one of the days ends with: *"and it was evening, and it was morning, the second (and third and fourth...) day."* We have a general rule stated by *Chazal*, לא בא הכתוב לסתום אלא לפרש, the verse does not come to obfuscate but rather to clarify, which Rashi mentions in many places (for instance *Bereishis* 10:25). According to this rule, when the Torah tells us facts, the purpose could not be to hide or obscure information. If it wanted to hide the information, it would not say anything to begin with.

Thus, there would be no point in the Torah saying exactly the same thing about each and every one of the days – *"and it was evening, and it was morning"* – if each one used a different definition of the nebulous term "day." It would turn out that Day One, Two and Three had one definition, and Four, Five and Six had another; yet, the Torah uses the same terminology for all. This approach is unacceptable to any thinking mind.

In addition, we find a statement of the Gemara that clearly refutes this entire approach.

אמר ר' יהודה אמר רב עשרה דברים נבראו ביום ראשון שמים וארץ, תהו ובהו, אור וחשך, רוח ומים, מדת יום ומדת לילה: (חגיגה י"ב ע"א)

Rabbi Yehudah said in the name of Rav: Ten things were created on the first day, and these are they: heaven and earth, toho vavohu, light and darkness, wind and water, and the measure of day and the measure of night. (Chagigah 12a)

Note this last set: "the measure of day and the measure of night." What does this mean? Rashi explains.

מדת יום ומדת לילה — עשרים וארבע שעות בין שניהם: (רש"י שם)

The meaning of "the measure of day and the measure of night" is that on the first day of Creation, HaKadosh Boruch Hu instituted that day and night would equal twenty-four hours between the two of them. (Rashi, ad loc.)

We do not find any statement of *Chazal* that disagrees with this. Therefore, the above Gemara with Rashi's explanation conclusively refutes any attempt to explain that Day Six was any shorter than Day One, as well as any attempt to divorce the concept of "day" from the measurement of twenty-four hours.

9 Torah and Science – The Correct Way to Resolve Contradictions

There are many different acceptable ways to resolve the apparent contradictions between the discoveries of science regarding the age of the world and the Torah description of Creation. I would just like to present one. I believe this is the simplest and most obvious way to approach the issue, obviating the need for all sorts of convoluted explanations.

Clearly, if an objective outsider were to observe *Adam HaRishon* shortly after he was created as he stood and looked around at the world that had been created before him, and would hypothesize as to how old Adam is, he would say: "Clearly, he is at least twenty-five. He is somewhere between that and forty."

Then he would be shocked to discover that Adam is not even a day old; he is just a few hours old! We think of someone a few hours old as an infant in a nursery. Yet, here was a grown man with tremendous stature. *HaKadosh Boruch Hu* did not have to create Adam as a baby and then wait for him to grow up. He created him as an adult from the start.

As Adam looked around and perceived his surroundings, he would have seen giant trees that existed around him and perhaps wondered of their age. If he would have cut down one of those trees, how many rings would we suppose the tree to have? No rings? Five rings? A hundred rings? It would be inconsistent with science and with the nature of the world to find a tree that looked like it was a hundred years old without a hundred rings. Yet, in truth, it was only a few days old. When *HaKadosh Boruch Hu* created the tree, He created it in its full form. The fruit trees were created with the ability to give forth fruit, and perhaps even with the fruit on them. Obviously, if Adam was placed in Gan Eden with fruit trees, he didn't have to wait for the trees to give forth their fruit. They had their fruit on them already. An objective outsider, taking a look at these trees, would have assumed them to have been in existence for decades! Yet, we know that they were only a few days old.

Let us assume that *Adam HaRishon* looked up into the sky at night and saw the stars. He might have contemplated how long it took the light of those stars to reach him. An objective observer might say: "Those stars are thousands of light-years away; the other ones are tens of thousands of light-years away and those over there are hundreds of thousands of light-years away!"

Even without a telescope, one can calculate the closest of stars to thousands of light-years away. It must have taken 5,000 years for that light to reach the earth. However, there is a tiny little problem: The stars were created this Wednesday. When *HaKadosh Boruch Hu* put the stars into the sky, He surely did not have to wait a few thousand years for the light to reach the earth before He would create Adam. Obviously, *HaKadosh Boruch Hu* created the light immediately on the earth, and created the ability of Adam to see those stars, even though in the normal course of events it would have taken thousands of years for the light to get there.

So let us take a look at this universe that *HaKadosh Boruch Hu* created. He created the first man to look like an adult, trees that are totally developed and a world in its most completed fashion. All the diamonds are already placed in the earth. Do you know what it takes to develop diamonds from graphite and then make them available to be found by man? According to modern science, millions of years ago, a pressure of 55,000 atmospheres and a temperature near 2,700 degrees Fahrenheit, as exists fifty miles below the surface of the earth, was needed. Pressure built up causing volcanic eruptions that brought the diamonds up to the surface. We see the stars with their twinkling lights, way up in the sky. Do we know how many years it takes for that light to get here? Light traveling at 186,282 mi/sec will take 4 light years from the nearest star, Proxima Centauri, to reach Earth. With sophisticated telescopes, we are able to see that far-away quasars are about 27 billion light years away! The light we see now was emitted when the quasar was about 4 billion light years away, taking into account the expanding universe. That is what modern science proposes, yet, we know that all of this wondrous nature was created immediately.

Parenthetically, let us discuss the scientific concept that the universe appears to be expanding. This concept is actually reflected in a statement of the Gemara.

ואמר רב יהודה אמר רב בשעה שברא הקדוש ברוך הוא את העולם היה מרחיב והולך כשתי פקעיות של שתי עד שגער בו הקדוש ברוך הוא והעמידו שנאמר עמודי שמים ירופפו ויתמהו מגערתו: והיינו דאמר ריש לקיש מאי דכתיב אני קל שקי אני הוא שאמרתי לעולם די: (חגיגה י"ב ע"א).

Said Rav Yehudah in the name of Rav: At the time that the Holy One Blessed be He created the world, it was continually expanding like two rolls of the warp of a loom, until the Holy One Blessed be He rebuked it and made it stand still. As it is written, "The pillars of heaven were loose, and they were stunned by His rebuke." This is like what Reish Lakish said: "What is the meaning of 'I am the G-d Sha--dai?' It means I am the One who said to the world: 'Dai' (enough)." (Chagigah 12a)

Now let us imagine the following scenario: A scientist goes and tests the material of the world and says, "Wait a second. It takes the light 4 billion years to get here from the far reaches of the universe and yet the universe seems to be only 1,000 years old; 2,000 years old; 5,000 years old; 5½ thousand years old! I tested it with carbon 14 dating and it tested only 5½ thousand years! There is an internal contradiction in the universe. The physical substance of world demonstrates youth, yet the physics of the world demonstrates an age of overwhelming proportions."

If this would have been the case, there would not have been much room left for the exercise of our free choice. Under those circumstances, it would have been pretty obvious that there was Divine design in Creation. Indeed, *HaKadosh Boruch Hu* chose not to create the world that way. He created a balanced world, where everything fits into its proper place. Just as He created Adam looking old, He created the rest of the world with an age that paralleled the age of Adam. This was reflected in the apparent age of the trees, the diamonds, the light from the stars, etc. All this *HaKadosh Boruch Hu* created immediately, in His infinite wisdom with His infinite ability.

Surely, Hashem can do as He wishes. He can and did create a full-blown world. Therefore, it is quite obvious that all of these scientific findings in no way contradict the fact that the world only actually exists for 5,767 years.

In addition to the above, we have the following teaching from *Pirkei Avos.*

בעשרה מאמרות נברא העולם. ומה תלמוד לומר, והלא במאמר אחד יכול להבראות:

(אבות ה':א')

The world was created through ten Divine utterances. And what does this teach us? Surely, the world could have been created through one utterance! (Pirkei Avos 5:1)

The point we may learn from here is that according to a true Torah outlook, the question is not how did the world come into being in such a short period of time, but rather why did it take so long? Why ten Divine utterances? Why seven full days?

From this clear lesson from *Chazal*, we see that whatever way we use to understand the Creation as taking a shorter time is more in line with true *emunah.* The greatness of our Creator is expressed by his ability to create the very complex in the most simplest of fashions, not vice versa. If this is so, any attempt on our own to add to whatever processes have been revealed to us, G-d forbid, limits our appreciation of the A-mighty[2] and, as we explained, this does not, in any way, have to contradict any scientific findings.

10. Binyan Av

רַבִּי יִשְׁמָעֵאל אוֹמֵר, בְּשְׁלֹשׁ עֶשְׂרֵה מִדּוֹת שֶׁהַתּוֹרָה נִדְרֶשֶׁת בָּהֶן:

(א) מִקַּל וָחֹמֶר.
(ב) וּמִגְּזֵרָה שָׁוָה.
(ג) מִבִּנְיַן אָב מִכָּתוּב אֶחָד, וּמִבִּנְיַן אָב מִשְּׁנֵי כְתוּבִים.

Among the first methods by which the Torah is interpreted is that of *binyan av,* the "prototype." This would appear not to be a matter of natural logic, like a *kal vachomer* is. The *kal vachomer* is called *a fortiori* reasoning, or inference from minor to major, and is universally accepted as an axiom of logic.

Neither is the *binyan av* just a *Halachah LeMoshe MiSinai*[3] like the *gezeirah shavah*[4] is. It is not just a Halachic tool of Scriptural interpretation meant to be viewed as a blind rule. Rather, it is fundamental to the way that the Torah is interpreted, and, in fact, is also fundamental to the very understanding of *B'rias Ha'Olam,* the Creation of the world. How is this so?

The *binyan av* seems to be the weakest of the thirteen methods of interpretation stated by Rabbi Yishmael. Nevertheless, it appears to be the very source from which all of the other methods after it flow.

This is because the true significance of *binyan av* stems from the Oneness and indivisibility of G-d Himself. As the Rambam points out in the beginning of *Mishneh Torah:*

המצוי הזה הוא אלקי העולם אדון כל הארץ, והוא המנהיג הגלגל בכח וכו'.

This existing Being is the G-d of the world, the L-rd of all the earth. He is the One who moves the globe with His strength...

וידיעת דבר זה מצות עשה וכו'.

And knowledge of this matter is a positive Torah mitzvah...

שזהו העיקר הגדול שהכל תלוי בו. אלוה זה אחד הוא ואינו שנים ולא יתר על שנים, אלא אחד, וכו'. אלא יחוד שאין יחוד אחר כמותו בעולם, וכו'.

This is the great principle upon which all depends. This G-d is One; He is not two or more than two, rather He is One... He is unified in a way that there is no other unity like His in the world...

לפיכך אי אפשר שיהיה אלא אחד, וידיעת דבר זה מצות עשה שנאמר ה' אלקינו ה' אחד: (הל' יסודי התורה פ"א הל' ה'-ז')

Therefore, it is impossible that He could be anything other

---

3   A protocol of Torah law whereby a commandment or explanation was transmitted by Moshe orally from Hashem to K'lal Yisrael.

4   A method of exegesis whereby two independent topics shed light on each other due to the placement of similar words or their juxtaposition.

than One, and the knowledge of this matter is a positive Torah
mitzvah, as it is written: "Hashem is our G-d; Hashem is One."
(Hilchos Yesodei HaTorah 1:5–7)

Rambam is telling us that G-d's Oneness is simple and indivisible. It is a Oneness from which emerges everything that we understand, and everything that exists.

The *Me'or Einayim* writes in his commentary on *Parshas Tetzaveh*[5] that the thirteen interpretive methods of the Torah flow from the thirteen Divine traits of mercy. These are the traits of "*Hashem, Hashem, Keil rachum vechanun...*"[6a] Through learning the Torah in this way, a person comes to unite himself with Hashem's absolute Oneness. As the Zohar says (Part 3, 73a), *HaKadosh Boruch Hu*, the Torah and the people of Israel are all one.

The Torah and Hashem are one. This means that the Torah is not just a body of knowledge; it is Divine Wisdom. Hence, we have the fundamental assumption that when we come upon two divergent concepts within the context of a Torah discussion, those two concepts are fundamentally the same. In other words, everything in the Torah is the same until proven that it is different.

This is the principle of the *binyan av,* that one area of Torah can serve as a prototype for other areas of Torah, since all is assumed to be the same until proven different. It is also the idea behind the בנין אב משני כתובים, otherwise known as the *tzad hashaveh* , the "common denominator."[6b]

The notion of a "common denominator" between very diverse laws of the Torah, upon which *Chazal* base many halachos, seems at first to be strange. Yet, this is the underpinning of the *binyan av* and the *tzad hashaveh*. This is how it works: If we see two different laws that have a common thread called "A", but one contains an "x" factor and the other a "y" factor in addition to the common thread, we assume that the common thread "A" does not come

---

5   אמנם יובן עם האמור למעלה שהמדות הם שנתצמצמו על ידי התלבשותו יתברך באור הוד מעטה לבושו יתברך שהיא התורה
בהם י"ג מדות שהתורה שבעל פה נדרשת בהן מהתורה שבכתב והן הן הי"ג מדות שנזכרים בפסוק וכו'. (שמות ל"ד, ו')

6a   וכן מצאתי בפרי צדיק מאמר קדושת שבת מאמר ז' בא"ד וזהו הקירון אור

6b   This is where a ruling is derived from a combination of two concepts rather then one.

either from the "x" or from the "y." Why is that? Why can't we say that one law has the "A" aspect because of factor "x", and the other, coincidentally, has the same "A" aspect but because of "y?" What is it that logically drives us to posit a shared characteristic of "z" as the source of "A?"

The answer is now simple: Everything is the same until proven different. If there is a common thread, there is a common reason for that thread. That is what underlies a *tzad hashaveh*.

From the perspective of pure logic, this is not necessarily so. It is a very unconvincing proof. However, in Torah it has to be so because of *binyan av*. When we find that there is a *gezeirah shavah* or a comparison of juxtaposed concepts (*hekesh*) contradicting our analysis, then and only then can we assume that there is a fundamental difference between one law of the Torah and another.

This profound unity and indivisibility is described as the philosophical concept of *pashtus*, "simplicity." There is a built-in simplicity. Torah matters are simple until they are proven complex.

Likewise, we have the rule of תפסת מרובה לא תפסת, תפסת מועט תפסת. "If you claim too much, you have claimed nothing. If you claim a little, you have successfully claimed." This is not just simple logic, requiring us to use the least possible or smallest derivation since otherwise there is no end to it. (That is actually the philosophical principle called "Occam's razor.") Rather, it is based on the Torah's "simplicity," its *pashtus*. Torah stances and ideas are deemed to be more alike than different. Consequently, if we see that they are in fact different, *binyan av* teaches us that they are different only to the minimum, not the maximum.[7]

This also explains דיו לבא מן הדין להיות כנדון.[8] This means that if we are going to compare two laws, even with the solid logic of a *kal vachomer*, all we may conclude is that the same conditions apply in all cases. They are going to be as much the same as possible, and only as un-alike as logic permits.

---

7   ע"ע רש"י סוכה ה' ע"ב ד"ה תפשת וחגיגה י"ז ע"א ד"ה תפשת ותוס' סוכה שם

8   ב"ק י"ח ע"ב

This will also explain the principle of אם אינו ענין, וכו' תנהו ענין. This means that if a law derived from a Torah verse is seemingly superfluous as regards topic "a", where the verse appears, we apply the law to topic "b", which is the topic most closely related to "a." Ostensibly, this seems incomprehensible. Why should an extra law in one topic have a halachic impact on another topic, even one closely related? Based on what we have said it makes perfect sense. It is simple: All of Torah is essentially one topic!

That is the way we approach ideas in Torah. If we can explain the actions of Hashem in a simple way, then without compelling evidence to the contrary, we must assume that *HaKadosh Boruch Hu* actually did it that way, and we do not look for a more complex explanation. There is no redundancy with the *Borei Ha'Olam*. A delightfully, fancifully complex creation is left to the imagination of finite humans who are impressed by its complexity, whereas the greatness of our Creator is His astounding simplicity in the creation of what appears exceedingly complex. Hypothesizing fanciful explanations actually detracts from belief in His perfection and *pashtus*.

> וזהו שאמרו רז"ל שנברא אדם יחידי, כדי שלא יאמרו המינים שתי רשויות, כי יאמרו שהם שתי התחלות ח"ו.

This is the meaning of what Chazal taught, that mankind was created as a single individual so that the heretics will not say that there are two divine forces. For they will say that there are two beginnings.

> והנה דקדקו בדבריהם כדי שלא יאמרו המינים, כי לפי האמת אין בדבר זה ממש, וכו'. מאחר שהוא ברצון ולא בחיוב יכול להיות הכל. רק כדי שלא יטעו המינים הוא האמור: (השל"ה הקדוש פסחים דרוש ששי ל"ז)

But it is implied that all this is so that the heretics will not make such a claim, whereas there is no substance to it... Since Hashem acts according to His will, freely choosing, anything could be. It is only so the heretics will not make this error that it was said. (Shelah, Pesachim, Drush 6:37)

If we can understand that the entire universe came about though one Divine utterance, we do not search for a more complex way. Some ancient peoples believed that there were two divine forces at work, as reflected in the citation above from the *Shelah HaKadosh*. Nowadays people entertain theories involving a confluence of various factors that would seem to fit with the approach that some natural selection or development or evolutionary process was at work. Why, though, should we try to explain everything the hard way around? Why should we even entertain such an idea? It is thoroughly unnecessary, superfluous and not in keeping with the perfection of *HaKadosh Boruch Hu.*

It is not my intention to propose that there were absolutely no processes in the development of Creation, since clearly we can see otherwise from a close reading of the relevant verses and statements of *Chazal*. As an example:

אבן היתה שם מימות נביאים ראשונים ושתייה היתה נקראת: (יומא נ"ג ע"ב)

There was a stone there from the days of the early Prophets, and it was called Shesiyah. (Yoma 53b)

ושתיה היתה נקראת. תנא: שממנה הושתת העולם. תנן כמאן דאמר מציון נברא העולם. דתניא, רבי אליעזר אומר: עולם מאמצעיתו נברא, שנאמר (איוב ל"ח:ל"ח) בצקת עפר למוצק ורגבים ידבקו?

*"And it was called Shesiyah." It was taught: [This name was] because from it, the world was created. This was taught according to the one who says that **from Zion, the world was created.** For it was taught: Rabbi Eliezer says: The world was created from its middle, as it says (Iyov, 38:38), "Who spread out the ground, and joined the clumps of earth together?"*

רבי יהושע אומר: עולם מן הצדדין נברא, וכו'. (שם נ"ד ע"ב)

*Rabbi Yehoshua says: **The world was created from the sides...** (ibid., 54b)*

In this *Chazal* we see a dispute between the Sages on whether the world's creation began from the middle of the world (the Temple Mount) or from the sides of the world. Rashi, (ad loc.) explains:

מציון נברא — ציון נבראת תחילה, וסביביה נדבקו רגבים עד סוף העולם מכל צד.

"From Zion, the world was created" — Zion was created first, and around it joined together the clumps of earth until the end of the world, from every side.

בצקת עפר למוצק — מוצק אחד היה לו, ומשם נדבקו רגבים סביביו.

"Who spread out the ground?" — *It was one unit, and from there all the clumps of earth joined together around it.*

מן הצדדין נברא — ארבע מוצקות היו לו, ונמתח והלך מכל צד, עד שנדבק באמצעיתו: (רש"י שם)

"The world was created from the sides" — *It had four units, and it stretched out toward every side, until it joined together in its middle.*

Thus we see here a deep discussion about whether the initial impetus of Creation was in one unit spreading out in four directions, or four units spreading inwards toward the center.

Indeed, the world could easily have been created with one single Divine utterance. Yet, the unfathomable Divine wisdom saw fit to do otherwise.

בעשרה מאמרות נברא העולם. ומה תלמוד לומר, והלא במאמר אחד יכול להבראות, אלא להפרע מן הרשעים שמאבדין את העולם שנברא בעשרה מאמרות, ולתן שכר טוב לצדיקים שמקימין את העולם שנברא בעשרה מאמרות: (אבות ה':א')

The world was created through ten Divine utterances. And what does this teach us? Surely, the world could have been created through one utterance! Rather, it was to punish the wicked who destroy the world, which was created through ten utterances. And it is to give reward to the tzaddikim who maintain the world, which was created through ten utterances. (Avos 5:1)

For us to attempt with our limited human knowledge to expand upon what has been revealed to us of the Divine plan is not just presumptuous, but wholly irrational.

11 Chochma, Bina and Da'as

וּמֵעֵץ הַדַּעַת טוֹב וָרָע לֹא תֹאכַל מִמֶּנּוּ וכו'.

And from the Tree of Knowledge of good and evil, you shall not eat from it... (Bereishis 2:17)

Adam and Chavah were given a precept not to eat from the *Eitz HaDa'as.* The Rambam explains (*Moreh Nevuchim* 1, ch. 2) that even before eating from the tree, Adam knew the difference between truth and falsehood. Although he did not have a *yetzer hara,* and lacked understanding of good and evil, he did understand the concepts of truth and falsehood. After they ate, the Torah does not say that they gained knowledge of truth and falsehood — only of good and evil.

How is this to be understood? Clearly, good and evil are intimately connected to truth and falsehood. To grasp how Adam had one without the other requires explanation.

Furthermore, it is strange that we are allowed to eat freely from this tree today, although it was forbidden to Adam on the pain of death. If we would find someone eating *treif,* we surely would not say to him that he might as well keep on eating since he already took a bite! Yet, *Chazal* identify this tree (*Brachos* 40a): It is either the grapevine, the fig tree or wheat, all of which are fully permitted to us.

We could answer that it was only the fruit from that specific grapevine or fig tree or wheat stalk that was forbidden. If so, what was the great enticement? If one can have grapes anywhere, why would one feel compelled to eat from that vine specifically?

To answer these questions we have to understand the term *da'as* in *Eitz HaDa'as.* What exactly is *"da'as?"* The tree was not called *Eitz HaChochmah* or *Eitz HaBinah.* It was *Eitz HaDa'as.*

Chochmah denotes encyclopedic knowledge; it is the knowledge of facts.

Binah denotes information that is transferred and applied, transitive inference; it means to understand "A" based on knowledge of "B" and "C." An example of this: You teach a child that fire is hot. That is a piece of information — pure *chochmah*. Now you teach the child that metal conducts heat. Again, another piece of information — more *chochmah*. Now the child notices a long piece of metal, part of which is over the fire and part of which is not. Without having to touch the metal, he comes to the mental conclusion that the part not over the fire is also hot. That is *binah*. He transferred the information and applied it. He has taken the two pieces of information, connected them and created a third piece of information that he now clearly and intellectually understands.

Yet, this is all just theoretical and academic. Knowing this information has no real life significance to the child whatsoever until his intellectual inquisitiveness and curiosity brings him to actually touch that piece of metal. He could know that fire possesses a quality described as "hot," yet not know what "hot" really means. He could know that metal conducts "heat," and understand what that means also. However, all this is without comprehending the true consequences of his knowledge. When he touches that piece of metal and burns himself, that is *da'as*! That is knowledge based on pragmatic, practical, experiential information. That is a comprehension of fact that is deeper than any *chochmah* or *binah* could possibly be.

(Regarding the experience of the Giving of the Torah, a revelation of Hashem on the experiential level of "face to face," as described in *Devarim* 5:4, the Torah says: *"Attah hor'eisa **lada'as**."* [*Devarim* 4:35] Similarly we find that the Torah writes: "In order to afflict you, to test you, to know [*lada'as*] what is in your heart." [ibid., 8:2] Hashem surely knows what is in our hearts, but He chooses to wait for us to express our intent in actuality, and bring it into the physical realm of experience. So, too, with all the verses in which we find reference to *da'as*.)

As we mentioned before, *Adam HaRishon* had the ability to understand what was true and what was false. Truth is what Hashem says is true. Falsehood is what Hashem says is untrue. Truth is not a man-made concept; we are not the ones who determine what is true and what is not. There is no subjective morality. In the area of truth and falsehood, *emes* and *sheker,* it is objective and absolute, and only Hashem is objective and absolute. Adam understood that if Hashem said that something is to be a certain way, then that way is true.

Whatever is not the way Hashem said it is to be is falsehood. Adam understood this clearly and could intellectually grasp this to the fullest extent.

However, the meaning of evil, i.e., doing actions that are contrary to Hashem's will, and their attendant ramifications, was something that Adam could not know because he had never experienced it. Thus, he lacked understanding of good as well. One can know what is right and good only in light of what is wrong and evil.

It emerges that Adam had intellectual knowledge of truth and falsehood. He knew what Hashem's will was and what was contrary to Hashem's will. The significance of taking that information and putting it into practice, actually violating Hashem's precept to guard and keep Gan Eden, was something that was outside Adam's reality before the sin. It was a perception that lay outside the realm of his experience until he ate from the *Eitz HaDa'as*. He knew it was falsehood, but what were the ramifications of falsehood? He could not know that the ramifications of falsehood are that it is evil; he could only speculate this without any way of truly appreciating its consequences.

Once Adam ate from the *Eitz HaDa'as*, which was violating Hashem's will, he understood the ramifications. He realized on an experiential level what it means to violate *HaKadosh Boruch Hu*'s precept. The fruit itself might have been innocuous and neutral, containing no inherent negative qualities, or perhaps it was spiritually toxic only for a person in the sinless state that was Adam's. This is not the real issue. It has become irrelevant. The issue was that Hashem said not to do this, and Adam violated Hashem's will.

We could relate to this as follows: In our terms, eating *treif* food is spiritually damaging to a Jew's heart. It is inherently evil, negative and inherently destructive to a Jew. That was not necessarily true of *Adam HaRishon* regarding the *Eitz HaDa'as*. His trial, unlike ours, was not to confront something that was inherently destructive to him but to confront something that was contrary to Hashem's will.

Therefore, the "forbidden" item remained permitted to him: It had no inherent negative qualities. After he ate from the *Eitz HaDa'as,* there was no more Divine precept not to eat from it. He was in a new situation in which this precept was not relevant. The prohibition was relevant only to the experience of evil that is defined by acting contrary to Hashem's will, and he already experienced it. Now Adam was in a new universe. The *yetzer hara*, with its physical drives and human needs, became part and parcel of his being and was no longer just an intellectual pursuit or scholarly speculation.

Thus, Adam now had to be put into a new area — both in location and in the way he was to deal with these new realities.

12 Why People Act Contrary to Hashem's Will

Continuing on the previous theme, I would like to speak of an additional aspect in the makeup of Adam and Chavah before the sin. If Adam did not have a *yetzer hara,* then how can we say he was enticed to eat from the *Eitz HaDa'as?* If there was no force or drive that pulled him to it, then why would he eat?

We may assume that most, if not all, of the factors that draw a person to act contrary to the will of Hashem came into being through the eating from the *Eitz HaDa'as.* If so, how were Adam and Chavah seduced by the *Nachash* to violate Hashem's will, if they originally lacked these factors?

It is written:

ותרא האשה וכו'. (בראשית ג':ו')

And the woman saw... (Bereishis 3:6)

ראתה דבריו של נחש והנאו לה והאמינתו: (רש"י שם)

She saw value in the words of the Nachash, and they gave her pleasure, and she believed him. (Rashi, ad loc.)

What was the pleasure that she derived from the words of the *Nachash?*

Although Adam and Chavah had no internal physical drives before the sin, this does not mean that they had no emotional aspect to their makeup. To the contrary, they possessed physical perfection! Are appreciation of music and art purely intellectual? Were they not capable of experiencing pleasure from these non-academic activities? Surely, there was an emotional component to

Adam and Chavah, but without the normal drives and desires that are now associated with them. This allowed for their perfection as humans while they still lacked the understanding of good and evil. Chavah could have pleasure, even though she had no concept of good and evil.

From this perspective, Rashi seems to be telling us that the pleasure that Chavah experienced had clouded her rational ability to properly analyze the truth. Chavah wanted to believe what the *Nachash* was saying to her. Therefore, she believed it. Although it was pure falsehood, she believed him because she wanted to believe him.

ותרא האשה כי טוב העץ למאכל וכי תאוה־הוא לעינים: (בראשית שם)

> *And the woman saw that the tree was good as food and was desirable (ta'avah) to the eyes. (Bereishis, ibid.)*

Chavah saw that there was benefit to be gained, and she believed it was true. Without question, this form of pitfall is something very real and present in our world of "after the sin," and similarly causes people today to act contrary to Hashem's will.

Desire, *ta'avah,* would not appear to be relevant to Chavah before the sin. The verse is therefore informing us that she did experience permitted pleasure of a type we cannot quite understand, and that she was drawn to believe that she would have more of the same as the result of "and your eyes will be opened" (ibid.), as the *Nachash* promised her. This was something that appealed to her; she had pleasure from it. Therefore, she wanted to believe the *Nachash.*

13   Not Part of the Punishment

We find that after Adam sinned, Hashem punished all those responsible. He designated a specific punishment for each. To the *Nachash,* Hashem says:

כי עשית זאת ארור אתה מכל הבהמה ומכל חית השדה על גחנך תלך ועפר תאכל כל

ימי חייך: ואיבה אשית בינך ובין האשה... (בראשית ג':י"ד-ט"ו)

Because you did this, you are more cursed than all the ani-
mals and all the beasts of the field. You shall go on your belly
and you shall eat dust all the days of your life. And I will place
enmity between you and the woman... (Bereishis 3:14–15)

To the woman (her name is not yet disclosed), Hashem metes out a different punishment:

הרבה ארבה עצבונך והרנך בעצב תלדי בנים ואל אישך תשוקתך והוא ימשל בך: (שם ט"ז)

"I will greatly increase your pain and that of your pregnancy.
In pain you shall give birth to children. And your longing shall
be to your husband, and he shall rule over you." (ibid., v. 3:16)

Thereafter, Adam is accorded his own, unique punishment:

ארורה האדמה בעבורך בעצבון תאכלנה כל ימי חייך וקוץ ודרדר תצמיח לך ואכלת
את עשב השדה: בזעת אפיך תאכל לחם... (שם י"ז-י"ט)

"The ground is cursed for you. In pain shall you eat from it all
the days of your life. And it shall sprout for you thorns and
thistles, and you shall eat the herb of the field. By the sweat of
your face shall you eat bread..." (ibid., vv. 17–19)

After this, we find Adam giving his wife the name of Chavah (ibid., v. 20),
and the passage ends with the description of Hashem giving clothing to Adam
and Chavah. That is basically the end of the story, but a very significant event is
absent. There is no mention at this point of Adam and Chavah having to leave
Gan Eden!

The Torah later discusses this event, but in a different context:

ויאמר ה' אלקים הן האדם היה כאחד ממנו לדעת טוב ורע ועתה פן ישלח ידו ולקח
גם מעץ החיים ואכל וחי לעלם: וישלחהו ה' אלקים מגן עדן לעבד את האדמה אשר
לקח משם: (שם כ"ב)

And Hashem, G-d, said: "Behold, the man has become as one
of us, to know good and evil. And now, lest he stretch forth his
hand and take also from the Tree of Life and eat, and live for-
ever." And Hashem, G-d, sent him from Gan Eden to work the
earth from which he was taken. (ibid., v 22)

Let us note that this is no longer part of the punishment, the account of which was finished long before. Therefore, we must ask: On what basis was Adam given this new mission? Hashem banished Adam from Gan Eden, never to return. What did Adam do now to deserve this new punishment? This is not part of the atonement for eating from the *Eitz HaDa'as*.

The most basic principle of our life in this world is the fact that Hashem granted us the faculty of free choice. Hashem created us with this method of serving Him. The *Ramchal* explains that the purpose of Creation is to enable Hashem to bestow goodness on others. (*Derech Hashem* 1:2)

This purpose necessitates the existence of free choice. That is why originally, Hashem thought to create the world through *midas hadin* but He later chose to incorporate the *midas harachamim*. (Rashi, ibid., 1:1) If the world would consist exclusively of *midas hadin*, without *midas harachamim*, there would be no room for free choice. Everyone would see the immediate consequences of their actions and no one would ever dare to do anything wrong! Therefore, *midas harachamim* had to be incorporated, so there could be a lapse of time between when a person sinned and when he was punished.

This created the possibility for people to not see the cause-and-result relationship between sin and punishment. A person could fool himself into thinking that they were not related, and that allows for free choice to exist. (See Rashi, ibid.)

The *Abarbanel* (*Bereishis* 2:5) lists six trials, six aspects of the human condition, that bring a person to sin and allow free choice to exist. Hashem originally created a world for Adam where none of these would exist. That was the state in Gan Eden.

The first cause of sin is pride of one's ancestry, the second is a land that is conducive to sinning, the third is pressure to earn a livelihood, the fourth is pressure to retain one's standard of living, the fifth is ignorance of the halacha and the sixth is negative peer pressure. None of these six existed for Adam in Gan Eden. There was nothing in the context of such a life that created the necessary conditions for free choice.

That is why Hashem had to remove Adam from Gan Eden. It was not a punishment, but rather a prerequisite for his service of Hashem. Adam was thus placed in a new situation and given a new set of precepts. He had either six or seven of these precepts, according to the various views expressed in Tractate *Sanhedrin*. However many there were, they necessitated that Adam now be in a new environment. The circumstances of his free choice changed; therefore, his environment changed accordingly.

Adam could not stay in Gan Eden, nor be allowed access to the Tree of Life, which was the essence of the Torah, of Hashem's will and His revealed wisdom to the world. As it is written: "For it is a Tree of Life for those who take hold of it." (*Mishlei* 3:18) It afforded the complete and total knowledge that perhaps only a *malach* has. However, Adam could not be allowed this, so that he could continue to serve Hashem in the path of free choice. If Adam would eat from the Tree of Life — if he would have such a clear and pure spiritual vision that there could be no more free choice—he would be coerced to do the good by the sheer force of his spiritual perception. In such a state he would live forever, and there would be no more real challenges and consequently no further point to the existence of creation. That is why Hashem required Adam to leave Gan Eden.

14 Failing to Get the Message

אַף עַל פִּי שֶׁרָאוּ בְּאָבְדָן שֶׁל דּוֹר אֱנוֹשׁ, שֶׁעָלָה אוֹקְיָנוֹס וְהֵצִיף שְׁלִישׁ הָעוֹלָם, לֹא נִכְנַע דּוֹר הַמַּבּוּל לִלְמוֹד מֵהֶם: (רש"י בראשית ו':ד')

Although they saw the destruction of the generation of Enosh, when the ocean rose and washed away a third of the world, the generation of the Great Flood was not moved to learn from them. (Rashi, Bereishis 6:4)

We might wonder how such a thing is possible. How could they not get the message? However, we need look no further than our own time.

The great Indian Ocean tsunami of 2004 caused the deaths of hundreds of thousands of people, and millions more were homeless in eleven countries. The earthquake that generated this disaster is estimated to have released the energy of 23,000 Hiroshima-type atomic bombs, according to the U.S. Geological Survey (USGS). (*National Geographic News*, January 7, 2005)

Although this did not affect one third of the world percentage-wise, as was the case with the generation of Enosh, in sheer numbers it was probably a greater disaster. Yet, the world continues on as if nothing happened. It brought about no change, no lesson, no soul-searching. It seems that the more things change, the more they stay the same...

נח

NOACH

1 Guilt by Association

צַדִּיק תָּמִים הָיָה בְּדֹרֹתָיו וכו'.

He was perfectly righteous in his generations... (Bereishis 6:9)

⌣

Noach was a tzaddik, as the Torah clearly says about him. He earned many praiseworthy titles. Yet, there is one title that seems most appropriate to Noach, which seems to fit him perfectly—yet, he did not receive it!

We know that *Avraham Avinu* is called *Ivri*, "the one who passed to the other side." (Psikta Rabasi, 33)

עברי שכל העולם כולו לעבר אחד והוא היה לעבר אחר: (פסיקתא רבתי פרשה ל"ג)

This term implies that the whole world was on one side while he was on the other. What about Noach? If there was anyone in history who is perceived as standing up alone against an entire world, it was surely Noach. He should be described as *Ivri*. All of humanity was on one side and Noach on the other.

However, if the Torah does not call Noach by the title *Ivri*, there is a reason. In order to understand this point, we need to understand what the idea of *Ivri* really means. *Avraham Avinu* did not acquire this special distinction of *Ivri* just because he refrained from doing what everyone else did. He did much more than that; he created a unique environment for himself. *Avraham Avinu* extended his spiritual boundaries and surrounded himself with a force that protected him. This prevented him from being impacted, influenced or in any way "acculturated" by society around him.

In other words, *Avraham Avinu* did not merely do what was appropriate. He put up an impenetrable spiritual barrier around him. This enabled him to grow and develop, to become the first of the great *Avos* of the Jewish people. He totally refused to be impacted in any way by the world around him. For instance, he took immediate action to separate himself completely from Lot when he saw that Lot was not acting appropriately. *Avraham Avinu* did not waste any time with Lot. He said to him right away:

הלא כל־הארץ לפניך הפרד נא מעלי אם־השמאל ואימנה ואם־הימין ואשמאילה:

(בראשית י"ג:ט')

"Please separate from me. If to the left, I will go to the right. And if to the right, I will go to the left." (Bereishis 13:9)

Avraham Avinu did not allow himself to be in the proximity of evil if he felt this would have any sort of negative impact on him. Noach, on the other hand, was affected by the world at large. The Noach that we see at the beginning of the story is not the Noach that we see at the end. This is readily seen from the incident that took place when he left the *Teivah*.

Noach begins his relationship with Hashem with what is written at the end of *Parshas Bereishis*:

ונח מצא חן בעיני ה': (בראשית ו':ח')

Noach found favor in the eyes of Hashem. (Bereishis 6:8)

Noach acted according to Hashem's will. Therefore, he is described as perfectly righteous! At the same time, we cannot say that Noach was not impacted by the spiritual state of his generation because we find that when Noach comes out of the *Teivah*, right after building an altar and bringing offerings that pleased Hashem, he takes a respite.

Noach is now relieved of the strain he has been under all these years and has time to sit back and relax. He is not being challenged by anyone else around him. He does not have to stand strong to protect himself. Now, let us take a good look: What occurs to Noach when there is no one else around?

As the Torah says:

ויחל נח איש האדמה ויטע כרם: (בראשית ט':כ')

And Noach, who was a man of the earth, began to plant a vine-yard. (Bereishis 9:20)

The Torah tells us clearly: "*a man of the earth.*" Rashi (loc cit.) comments that Noach's choice to first plant a vineyard expressed a mundane (*chol*) approach. From an *Ish Elokim*, a man of G-d who spoke to Hashem and whom Hashem spoke to and instructed, from a perfect tzaddik, he devolved to "*a man of the earth.*" The aura of greatness, of *kedushah*, of holiness, leaves.

How did that happen? It could only have happened because Noach allowed his defenses to fall. He allowed a certain small amount of antediluvian influence to seep into the fibers of his being. However minute the amount was, he let it in. He allowed himself to be influenced by the generation that had preceded him, by the generation that had been destroyed — and that influence caused Noach to fall.

This is why Noach was not deserving of the title of *Ivri*. We cannot say unequivocally that he was on one side, while the entire world was on the other. For a certain part of him was still on their side, connected to the previous generation.

Avraham Avinu, however, distinguished himself by reaching out to idol worshippers on his own terms. Rather than go to their locale to pursue *kiruv*, he brought them in under *his* roof. In this way, he ensured that his contacts with the outside world were governed by *his* rules, protecting *his* values of propriety and holiness. This is what made *Avraham Avinu* the archetypal *Ivri*.

2 Opening the Floodgate

כִּי מֵי נֹחַ וכו'.

For these are the waters of Noach... (Yeshayahu 54:9)

⁓

We find that the name of Noach is associated with the *Mabul* – "the waters of Noach." This is generally viewed to his discredit, and is attributed to his failing to pray for the people of his generation.[9] However, this explanation presents the following problem.

When *Avraham Avinu* prayed for the people of Sedom, he is hailed as the paradigm of the tzaddik praying for his generation. He pleaded to Hashem to save Sedom if it contained fifty tzaddikim. When this request was granted, he proceeded to plead for Sedom even if it contained only ten tzaddikim. Yet, *Avraham Avinu* did not pray for Sedom if less than ten tzaddikim could be found there. Rashi explains:

אוּלַי יִמָּצְאוּן שָׁם עֲשָׂרָה. עַל פָּחוֹת לֹא בִּקֵּשׁ, אָמַר, דּוֹר הַמַּבּוּל הָיוּ שְׁמוֹנָה, נֹחַ וּבָנָיו וּנְשֵׁיהֶם, וְלֹא הִצִּילוּ עַל דּוֹרָם (ב"ר מט:יג). וְעַל תִּשְׁעָה עַל יְדֵי צֵרוּף כְּבָר בִּקֵּשׁ וְלֹא מָצָא:
(רש"י בראשית י"ח ל"ב)

For a smaller number he did not plead. He said to himself: "In the generation of the Mabul there were eight tzaddikim – Noach, his sons and wives – and they could not save their generation." (Bereishis Rabba 49:13). And for nine together with Hashem, he (Avraham) had already pleaded, but had not found acceptance. (Rashi, Bereishis 18:32)

Thus, we see that when *Avraham Avinu* considered Noach, he understood that his prayers would not have helped if there had been less than ten tzaddikim. Consequently, he did not daven for Sedom.

This is truly astounding! What then is the complaint against Noach?

---

9   עיין זוהר חלק א' דף ס"ז ע"ב

If *Avraham Avinu* did not daven for less than ten because he learned from Noach, how can Noach himself be criticized for not davening for his generation? After all, Noach did not have ten tzaddikim!

I would suggest that the objection to Noach's conduct was not that he failed to daven for the generation, but rather that he did not do enough to ensure that there would be a tenth person, to make prayer possible. In contrast, *Avraham Avinu* actively publicized the existence of Hashem and did everything in his power to bring others close to Him. Thus, he was not censured because Sedom lacked ten tzaddikim.

This now resolves one more issue.

Rashi comments on the verse of *"These are the generations of Noach. Noach was a tzaddik,"* (*Bereishis* 6:9) and he says:

למדך שעיקר תולדותיהם של צדיקים מעשים טובים: (רש"י בראשית ו:ט)

This teaches that the real progeny of tzaddikim are their good deeds. (Rashi, ibid.)

Rashi also comments, in *Parshas Mishpatim,* on the verse of *"And these are the judgments that you shall put before them,"* (*Shemos* 21:1) and he says:

כל מקום שנא' אלה פסל את הראשונים ואלה מוסיף על הראשונים מה הראשונים
מסיני אף אלו מסיני: (רש"י שמות כא:א')

Wherever the word "eileh" (these) is employed by the Torah, it serves to sever the previous section of text. Wherever "ve'eileh" (and these) is used, it adds something to the former section. (Rashi, ibid.)

Now, the Torah states at the end of *Parshas Bereishis*:

ויהי נח בן חמש מאות שנה ויולד נח את שם את חם ואת יפת: (בראשית ה:ל"ב)

Noach was five hundred years old; and he had Shem, Cham and Yefes. (Bereishis 5:32)

Thus, it would seem that *Parshas Noach* is a continuation of *Parshas Bereishis*. This being so, why does *Parshas Noach* not begin with the word *"ve'eileh,"* implying continuity?

When the Torah starts *Parshas Noach* with the word "*eileh,*" implying the beginning of a new topic, there is a significant lesson to be learned from the sequence of events. It is coming to instruct us that the "generations" of a person are only those actions or children who are an extension of the person himself and that continue to endure. However, the good deeds of the first six hundred years of Noach's life "drowned," so to speak, in the *Mabul*. The only "generations" of any significance that issued from Noach are those that he took into the *Teivah* with him and that lived on after the destruction. Thus, only "*eileh*" (these) are the true generations of Noach. (See also *Ohr HaChayim* on v. 6:9.)

Even with this explanation we still have the following problem. Ramban – (and, as the Ramban himself notes, Rashi brings a similar point with this view in 5:32) – makes the following observation:

ואלה תולדת בני־נח שם חם ויפת ויולדו להם בנים אחר המבול: (בראשית י"א)

And these are the generations of the sons of Noach, Shem, Cham and Yafes. And children were [first] born to them after the flood. (Bereishis 10:1)

וטעם ויולדו להם בנים אחר המבול לרמוז כי אף על פי שהיו ראוים לבנים קודם המבול, כי דרך הדורות ההם להוליד כבני ששים, אלו לא נולדו להם גם למאה רק אחר המבול, כי כבש השם את מעיינם שלא יולידו ויאבדו במבול, או שיצטרך להציל רבים בתיבה וכו'. (רמב"ן בראשית י"א)

The reason [for the emphasis] that "children were [first] born to them after the flood" is to allude that even though they were [physically] capable of having children before the flood, for the norm of those generations was to give birth in their sixties, [nonetheless,] they did not have children even at [the age of] one hundred. [They first had children] only after the flood. [The reason for this was because] Hashem restrained their faculties for reproducing in order that they not give birth to children only to be destroyed in the Mabul or in order [not] to trouble him (Noach) to save many more in the Teivah, etc. (Ramban, ibid., 10:1)

In light of what we said above, how can we understand this? If Noach would have fathered even one more righteous child, then there would have been the minimum ten tzaddikim and there would not have been a *Mabul* at all! So why does the Ramban (and Rashi based on *Midrash Rabba*) state that having more children would have forced Noach to save them all in the *Teivah*?

This issue requires further thought. *Tzarich iyun.*

3 Middah Kenegged Middah

W e know that one of the ways that Hashem conducts His world is to make the punishment fit the crime – middah kenegged middah ("measure for measure"). If the only purpose of this conduct is to impress upon us the justice of Hashem, then a person ought to be aware of this quality when he is punished.

However, it would seem otherwise. When the Creator acts *middah kenegged middah,* it is independent of and detached from the awareness of any created being. Rashi comments:

ביום הזה נבקעו כל־מעינות תהום רבה וארבת השמים נפתחו: (בראשית ז':י"א)

On that day, all the fountains of the great deep burst and the windows of heaven opened. (Bereishis 7:11)

מדה כנגד מדה, הם חטאו ב"רבה רעת האדם" (לעיל ו:ה) ולקו ב"תהום רבה": (רש"י שם)

This is middah kenegged middah: They had sinned with "great was the evil of man" (above, v. 6:5), therefore, they were punished by "the great deep." (Rashi, loc cit.)

Obviously, the victims of the *Mabul* could not have been aware of the method of destruction being wrought upon them. Certainly they were unaware that their punishment was a reflection of their crime and at this late juncture the significance of that fact would surely have been lost on them anyway. Thus, we learn from Rashi that Hashem's conduct is independent of man's knowledge or understanding.

4   Withheld Rain

וַיִּסָּכְרוּ מַעְיְנֹת תְּהוֹם וַאֲרֻבֹּת הַשָּׁמָיִם וַיִּכָּלֵא הַגֶּשֶׁם מִן הַשָּׁמָיִם:

And the fountains of the deep and the openings of heaven were sealed; and the rain was withheld from the heavens.
(Bereishis 8:2)

It states in verse 7:12 that the rain of the *Mabul* fell for forty days and nights. After this, we are informed (v. 7:24) that the waters grew stronger upon the earth for a hundred and fifty days. Therefore, it is understandable that the fountains of the deep were closed up after this latter period. What, though, does the Torah mean by "*the rain was withheld from the heavens?*" Surely, it had already stopped raining after the first forty days!

Perhaps the meaning is that it did not rain at all afterwards. During the course of the rest of the entire year, Hashem did not allow it to rain any longer and add any more water.

5   Lesheim Shamayim

First, Noach dispatched a raven, which proceeded to circle around the *Teivah*. Then he sent out a dove, which then returned. A week later, the dove was re-dispatched and it returned carrying an olive branch. Then Noach knew that the land was dry. He proceeded to take the roof off the *Teivah*. However, he did not leave the *Teivah*. Why? Because Hashem had not yet told him to leave.

If Noach was not permitted to depart from the *Teivah* until receiving Hashem's command, then what was the point of sending out the birds? What information did the dove provide that was of any significance or consequence? Surely, it was superfluous for Noach to know that the land was dry, since anyway he was not going to leave until he was instructed to do so.

The answer lies in the fact that Noach wanted his failure to leave the *Teivah* to be dependent solely on the Divine command. If he had not sent out the birds, it could be claimed that the reason he didn't leave was because of lack of knowledge; maybe he thought the floodwaters were still present or that the land was uninhabitable, making it impossible to leave. Thus, in order to ensure that his sitting in the *Teivah* was being done *lesheim Shamayim,* fulfilling the Divine mandate—rather than because of any personal agenda or bias—he had to *know* that the land was dry.

Once Noach knew the land was dry yet stayed inside, he had demonstrated his willingness to sit in the *Teivah* even if there had been no rain at all. What Hashem decrees, Noach obeys. In this way, it became retroactively apparent that his entire stay in the *Teivah* was solely in fulfillment of Hashem's will.

Perhaps this was a rectification for his failure to enter the *Teivah* in the beginning, when Hashem had instructed him to. At that time, he only entered when the waters drove him in. Thus, by waiting to leave the *Teivah* he demonstrated his obedience to Hashem, effectively correcting his mistake at the time of entering the *Teivah.*

(After resolving this question, I found that our great Rosh Yeshiva, Maran HaRav HaGaon Moshe Feinstein, *ztzvk"l.,* had given the same answer, as cited in the work *Kol Ram* by Rav Avraham Fishelis, *zatzal. Boruch shekivanti ledivrei Mori!*)

6 A Bris Made in Heaven

וַאֲנִי הִנְנִי מֵקִים אֶת בְּרִיתִי אִתְּכֶם וכו'.

I am establishing my covenant with you... (Bereishis 9:9)

After exiting the *Teivah*, Hashem makes a covenant with Noach and the entire Creation that He will never again bring a *Mabul* on the world. As confirmation of this covenant, Hashem set a rainbow in the sky.

Similarly, in *Parshas Lech Lecha*, Hashem makes an everlasting covenant with *Avraham Avinu*. What makes these two covenants qualitatively different?

First and foremost is the fact that the covenant with Noach is an entirely unilateral declaration. It is left entirely in Hashem's hands. Hence, it is entirely appropriate that Hashem puts the rainbow in the sky as an expression of this. In contrast, the covenant with *Avraham Avinu* requires input and action by man. We will suggest a reason for this.

There is a fundamental difference between *K'lal Yisrael* and non-Jews in terms of what they can achieve in this world. It is true that Hashem affirms the *Bais HaMikdash* as a place of gathering, prayer and offering for the whole world. As the verse states:

כי ביתי בית תפילה יקרא לכל־העמים: (ישעיהו נ"ו:ז')

For My house shall be called a house of prayer for all peoples.
(Yeshayahu 56:7)

Nevertheless, non-Jews are limited in what they can bring to the *Bais HaMikdash*. They may bring only the *olah* offering, which is entirely consumed on the *mizbey'ach*.

K'lal Yisrael, however, has the special privilege to also bring the *shelamim* offering. This "peace" offering is consumed by three: the Altar, the Kohen and the owner (i.e., the person who brought the offering). It is considered as if a person has merited eating from the table of Hashem because the person brings the offering to Hashem and then He shares it with him, so to speak.

Non-Jews cannot do this. For them, the spiritual is totally separated from the mundane. Once the offering is brought it is a completely spiritual entity and stays in the spiritual world. In contrast, *K'lal Yisrael* has the ability to take something in the physical realm and infuse it with holiness, even while it remains in the material world. They are able to be *mosif me'chol al hakodesh*, to take Shabbos and spread it out over part of Friday; to take Erev Yom Kippur and make it like Yom Kippur. This is a special quality of sanctifying everything we have, of creating a spiritual reality in *this* world.

When a Jew eats in order to derive strength for serving Hashem, he imbues the food with holiness. He eats from the physical world and thereby creates from it a spiritual entity.

This is one of the meanings of the *bris milah* of *Avraham Avinu*. It is an expression of sanctifying the *taivos*, the physical desires of this world. This extends even to those areas that are normally considered under the rule of the *yetzer hara*. Only *K'lal Yisrael* can take the *taivos* of the world and elevate all of them in the service of Hashem. This is what the Shema is telling us: A Jew must serve Hashem with "all your heart."

בכל לבבך – בשני יצרך: (רש״י דברים ו׳:ה׳ ע״פ ברכות נ״ד ע״א)

As Rashi states there (Devarim 6:5) from the Gemara (Brachos 54a), this means that one must serve Hashem with the *yetzer hara* as well as the *yetzer hatov*. A Jew takes something of *olam hazeh*, this world, and elevates it to something significant, as if it was in Heaven above.

Such a concept does not exist among non-Jews. On the contrary, as far as they are concerned, anything spiritual has to be under Hashem's exclusive direction – and it has to stay there. Therefore, the only offering that they are capable of bringing is the *olah*—an exclusively spiritual offering dedicated entirely to the Altar. So it was with the symbol of the covenant that Hashem made with Noach and the entire world. It was a covenant restricted to the spiritual domain alone, fittingly symbolized by a rainbow, a creation of Hashem in the sky above.

In startling contrast is the symbol of the covenant that Hashem made with *K'lal Yisrael*. The *bris milah* of *Avraham Avinu* represents a creation of spirituality in this world, and its sign is sealed in the flesh. This represents a much higher accomplishment, one that is exclusive to *K'lal Yisrael*. It is an act of creation performed by a human being! The entire concept of *bris milah* is the elevation of the physical to the spiritual, the re-creation of something in this world into a spiritual existence.

Don't Even Look

וַיִּטַּע כָּרֶם... וַיֵּשְׁתְּ מִן הַיַּיִן וַיִּשְׁכָּר:

He planted a vineyard...drank from the wine and became drunk. (Bereishis 9:20–21)

The Gemara tells us the following:

כל הרואה סוטה בקלקולה יזיר עצמו מן היין: (נזיר ב' ע"א)

Anyone who sees a sotah in her disgrace should take a vow of abstinence from wine. (Nazir 2a)

This teaching of *Chazal* is puzzling. When one sees a *sotah* subjected to such a horribly disgraceful ordeal, this ought to be enough deterrent for anyone who might harbor the wrong ideas. So why is one also required to separate from wine in order to avoid these possible deleterious effects?

It is clear from here that a negative impact is made on a person who sees someone else who has transgressed, and this impact remains even after the person sees them punished for that transgression! This finds expression in the incident of Amalek.

When Amalek attacked *K'lal Yisrael* after leaving Egypt, we are told that he cooled off from the notion that *K'lal Yisrael* was invincible from attack. The expected reaction by the nations of the world should have been: "How could anyone do such an abhorrent act, to attack the people of Hashem?" The ensuing defeat of Amalek should certainly have reinforced the deterrent. Instead, we find that their witnessing Amalek's initial attack (regardless of Amalek's subsequent loss in battle) actually strengthened the resolve of the nations to transgress Hashem's will and harm Israel.

From this perspective we can understand the Torah's criticism of Noach that his first act upon exiting the *Teivah* was to plant a vineyard.

Noach had survived the *Mabul.* He had been a witness to Hashem's destruction of all Creation, as punishment for their improper conduct. One would have expected that this would have made a sufficient impression on Noach. He ought to have carried this staggering vision of punishment with him at all times, distancing him far from any transgression.

Yet, *Chazal* teach us differently: "Anyone who sees a *sotah* in her disgrace should take a vow of abstinence from wine." As great as Noach was, he did not practice this principle. After leaving the *Teivah,* the first thing he planted was a vine and the first thing he drank was the intoxicating wine from those grapes, in spite of its known effects. He violated the rule that "one should take a vow of abstinence from wine" when seeing transgressions of immorality—and he suffered the ignomy that followed.[10]

8 What Happened to Put?

ואלה תולדת בני־נח שם חם ויפת וכו'. בני יפת גמר וכו'. ובני גמר אשכנז וכו'.

(בראשית י':א'-ג')

These are the progeny of the sons of Noach – Shem, Cham and Yefes... The sons of Yefes: Gomer... And the sons of Gomer: Ashkenaz... (Bereishis 10:1-3)

ובני חם כוש ומצרים ופוט וכנען: (בראשית י':ו')

And the sons of Cham: Cush, Mitzrayim, Put and Canaan. (Bereishis 10:6)

From the Mishnah (*Negaim* 2:1), we learn about the various races of humanity. The Mishnah mentions that Germanic peoples, whom we call Caucasians, are white. Since Ashkenaz, or Germany, is a son of Gomer, we may deduce that white skin is a characteristic of Yefes, progenitor of the so-called Greek and Aryan nations. We know that from Cham issued the black

---

10 Subsequently I discovered an allusion to this idea in the Ramban (*Bereishis* 9:26) בא״ד ונכתב ענין היין בנח

people of Africa. The Mishnah tells us that the Semitic people, those coming from Shem, have a skin color that is in-between the two extremes.

This presents us with a question: From whom descended the Orientals of the Mongoloid race: the Chinese, Japanese, Koreans and so on? To answer, perhaps we could make a deduction from a seeming anomaly.

We find that the Torah (ibid., 10:6-18) lists the children of Cham and then delineates their generations, who are the descendants of Mitzraim, Cush and Canaan. Noticeably absent are the descendants of Put, who was the third son of Cham.

We might conclude that Put had no children. However, this cannot be, for in *Yechezkel*, Chapter 38, we find that Put is listed among the nations that Gog and Magog will gather for war at the end of days. Put certainly must have had children, since he personally can't possibly have lived from Noach's time until the days of Gog and Magog. Thus, we must conclude that the Torah does not list the children of Put, as for some reason it is not relevant.

Indeed, the *Seforno* addresses this issue in his commentary on the Torah:

לא הזכיר בני פוט כי היו כל בניו לגוי אחד נקרא על שמו כאמרו (יחזקאל ל"ח:ה') פרס
כוש ופוט אתם: (ספורנו בראשית י':ו')

Put's children are not mentioned because all his children formed one people that were called by his name, as it states (Yechezkel 38:5): "Among them shall be Persia, Cush and Put." (Seforno, v. 10:6)

I would propose that the Oriental peoples are, in fact, the descendants of Put, and the reason that the Torah does not discuss them is because they did not live in the ancient world of *K'lal Yisrael*. It was not until modern times that they became integrated into the Western world, now playing out their present role in the world scheme until messianic times. Whenever the final war of Gog and Magog will take place, the Japanese, Chinese and Koreans will all take part in the battle against *K'lal Yisrael* and will be defeated.[11]

Subsequently, I saw that the Ramban was similarly puzzled by the disappearance of Put. He gave the following explanation, according to *peshat* and *derush*:

ובני כוש סבא וחוילה היו אלה ראשי אומות, ובני רעמה היו שני לאומים, אבל נמרוד
לא היה לאום, על כן כתב אחר כך וכוש ילד את נמרוד, ולא אמר "ובני כוש נמרוד
וסבא וחוילה:

Seva and Chavilah, the sons of Cush, were heads of nations.
The sons of Ra'amah became two peoples. Nimrod, however,
did not found a separate people. Therefore, the verse states
afterwards that Cush fathered Nimrod; it did not state (in the
previous verse): "The sons of Cush: Nimrod, Seva, Chavilah,
"...[[Savtah, Ra'amah and Savtecha

אבל פוט היה לגוי אחד ולא היו ממנו אומות שונות כמצרים וכנען, על כן לא החזירו
הכתוב. ובבראשית רבה (ל"ז:ב') אמר ריש לקיש היינו סבורים שנבלעה משפחתו של
פוט, ובא יחזקאל ופירש, פוט ולוד וכל הערב וכו'. (יחזקאל ל':ה')

But Put was one nation. Different nations did not form from him
in the same way as with Mitzrayim and Canaan. Therefore, the
verse did not speak of his [descendants]. And in Bereishis Rabba
(37:2) it states: "Reish Lakish said: We would have thought that
the family of Put petered out. However, Yechezkel came and
explained (v. 30:5): 'Cush and Put, and Lud, and all who support
her...'"

כי מפני שלא החזירו הכתוב היינו סבורים שנתערב זרעו בבני כנען, ולא היו אומה
ולא ירשו להם ארץ שתקרא על שמם אבל גם במגוג ומדי ותובל ומשך ותירס בני
יפת לא הזכיר משפחות בתולדותם, וכן בבני שם עילם ואשור וארפכשד ולוד, ראשי
אומות, ולא הזכיר להם תולדות, כי כל אחד היה לגוי אחד בארץ ולא הוליד אומות
שונות: (רמב"ן בראשית י':ו')

Since the verse did not go back [to relate the genealogy of Put], we
would have thought that his (Put's) children became assimilated
with Canaan. We would have supposed that they did not become
a people and did not inherit a land of their own. But [the truth is
that] there was similarly no mention of the family genealogy of
the sons of Yefes — Magog, Maddai, Tuval, Meshech and Tiras.

---

11   Interestingly, Rav Aharon Marcus in Keses Hasofer conjectures that the descendants of Magog, one
of the children of Yefes, may be identified with the Mongol people who lived near China. (Cited in the
ArtScroll Gemara, Yoma Daf 10a, end of note 6.)

Similarly, the sons of Shem – Eilam, Ashur, Arpachshad and Lud – all founded nations, but no mention is made of their genealogy. For each one was a separate nation in the land, rather than giving rise to different nations. (Ramban, Bereishis 10:7)

Perhaps this was also the intent of *Seforno*.

9 Paganism in the Far East

There is another point that needs clarifying in regard to the Oriental people inhabiting the Far East and South Asia. How is it that their religions have such a strong history of pagan metaphysics, holding views that are entirely contrary to Torah belief?

Perhaps this striking anomaly can be explained by way of Rashi's comment in *Parshas Chayei Sarah*:

ולבני הפילגשים אשר לאברהם נתן אברהם מתנת וישלחם מעל יצחק בנו בעודנו חי קדמה אל־ארץ קדם: (בראשית כ"ה:ו')

And to the sons of the concubine that Avraham had, Avraham gave gifts. And he sent them away from his son Yitzchok while he was still alive, eastward, to the land of the east. (Bereishis 25:6)

פרשו רבותינו, שם טמאה מסר להם: (רש"י שם)

Our Sages explained that he transmitted to them the names of impure things. (Rashi, ibid.)

From this we see that *Avraham Avinu* gave them the metaphysical know-how that eventually led to their pervasive knowledge of *kochos hatumah*, impure forces. This knowledge (in its present, greatly degenerated form) continues to permeate that entire region to the east.

10 The Significance of Aramaic

Sefer Daniel and Sefer Ezra are written in Aramaic. Basic Jewish texts such as the Talmud and the Zohar, as well as parts of the tefillah, are written and learnt in Aramaic. This language continues to occupy a central place in Jewish life. How did Aramaic acquire this distinction?

Another astonishing fact is that the written form of our Hebrew letters, the *kesav* that appears in the *Sefer Torah*, is known as "Assyrian script," or *kesav Ashuris*. Why is it not termed Hebrew script, *kesav Ivri* or *kesav Yisraeli*?

The Gemara discusses this latter point:

למה נקרא אשורית, שעלה עמהם מאשור וכו'. למה נקרא שמה אשורית, שמאושרת
בכתב. (סנהדרין כ"ב ע"א)

Why [is the form of the Hebrew letters] termed Ashuris? Because it came up with them from Ashur (Assyria or Babylon)... Why is its name Ashuris? Because it is rich (ashir) in form. (Sanhedrin 22a)

From the Gemara's first answer it would seem that the ancient Assyrians actually wrote in *kesav Ashuris*. Historically speaking, we find corroboration of this and of the fact that the language in use at that time was Aramaic. A Jew can actually read and understand ancient artifacts found from that period. So how are we to explain the adoption of the Assyrian *kesav, Ashuris*, by *K'lal Yisrael,* to the extent that we even use it to write the *Sefer Torah*?

The answer is found in the Torah's discussion of the children of Cham. In the middle of the narrative we are told (*Bereishis* 10:11) that Ashur left and built Nineveh. Rashi explains that Ashur departed from the area because he saw his sons heeding Nimrod, the king of Bavel, and building the Tower of Bavel in rebellion against Hashem.

Let us examine this. The language that everyone spoke before the Tower of Bavel was *lashon hakodesh*, Hebrew. Now, it is known that when you have many different kinds of people speaking the same language, spread out over large areas, the language inevitably changes, developing into different dialects.

Thus, *lehavdil*, the English spoken in America is not identical to that of Australia or South Africa or England. Variations occur not only in accents, but also in vocabulary and usage of words. We could assume the same was true of *lashon hakodesh* when it served as the vernacular of all nations.

Indeed, *lashon hakodesh* was the language with which the world was created. However, with the different groups of people that formed after Noach came out the *Teivah,* split up into many different areas, it stands to reason that variations of the language arose. Thus, Aramaic developed as a parallel to the pure, original *lashon hakodesh.* It follows the same grammar, and has parallel words with certain letters changing consistently with others.

Similarly, the form of the *kesav* in use before the Tower of Bavel was the same as that which Hashem used to create the world.

Thus, we may venture to say that Ashur preserved Aramaic, along with the original *kesav,* when he wisely chose to part ways with the wicked Bavel of Nimrod, before the tower was built and, more importantly, before the seventy languages of the world came into being. Therefore, as a reward for this, the *kesav* we use continues to bear his name, *kesav Ashuris.*

Aramaic was thus preserved by Ashur as a national language with its original national *kesav.* This is how Aramaic became the language of the Chaldeans, the language of both Bavel and Ashur. Consequently, *Avraham Avinu,* who came from *Ur Kasdim* (*Ur* of the "Chaldeans"), knew the language of Aramaic. He also knew the *kesav* of *lashon hakodesh* as we have it today. Perhaps he received *lashon hakodesh* directly from Noach, or perhaps after his first prophesy from Hashem.

Chazal say, cited by Rashi:

אלה תולדות האדם בהבראם (בראשית ב':ד')

These are the products of the heaven and the earth בהבראם *(when they were created). (Bereishis 2:4)*

בה' בראם שנאמר "בקה ה' צור עולמים" (ישעיה כו:ד) וכו'. ולמדך כאן שהעולם הזה נברא בהֵ"א: (רש"י שם)

This means that with the letter ה*, He (Hashem) created the world. As it states: For the L-rd (kah) G-d is an eternal Rock.*

(Isaiah 26:4)...and it teaches here that this world was created with a ה. *(Rashi, ibid.)*

According to what we have explained, this ה was of *kesav Ashuris*.

In summary: *Avraham Avinu* preserved *lashon hakodesh* in its original form, and became the ancestor of *K'lal Yisrael*. Aramaic has *kedushah*, sanctity, because it was a dialect of *lashon hakodesh,* pre-dating the Tower of Bavel. *Kesav Ashuris* is our *kesav* because the world was created with it. It is called *kesav Ashuris,* after that act of courage performed by Ashur when he left Bavel and its wickedness.

לֶךְ לְךָ

LECH LECHA

1 Not Everything is as It Seems

There are two great lessons to be learnt from the travels of *Avraham Avinu* to Egypt. First, we see that an occurrence that appears negative might in reality not be so. Second, an occurrence that appears quite good and positive might not turn out to be for our benefit in the long term.

When *Avraham Avinu* came to *Eretz Yisrael*, he was almost immediately forced to go to Egypt. This was one of his ten trials, and it must have appeared to him as something very negative. However, as events unfolded, we see that what originally appeared to be detrimental turned out to be extraordinarily good. His fears of what would occur never materialized because Hashem protected him. In fact, his departure for Egypt set the stage for him to become a wealthy man. He was greatly respected and honored amongst the Canaanites because of the great wealth he accrued in Egypt. In addition, when Avraham went to Egypt, he prepared *K'lal Yisrael*, of the future, for their journey there. This is the great principle of *"ma'aseh avos siman lebanim."* The acts of the *Avos,* the Patriarchs, served to set the pattern of events for their descendants, *K'lal Yisrael*.

The same holds true with *K'lal Yisrael* going down into Egypt. This seemingly negative event was actually the prerequisite for *K'lal Yisrael* receiving the Torah and taking possession of *Eretz Yisrael*. As the verse states, Egypt was the "iron crucible" for forging the people as a nation; it is called the *kur habarzel* (*Devarim* 4:20) of *K'lal Yisrael*. The Midrash refers to the servitude

69

in Egypt as a *shtar chov,* a document of debt, that *K'lal Yisrael* had to pay before receiving *Eretz Yisrael* (Rashi *Bamidbar* 20:14, based on *Bereishis Rabba* 83:13). Eisav rejected the responsibility for paying this *shtar chov* and thereby relinquished his claim to *Eretz Yisrael.*

We see that the servitude and suffering in Egypt emerged in the long term as something very positive for us. This was not at all apparent at the time, for it was an extraordinarily difficult ordeal. While *K'lal Yisrael* was experiencing it, they likely had no idea of the purpose of their tremendous persecution, pain and anguish. Nevertheless, it turned out for *K'lal Yisrael* to be quite a positive process.

What about the second lesson, that an occurrence that appears quite good and positive might not turn out to be for our benefit in the long term? The good that *Avraham Avinu* received by going to Egypt appears to have had quite a negative consequence in the end. Included in the wealth was Hagar, the daughter of Pharaoh (Rashi, *Bereishis* 16:1), who came as a maidservant and from whom issued Yishmael.

If *Avraham Avinu* would not have gone to Egypt, he never would have received the wealth he never would have married Hagar and he never would have fathered Yishmael. Thus, his Egyptian wealth turned out to be quite problematic in the long term for *K'lal Yisrael*, something that we are paying for until this very day.

This can be seen regarding Lot as well. Lot went down to Egypt along with *Avraham Avinu* and consequently became wealthy. Rashi (ibid., 13:5) tells us that this wealth was granted to him by Heaven, in the merit of *Avraham Avinu.* Nevertheless, the wealth that Lot received turned out to be his downfall. It was because of that wealth that he developed pride and chose to leave *Avraham Avinu,* ending up in Sedom. This brought about his destruction. Besides being taken captive by the Four Kings, Lot suffered serious spiritual consequences as a result of moving to Sedom. As Rashi states (ibid., *v. 11*), Lot was cut off "*miKadmono shel olam,*" from Hashem, as it were. If not for his Egyptian wealth, he would have stayed with *Avraham Avinu,* and who knows what great things could have developed.

What, then, could be the positive assessment of this episode? It is that Lot's destruction when he left for Sedom actually accomplished a tremendous boon for *K'lal Yisrael* because it was in Sedom (of all places) that the *Mashiach's* holy origin was to be found. From the ashes of Sedom came Ammon and Moav (born from Lot's daughters, conceived immediately after they escaped the overturning of Sedom) and from Ammon and Moav came Rus the Moabite and Na'amah the Ammonite. From all this, *K'lal Yisrael* received the *Mashiach*, born in the sovereign line of the House of Dovid. So what appeared to be overwhelmingly negative for Lot turned out to be quite positive for *K'lal Yisrael*. The House of Dovid and its eternal sovereignty came into being due to Lot's descent to Sedom.

2 Unquestioning Belief

It is important for us to understand and analyze where lay the test for *Avraham Avinu* in going to Egypt. Surely, it was a hard situation for him when he came to *Eretz Yisrael* and the famine immediately forced him to leave for Egypt. However, this seems to pale in comparison to the test of *Kiddush Hashem* that preceded his arrival in *Eretz Yisrael*. Then, *Avraham Avinu* unflinchingly stood up for his values and his faith in the Creator, against both his father and King Nimrod, and endured great suffering when he was ready to give up his very life in the fires of Ur Kasdim. Why would that great test be followed by what appears to be a smaller test?

Let us look more closely at this test of the famine. Certainly, it created a situation where *Avraham Avinu* could have questioned Hashem's motives. After all, Hashem had promised him *Eretz Yisrael* and then forced him to go down to Egypt (a poor substitute to be sure).

Yet, it seems there was a much greater objective to this test. In it, we find a Divine design to show to what an extent *Avraham Avinu* excelled in his unquestioning acceptance of Hashem's actions. The adversity expressed in this test was a striking assessment of the greatness of *Avraham Avinu*, and of his willingness to accept Hashem's *gezeiros*. What Hashem decreed, Avraham accepted unquestioningly.

For here, it was not a test solely for *Avraham Avinu*. Although people are often willing to take the extreme step of sacrificing themselves to sanctify Hashem's Name, it is different when it comes to sacrificing other members of their family. Then the equation changes. Going down to Egypt was not just a danger for *Avraham Avinu*. It entailed a significant danger for Sarah, the likelihood of the righteous Sarah being taken to the palace of Pharaoh and subjected to the worst type of humiliation. *Avraham Avinu* understood this as he was going down. That is why he set up the whole system of "*say that you are my sister,*" since he understood what awaited them in Egypt. He recognized the dangers that existed for both of them, which came very close to being realized.

Thus, we see that the test of *Avraham Avinu* going down to Egypt was extraordinarily great. Although he was previously found willing to give up his own life, he now demonstrated that his mind-set of "not questioning the actions of Hashem" was absolute. It would not have been surprising at all if Avraham *would* have questioned the Creator and said, "Hashem! It is one thing that I am not found worthy. I understand that You are treating me harshly, but my righteous wife Sarah — why is she being subjected to dangers that are surely not befitting her?" Nevertheless, *Avraham Avinu* accepted the Heavenly decree. He went down to Egypt without question.

As *Avraham Avinu*'s trials moved up from one level to the next, the final and ultimate test was the *Akeidah*, the Binding of Yitzchok. Here, even after *Avraham Avinu* showed his willingness to give up his own life and risk his wife's, too, the challenge became giving over his *own child* to sure death — and not just that, but the father himself must perform the act of slaughter. That was the ultimate test.

To reach the level of this tenth and final test of the *Akeidah*, it was necessary that *Avraham Avinu* first go through the test of the famine, in which his wife was put into danger. He grew from level to level in accepting the Creator's decree.

3

Go West

The Torah's account of the return of *Avraham Avinu* from Egypt presents us with a problem:

וילך למסעיו מנגב ועד בית־אל עד המקום אשר היה שם אהלה בתחלה, בין בית־אל
ובין העי: (בראשית י"ג:ג')

And he went on his journeys from the south to Bais El, to the place where his tent had been previously, between Bais El and Ai. (Bereishis 13:3)

Looking at a map of *Eretz Yisrael*, it is very clear that in order to travel from the area of Bais El to Sedom and Amorah, located in the plain that is now the Dead Sea, one must travel east. In fact, if you are going to travel to the Dead Sea from *anywhere* in *Eretz Yisrael,* you would not be traveling west. Sedom was somewhere near the border formed by the Jordan river, which feeds into the Dead Sea. So wherever Sedom, Amorah, Admah and Tzvoyim were, that entire area would have been south-east of wherever *Avraham Avinu* was. Of course, Bais El and Ai are north-west of that area.

This is fine until we get to the account of the fight that broke out between the shepherds of Lot and those of *Avraham Avinu*. Avraham tells Lot to make a decision where to go. The verse tells us:

ויבחר לו לוט את כל ככר הירדן ויסע לוט מקדם וכו'. (בראשית י"ג:י"א)

Lot chose for himself the entire Jordan plain... (he) traveled from the east. (Bereishis 13:11)

Assuming that *mikedem* means *from the east,* we are left with a perplexing problem. How could Lot have traveled from the east? Surely, at that time he was located to the west of the Jordan River valley!

Rashi gives two explanations of this verse, the first of which is quite difficult. He says that Lot actually traveled west. The *Sifsei Chachamim* cites the *Mizrachi* as asking the question we have, without offering an answer. The *Sifsei Chachamim* also cites the *Divrei Dovid* as saying that Lot first traveled west because he was too embarrassed for Avraham to know that he was actually headed for the ill-reputed Sedom.

Even with the *Divrei Dovid,* this first explanation of Rashi remains problematic. For we find earlier:

ויעתק משם ההרה מקדם לבית־אל: (בראשית י"ב:ח')

He (Avraham) moved on to the mountain east of Bais El. (v. 12:8)

Here, Rashi explains it simply:

מִקֶּדֶם לבית אל. במזרחה של בית אל, נמצאת בית אל במערבו וכו'. (רש"י י"ב:ח')

"To the east of Bais El." Thus, Bais El lay to his west... (Rashi, 12:8)

We are therefore left with the additional problem as to why Rashi would change the later explanation, in the story of Lot leaving *Avraham Avinu,* from its simple meaning of **to the east.** For the present, we must leave this question unanswered. *Tzarich iyun.*

Nevertheless, we can see how the second explanation of Rashi (v. 13:11) fully resolves the problem by redefining what *"kedem"* (ostensibly "east") actually means in our context.

הסיע עצמו מקדמונו של עולם אמר אי אפשי לא באברם ולא באלקיו (רש"י י"ג:י"א)

The Torah is alluding to us that Lot wandered away from "the Kadmono (Originator) of the world, saying: 'I do not want Avraham or his G-d.'"

Let us explain further what Lot did, and the meaning of distancing "from the *Kadmono* of the world."

If we look earlier in *Parshas Bereishis,* we find that when Hashem created Gan Eden the verse says (*Bereishis* 2:8) that He planted it in Eden *"mikedem."* Rashi explains *mikedem* exactly the way we would have expected: "In (or to) the *east* of Eden He planted the Garden." Clearly, the implication is that Eden is where Hashem resides, so to speak. For *Chazal* tell us that the Shechinah resides in the west (*Bava Basra* 25a) and that is where we find the *Kodesh HaKodoshim,* the Holy of Holies, in the Sanctuary and first and second Temples. Thus, Gan

Eden is slightly away from the place of the Shechinah and it is located to the east, for when one moves away from the Shechinah, one moves eastwards.

Similarly, when *Adam HaRishon* is driven from Gan Eden, the Torah tells us the following:

וַיֹּאמֶר ה' אֱלֹקִים הֵן הָאָדָם הָיָה כְּאַחַד מִמֶּנּוּ וְכוּ'. וַיְשַׁלְּחֵהוּ ה' אֱלֹקִים מִגַּן עֵדֶן וְכוּ'.
וַיְגָרֶשׁ אֶת הָאָדָם וַיַּשְׁכֵּן מִקֶּדֶם לְגַן עֵדֶן: (בראשית ג':כ"ב-כ"ד)

"Hashem said: 'Adam has now become like one of us...' And Hashem banished him (Adam) from Gan Eden... He drove Adam away and stationed at mikedem (east of) Gan Eden..." (Bereishis 3:22–24)

בְּמִזְרָחוֹ שֶׁל גַּן עֵדֶן חוּץ לַגָּן: (רש"י שם)

Eastward of Gan Eden, outside the Garden. (Rashi, ad loc.)

Further on we find:

וַיֵּצֵא קַיִן מִלִּפְנֵי ה' וַיֵּשֶׁב בְּאֶרֶץ־נוֹד קִדְמַת־עֵדֶן: (בראשית ד':ט"ז)

And Kayin went away from Hashem's presence and settled in the land of Nod, kidmas (east of) Eden. (Bereishis 4:16)

קִדְמַת עֵדֶן. שָׁם גָּלָה אָבִיו כְּשֶׁגֹּרַשׁ מִגַּן עֵדֶן, שֶׁנֶּאֱמַר (לעיל ג:כד) וַיַּשְׁכֵּן מִקֶּדֶם לְגַן עֵדֶן
לִשְׁמֹר אֶת שְׁמִירַת דֶּרֶךְ מְבוֹא הַגָּן, שֶׁיֵּשׁ לִלְמֹד שֶׁהָיָה אָדָם שָׁם, וְכוּ'. (רש"י שם)

"Kidmas Eden" – His father (Adam) was exiled there when he was banished from Gan Eden. As it says (v. 3:24): "And He (Hashem) stationed in the east of Gan Eden" a guard on the road that leads to the entrance of the Garden. [And from this] one may learn that Adam was there [in the east]. (Rashi, ad loc.)

Again, when the Torah describes the banishing of Kayin, we find him settling east of Eden.

On the surface, all of this is perplexing. Rashi is informing us that Kayin now settles near to where his father, Adam, had settled upon being banished from Gan Eden. But where had Kayin been living before this? Surely, if it is important to know where he is living now, then why were we not told where he was living previously? Why was he not living in close proximity to his parents before? Why did he move close to them now? What relevance does all of this have?

Here, too, the verse is telling us not about where Kayin resides physically, but rather his spiritual condition. Until now, Kayin was the man born in Gan Eden who still retained his great spiritual stature of Adam before the sin. Now, after killing his brother Hevel, he, too, finds himself driven away from the Shechinah. He is driven away from the west, arriving at the very place where his father found himself. Kayin, too, is expelled *mikedem* of Gan Eden.

Thus, we see that *mikedem* or movement to *mizrach,* "east," means to be further removed from Hashem. Similarly, the place of the Shechinah was in the tent of *Avraham Avinu,* as the Ramban explains in the beginning of *Shemos* that the tents of the *Avos* and *Imahos* were the places of the Shechinah. They were the "Tabernacle" of that period.

Rashi is explaining a vitally critical and fundamental point. The Torah is not just informing us of Lot's geographical location. Rather, when Lot chose to move away from *Avraham Avinu* and move to Sedom, he moved *mikedem* – further away from Hashem, the *Kadmono* of the world.

(As we mentioned earlier, in verse 12:8 we find *Avraham Avinu* traveling through *Eretz Canaan,* and it says "*He moved on to the mountain mikedem [east of] Bais El.*" As we pointed out, Rashi says that *mikedem* is "to the east of Bais El." It has to mean *to* the east because we find that it then says "having Bais El on the west." Thus, if he went *mikedem* of Bais El, they had to be traveling east in order that Bais El should be west of wherever he was. Further it says, "*and Ai mikedem [to the east].*" Again, *mikedem* must mean *to* the east, not *from* the east, since the Torah is pinpointing Avraham's location somewhere between Bais El and Ai. It is interesting to note that here, unlike the other places where it says *mikedem,* the *Targum* actually uses the word ממדנח, meaning *mizrach,* east, rather than מלקדמן, the wording meaning *mikedem,* which is used in other places. Yet, Rashi in his first, simple explanation [loc. cit., 13:11] says that *mikedem* means *from* the east, not *to* the east.)

Similarly, we find the following concerning the generation of the Tower of Bavel:

ויהי כל־הארץ שפה אחת ודברים אחדים: ויהי בנסעם מקדם וימצאו בקעה בארץ
שנער וישבו שם: (בראשית י"א:א'-ב')

"And the entire earth had one language with uniform words. And it happened that when they journeyed mikedem (from the

east), they found a valley in the land of Shinar and they settled there." (Bereishis 11:1–2)

Once again, this is a reference to their distancing themselves from Hashem, rather than their geographical movement.

Based on the model we have presented, we can understand the significance and intent of how the Israelites encamped at Mount Sinai.

ויבאו מדבר סיני ויחנו במדבר ויחן־שם ישראל נגד ההר: (שמות י"ט:ב')

And they (the Israelites) came to the Sinai desert and they encamped across from (neged) the mountain. (Shemos 19:2)

Rashi explains what it means to encamp *neged* the mountain:

למזרחו, וכל מקום שאתה מוצא "נגד" פנים למזרח: (רש"י שם)

To the east [i.e., facing west]. Whenever you find [the word] neged, it is [across from one] facing east. (Rashi, ad loc.)

Why is this important to know? Again, the answer is that the Shechinah is in the west. The Israelites did not encamp in a vacant mountain in the desolate Sinai wilderness, but rather they faced the mountain that was to host the presence of the Shechinah.

In *Parshas Terumah* we find "east" in connection with the *Mishkan*.

ורחב החצר לפאת קדמה מזרחה וכו'. (שמות כ"ז:י"ג)

The width of the Courtyard at the front side, to the east (keidmah mizrachah)... (Shemos 27:13)

Here again, Rashi goes out of his way to explain the exact directions:

פני המזרח. קדם לשון פנים. אחור לשון אחורים. לפיכך המזרח קרוי קדם שהוא פנים, ומערב קרוי אחור וכו'. (רש"י שם)

[It means to] the face of the east. Kedem means face and achor means the rear. Therefore, the east is called kedem because it is the front, and the west is called achor (rear)... (Rashi, ad loc.)

In *Parshas Bamidbar* we also find:

והחנים קדמה מזרחה: (במדבר ב':ג')

"And they shall encamp keidmah mizrachah." (Bamidbar 2:3)

קדמה. לפנים הקרויה קדם, ואיזו, זו רוח מזרחית, והמערב קרוי אחור: (רש"י במדבר ב':ג')

"Keidmah" – In front is termed kedem. And which side is this? The mizrach (east) side. And [correspondingly], the ma'arav (west) is termed achor, the back. (Rashi, ad loc.)

Here we see that *mizrach* is the front and *ma'arav* is the back. How are we to understand this, in light of the fact that *mikedem* is moving away from the Shechinah and *ma'arav* is the place of the Shechinah?

We can understand it as follows: When we experience and perceive the Shechinah "in the west," we are always to the east, in front of the Shechinah. Correspondingly, the perspective of *mikedem* is from the perspective of Hashem and it is in front of Him, so to speak. West, from the perspective of the King on His Throne, as it were, is behind the throne.

4   Eretz Canaan

It is surely puzzling why *Eretz Yisrael* is called *Eretz Canaan* throughout the Torah. It is given this perplexing title out of context to the situations and circumstances being discussed. Furthermore, throughout *Bamidbar* and *Devarim* where we find *Eretz Yisrael* described, all of the seven Canaanite people are enumerated by name, as if they have some sort of special significance.

What is the reason that the Canaanites have to be mentioned so frequently and why is the Holy Land referred to as *Eretz Canaan*?

Let us consider these nations at the time when Lot separated from *Avraham Avinu*. The verses say:

ויסע לוט מקדם ויפרדו איש מעל אחיו. אברם ישב בארץ כנען ולוט ישב בערי הככר

ויאהל עד סדם: (בראשית י"ג:י"א,י"ב)

And Lot journeyed eastwards and they parted from each other.
Avram lived in the land of Canaan, while Lot dwelt in the cities
of the plain, pitching his tent towards Sedom. (Bereishis 13:11–12)

It seems misleading to say that Avraham lived in *Eretz Canaan*, while Lot went to live in the cities of the plain. Surely, the plain containing Sedom and Amorah is also part of *Eretz Canaan*!

The *Seforno* addresses this. He says that even though Sedom and its sister cities are part of the territory of Canaan, nevertheless the inhabitants were not Canaanites. He goes on to explain:

אז אמר אם כן שאברם בחר לשבת באותו החלק מן הארץ שהיו יושבים בו בני כנען
שלא היו כל כך רעים כאנשי סדום ולא קרב לגבול סדום כלל: (ספורנו בראשית י"ג:י"ב)

Thus, it tells us that Avram chose to settle in that part of the land where the Canaanites lived, since they were not as wicked as the inhabitants of Sedom. He did not come close to the environs of Sedom. (Seforno, Bereishis 13:12)

It seems that the people of Sedom and Amorah were actually descendents of Shem. This can be deduced from Rashi elsewhere, who comments that, at that time, the Canaanites were taking over the land that had originally belonged to Shem. As the verse says:

והכנעני אז בארץ: (בראשית י"ב:ו')

"And the Canaanite lived then in the land." (Bereishis 12:6)

היה הולך וכובש את ארץ ישראל מזרע של שם: (רש"י שם)

They were progressively conquering Eretz Yisrael from the descendants of Shem. (Rashi, ad loc.)

Indeed, Canaanite culture was extraordinarily evil, compared by the Torah to Egypt. When Hashem warns us not to learn from their evil ways, both these nations stand out in terms of their corrupt, deviant culture. (See *Vayikra* 18:3, Rashi, loc. cit.) Still, the Canaanites were not as bad as Sedom and Amorah. Even the Canaanites had moral qualms about what was transpiring in the Jordan River plain, and they separated themselves from the people and culture of Sedom. We see clearly that only Sedom was destroyed, not the rest of Canaan.

Only the inhabitants of Sedom were so extraordinarily evil that they "merited" being destroyed in such a fashion, suffering utter obliteration from the face of the earth. In the meantime, the rest of Canaan continued in its normal fashion. To be sure, over the course of the next four hundred years, they, too, were going to be driven out. However, Sedom in its entirety lasted only fifty-two years. Its evil was so great that it did not even live to sixty, whereas Canaan took approximately five hundred years before deserving destruction — almost ten times as long.

We know that "Hashem does not withhold reward from any creature." (*Pesachim* 118a) What was the Canaanites' reward for not following the ways of Sedom?

Perhaps our question is the answer. The land of Israel is called *Eretz Canaan* by the Torah to show recognition to the Canaanites for their praiseworthy rejection of Sedom and its ways.

This continued until their time came to pay the price of their own wickedness, until *K'lal Yisrael* finally inhabited the land and took it over from them.

Thus, the Canaanites are given credit for protecting the Land from the evil of Sedom. Each one of the nations is mentioned individually, so as not to give a generalized credit, since each one of the seven individual nations deserves credit for having preserved *Eretz Yisrael* from the evils of Sedom.

This is what the above-mentioned *Seforno* alluded to when he wrote that Avram chose to live in the part of the land where the Canaanites lived, since they were not as wicked as the Sedomites. Avram could set up his tent, his *Eshel*, amongst the Canaanites and carry on his holy work there. This would have been incomprehensible amongst the Sedomites.

Let us note that in *Parshas Noach,* the verse defines the borders of the Canaanites in the following way:

ויהי גבול הכנעני מצידן באכה גררה עד עזה: (בראשית י':י"ט)

The Canaanite borders extended from Sidon toward Gerar until Gaza. (Bereishis 10:19)

This is the area along the west coast of *Eretz Yisrael,* along the Mediterranean. Then it says:

באכה סדמה ועמרה ואדמה וצבים עד לשע: (שם)

And toward Sedom, Amorah, Admah and Tzevoyim, until Lasha.
(ibid.)

The Torah here clearly states that the borders of the Canaanites included Sedom. So now we can understand why it says later in the verse in *Parshas Lech Lecha* that it is on the border of Canaan. It could very well be that the Canaanites were able to conquer and take it, but consciously chose not to have anything to do with it or its inhabitants.

5 Jewish Genes

לֹא יָבֹא עַמּוֹנִי וּמוֹאָבִי בִּקְהַל ה' וכו'.

עַל דְּבַר אֲשֶׁר לֹא קִדְּמוּ אֶתְכֶם בַּלֶּחֶם וּבַמַּיִם וכו'.

An Ammonite or Moabite may not enter the assembly of Hashem... since they did not greet you with bread and water... (Devarim 23:4-5)

———

The fact that Ammon and Moav may not marry into *K'lal Yisrael* even if they convert to Judaism emanates from the fact that spiritually speaking, in a sort of "spiritual genetics," they belong to a class of people that not only rejects *chesed* but is incapable of it.

That *"they did not greet you with bread and water"* is not just testifying to a lack of *chesed*. It is revealing that something was wrong in the national psyche of these two ancient peoples.

שלשה סימנים יש באומה זו הרחמנים והביישנין וגומלי חסדים וכו'. כל שיש בו
שלשה סימנים הללו ראוי להדבק באומה זו: (יבמות ע"ט ע"א)

There are three characteristics of this people (the Jews). They are merciful, have a sense of shame and bestow chesed... Anyone exhibiting these three characteristics is fitting to attach himself to this people. (Yevamot 79a)

It is not just a requirement for *K'lal Yisrael* to have these three characteristics. It is more than that: Ammon and Moav, by their very nature, are *contrary* to all of these. The fact that *"they did not greet you with bread and water"* shows a lack of mercy and *chesed*. Their shamelessness is quite evident from the incident following Bilaam's failure to curse the people, in which Moav sent out their women to snare the Israelites in immorality—although such behavior was unheard of at that time.

Their "spiritual genetics" not only lacked all the qualities necessary for *K'lal Yisrael*, but had the opposite effect. If a person is lacking all mercy, then by definition he is cruel. If a person is lacking all shame, then by definition he is shameless and immoral. There cannot be a neutral position. If a person does not do any *chesed* at all, then he is missing this quality in his nature, and perforce he will be opposed to *gemilus chasadim*. Such a person cannot be part of *K'lal Yisrael*.

How did Ammon and Moav get to be this way? Did it happen by itself? It seems that these were the qualities developed by Lot himself when leaving *Avraham Avinu*.

When Lot had been with *Avraham Avinu* he was developing proper traits and attitudes. However, once he left him, he became a *kafui tov,* inappreciative of good. In truth, he owed everything he had to *Avraham Avinu,* both his wealth and his spiritual development, but he turned around and denied everything he gained, nullifying all that he once was. This devolution of *midos* led to Lot becoming less merciful when he entered Sedom. He stood by as the people of Sedom "tarred and feathered" his very own daughter for her acts of kindness. The Midrash (*Sanhedrin* 109b) describes how they placed her on the roof, smeared her with honey and caused her to die a horrible, ruthless death. He could not even be merciful to his own child.

What about the quality of having a sense of shame? The offer Lot made to the people who surrounded his house is convincing proof of his lack of shame. In terms of doing *chesed*, Lot does appear good. It seems that Lot graciously took in the angels and went out of his way to show positive character attributes regarding them. He seemed to be the paradigm of hospitality in Sedom. Yet, his wife was opposed to all those activities. Thus, she was turned into a pillar of salt, and that part of her seems to have been implanted in her children. Consequently, even though Lot had this one positive attribute, it was cancelled out by his wife. As a result, the children of Lot also carried that negative "spiritual gene."

If so, why are the female descendants of Lot different, in that they are permitted to be part of *K'lal Yisrael?* The Torah only forbids the males of Ammon and Moav. Furthermore, how was it possible that Rus the Moabite and Na'amah the Ammonite developed to be outstandingly righteous, and became the predecessors of the *Mashiach?* They clearly contained within them the spark of holiness.

I would submit that their inherent spark of holiness emanates from Haran, father of Lot, who died in sanctification of Heaven's Name. Haran witnessed how *Avraham Avinu* was cast into the fires of Ur Kasdim for denying idolatry, and agreed that the same be done to him. Now, it is true that he saw Avraham come out unscathed and assumed the same would happen to him. Thus, although we do not find that he was willing to die for the sake of Hashem like Avraham was, nonetheless, we must admit that, de facto, he died *al Kiddush Hashem.*

That *Kiddush Hashem* of Haran made him worthy of many things. We find that *K'lal Yisrael* is descended solely from the three brothers: Haran, Avraham and Nachor, all sons of Terach. This is true even from our mother's side, for Sarah and Milkah were the daughters of Haran. Haran must have had a mighty *zechus* to produce the righteous women of *K'lal Yisrael.* Sarah, Rivkah, Rachel and Leah all issue from Haran, while Rivkah, Rachel and Leah also came from Nachor. Thus, we see that together with Avraham, the other sons of Terach also contributed to creating *K'lal Yisrael.* Even the royal line of Dovid came through Haran, by way of Lot and his daughters who gave birth to Ammon and Moav. Therefore, it seems that it was thanks to his father that Lot became the ancestor of the Davidic dynasty.[12]

Why is this positive trait carried only by the women? It is because only the daughters of Lot sacrificed for the sake of *chesed.* We find the following:

הרי שבנותיו מדה אחרת היתה להם שההזיקו בלחם לעני ואביון, ועל כן כל בנות
עמון ומואב מותרות לבוא בקהל וכו'. ולא בזכרים, ולך ראה שלשלת הקדושה שיצא
מנקיבות עמון ומואב וכו'. (באר מים חיים וירא פרק י"ט)

Lot's daughters showed a different trait. They supported the

---

12   After I wrote this, HaRav Yisrael HaCohen Chesir, *shlita,* showed me this explanation in the *Chasam Sofer (Parshas Veyeira)* and the *Sefas Emes (Parshas Lech Lecha).*

poor and destitute with bread. Therefore, all the women of Ammon and Moav are permitted to marry into the Jewish community [after conversion]... but not the males. You thereby see the progression of holiness that spreads out from the females of Ammon and Moav... (Beer Mayim Chaim, Parshas Vayeira, ch. 19)

It is clear that Lot's daughters were different from the males of his line. All this is while Lot himself brought only destruction and downfall upon himself and his family through abandoning *Avraham Avinu.* Hence, "a [male] Ammonite and Moabite may not enter the assembly of Hashem."

6   Walk, Don't Stand

הִתְהַלֵּךְ לְפָנַי וֶהְיֵה תָמִים:

Walk before Me and be perfect. (Bereishis 17:1)

Avram was ninety-nine years old when Hashem gave him the instruction contained in the above verse. Rashi explains the import of these words:

התהלך לפני. כתרגומו, "פלח קדמי", הדבק בעבודתי: (רש"י בראשית י"ז:א')

"Walk before me" – [We may understand this] as the Targum explains it: "Worship before Me." [In other words,] cleave to My service. (Rashi, Bereishis 17:1)

What did Rashi and the Targum see here that caused them to translate "walk" as "worship?" Why is this the simple meaning of the verse?

We may answer this question based on what we find in the book of *Zechariah*:

ונתתי לך מהלכים בין העמדים האלה: (זכריה ג':ז')

"If you walk in My ways... I will give you 'mahalachim' between those who are standing." (Zechariah 3:7)

ונתתי לך מהלכים – כתרגומו ובאחיות מיתיא אחיינך ואתן לך רגלין דמהלכין בין
שרפיא האלין: (רש"י שם)

"I will give you 'mahalachim'" – [We may understand this] as the Targum explains it: "And when the dead will be resurrected, I will resurrect you; and I will give you walkers that walk (mehalchin) among these seraphim." (Rashi, ad loc.)

Humans are called "walkers" and angels are called "standers." This is because a human being has to be constantly moving. Obviously, we are referring to moving in *ruchnius* — spiritual progression and intensification.

Now, we see that the simple meaning of the verse in our *Parshah* is exactly as the Targum translates it. When one "walks" before the Al-mighty, we are not speaking of walking a block or two, or even all the way to Mount Moriah. The "walker" in this verse is walking in *ruchnius*, just as in the above verse from the Book of *Zechariah*. This can only be accomplished by "worship before Me," by serving Hashem.

אמר רבי חייא בר אשי אמר רב תלמידי חכמים אין להם מנוחה לא בעולם הזה ולא
בעולם הבא שנאמר ילכו מחיל אל חיל וכו'. (ברכות דף ס"ד ע"א)

Rabbi Chiya bar Ashi said in the name of Rav: Torah scholars experience no rest, not in this nor the next world. For it states (Tehillim 84:8): "They walk (i.e., go) from strength to strength." (Brachos 64a)

In truth, this teaching of *Chazal* speaking of non-stop walking is referring to learning Torah in the next world. Nevertheless, the teaching's impact extends to all areas of spiritual accomplishment in this world, which is called the *Olam Ha'Asiyah*, the World of Action. For only here exists an arena for exercising free will and serving Hashem — "Worship before Me"!

וירא

VAYERA

1 The Eyes Have It

אֶשָּׂא עֵינַי אֶל הֶהָרִים וכו'.

I lift up my eyes to the mountains... (Tehillim 121:1)

There are numerous places in *Tanach* where the expression *"he lifted up his eyes"* appears. In *Parshas Lech Lecha,* we found that:

וישא לוט את עיניו וירא את כל ככר הירדן: (בראשית י"ג:י')

Lot lifted up his eyes and saw the Jordan plain. (Bereishis 13:10)

Here, in the beginning of *Parshas Vayera,* it says:

וישא עיניו וירא והנה שלשה אנשים נצבים: (שם י"ח:ב')

He (Avraham) lifted up his eyes and looked. And, behold, there were three men standing. (v. 18:2)

Similarly, at the *Akeidah,* we find it said twice that *"he (Avraham) lifted up his eyes."*

וישא אברהם את עיניו וירא את המקום מרחוק: (שם כ"ב:ד')

He (Avraham) lifted up his eyes and he saw the place from afar. (v. 22:4)

וישא אברהם את עיניו וירא והנה איל אחר נאחז בסבך: (שם כ"ב:י"ג)

He (Avraham) lifted up his eyes and looked, and behold behind him a ram caught in a thicket. (v. 22:13)

When Eliezer was returning with Rivkah, it says concerning Yitzchok,

וישא עיניו וירא והנה גמלים באים: (שם כ"ד:ס"ג)

And he lifted up his eyes, and saw, and, behold, the camels were coming. (v. 24:63)

Lest we think that only men "lift up their eyes," we find that:

ותשא רבקה את עיניה ותרא את יצחק: (שם כ"ד:ס"ד)

Rivkah lifted up her eyes and saw Yitzchok. (ibid., v. 64)

Lehavdil, it is written:

ותשא אשת אדוניו את עיניה וכו'. (שם ל"ט:ז')

*The wife of his master lifted up her eyes to Yosef, and said...
(v. 39:7)*

Throughout *Tanach,* we find this term used in different situations. Many commentators agree that "lifting up the eyes" is stressing a change from originally "looking down." It seems that the Torah used this term when it wanted to highlight the fact that the individual in question was originally looking down. Sometimes, the commentators say that the eyes were focused downward out of modesty and the person raised his or her eyes because they wanted to see something. This highlights the fact that their eyes were always modestly down. However, we find such a grand mixture of people and situations to which this term is applied that it is hard to say that it always implies positive qualities such as modesty or the like.

The leitmotif that emerges is that a person sees what he wants to see and seeks what he wants to seek. There is a prior intention and desire that informs one's visual perceptions. Lot was looking for *gashmius,* for the life of this world. He was looking for the negative and lifted up his eyes and found it, in Sedom. Avraham was looking to provide hospitality to wayfarers, *hachnasas orchim.* He was looking for travelers, and he lifted up his eyes and he, too, found what he was looking for. Yitzchok was waiting for the return of Rivkah; and Rivkah was waiting to see Yitzchok. In each of these cases, the person was raising his or her eyes to find what they were seeking. That is what we find by the wife of Potiphar as well. So it is with each of the verses mentioned above, as well as with many others that are beyond the scope of this work to examine.

This principle is best expressed in *Parshas Vayeitzei*. The verse there has nothing to do with eyes, but it sheds light on our subject nonetheless. It tells of Yaakov's reaction to what Hashem had promised him in the vision of the ladder ascending to heaven:

וישא יעקב רגליו וילך ארצה בני קדם: (שם כ"ט:א')

Yaakov lifted up his feet and went to the land of the people of the east. (v. 29:1)

Rashi comments:

משנתבשר בשורה טובה שהובטח בשמירה נשא את רגליו ונעשה קל ללכת:
(רש"י שם)

Once he received the good news – that his safety was guaranteed – his heart lifted his feet, making it easy to walk. (Rashi, ibid.)

Rashi is saying that the heart, which is the seat of emotion, made the walking easier. It lifted him up. A yearning that exists in the heart and motivates it, the emotional drive of the heart, moves the rest of the body. This is the meaning of *"Yaakov lifted up his feet,"* and we may also apply this explanation to cases of "he (or she) lifted up his eyes." It implies that whatever was in their heart, drove their body to action. Whatever was in their heart, directed their eyes.

That is also what it means in the third paragraph of the Shema:

לא תתורו אחרי לבבכם ואחרי עיניכם וכו'. (במדבר ט"ו:ל"ט)

"Do not go after your heart and after your eyes..." (Bamidbar 15:39)

This is because, as Rashi explains,

הלב חומד והעינים רואים: (רש"י שם)

The heart desires and the eyes see. (Rashi, ibid.)

On a deeper level, this means that whatever the heart desires, that is what the eye will want to see. When it is for the good, then you have *Avraham Avinu* looking for *hachnasas orchim*. When it is for the bad, you have Lot looking for Sedom.

A person sees what he wants to see.

2 What It Takes to Save a City

I n *Parshas Vayeira,* we find that Lot is saved from the city of Sedom. The angels take him out, with his unmarried daughters and his wife, and they instruct him to run to the mountain.

Rashi explains that the mountain is actually an allusion to *Avraham Avinu,* but Lot pleads with Hashem that he should not be required to run to *Avraham Avinu.* Lot is afraid. He is concerned that should he be juxtaposed to Avraham he would be judged as an evil person and, consequently, be destroyed. Rather, Lot prefers the city of Tzo'ar. Lot prays that the city of Tzo'ar should be saved in order that he should have a refuge there. However, Lot doesn't even stay in Tzo'ar. He is so terrified of Sedom's overturn that he immediately heads for the hills and hides in a cave.

This entire episode is quite puzzling. We know that the merit that saved Lot was from Avraham:

וַיִּזְכֹּר אלקים את אברהם וישלח את לוט מתוך ההפכה: (בראשית י"ט:כ"ט)

And G-d remembered Avraham, and sent him (Lot) out of the overturning. (Bereishis 19:29)

Avraham Avinu had prayed for Sedom and Amorah. While he was not answered regarding the saving of the cities, he was answered regarding the saving of his nephew Lot. Another reason for saving Lot was that Hashem was interested in the royal line of *Dovid HaMelech,* which was destined to come from him. However we look at it, the merit came either from *Avraham Avinu* or from Lot's future descendants.

Yet, Lot, the man without enough merit to save himself, seems to outdo *Avraham Avinu* in his power of prayer! Avraham prays for the five cities. He asks if there are fifty, if there are forty-five, if there are forty tzaddikim.

"No," says Hashem.

"Thirty, twenty…" *Avraham Avinu* says, "Even if there are just ten, save at least one city."

"No, we cannot save even one city," says Hashem. The prayer of the tzaddik, *Avraham Avinu,* cannot save a single city. Yet here, Lot, who is absolutely nothing compared to *Avraham Avinu,* makes a simple request for Tzo'ar and seems to be worthy enough to save the whole city—even though he doesn't even stay there in the end! How did that happen?

Perhaps the answer is in this Rashi from *Sefer Bamidbar:*

אַךְ אֶת מַטֵּה לֵוִי לֹא תִפְקֹד וְכוּ'. (במדבר א':מ"ט)

But do not count the tribe of Levi… (Bamidbar 1:49)

צָפָה הַקָּדוֹשׁ בָּרוּךְ הוּא שֶׁעֲתִידָה לַעֲמֹד גְּזֵרָה עַל כָּל הַנִּמְנִין מִבֶּן עֶשְׂרִים שָׁנָה וָמַעְלָה שֶׁיָּמוּתוּ בַּמִּדְבָּר, אָמַר אַל יִהְיוּ אֵלּוּ בַּכְּלָל, לְפִי שֶׁהֵם שֶׁלִּי, שֶׁלֹּא טָעוּ בָּעֵגֶל: (רש"י שם):

The Holy One Blessed be He saw that, in the future, there would be a decree against all those who are counted from the age of twenty and above, that they will die in the Wilderness. He said: "May these people (the Tribe of Levi) not be included, as they belong to Me. For they did not go astray after the Golden Calf." (Rashi, ad loc.)

Rashi reveals to us a deep insight into how Hashem applies His decrees to the community. The decree on the generation that left Egypt that they will wander and die in the Wilderness was a result of both the sin of the Golden Calf *and* the sin of the Spies.[13] Nevertheless, once this decree was made against the community as a whole, it would encompass even those who were not guilty of both sins. It would affect even the Tribe of Levi. It was only the fact that this tribe was specially separated and not counted with the others that saved them.

Let us now return to our topic — Lot's feat of saving the city of Tzo'ar. *Avraham Avinu,* who was far removed from these cities, prayed for all the

---

13 ע"ע רש"י במדבר י"ד:ל':ל"ג בד"ה ארבעים שנה

cities together. In truth, they were united as five cities. They were all one con-glomerate, one "united states." Therefore, when four of the five were fully deserving of destruction, all five would be destroyed as one unit. *Avraham Avinu* prayed for the entire unit, yet, it could not be saved this way, since it was worthy of total and complete annihilation.

However, Lot was there among them and was privy to the inner workings of the cities. He understood that Tzo'ar was in existence for only fifty-one years and had not yet grown quite as evil as the other four. Therefore, Lot asked for Tzo'ar on its own. He did not place it in the general context. Since Lot's prayer was applied to a specific issue, it surpassed even the prayer of *Avraham Avinu* and accomplished what *Avraham Avinu* was unable to.

If we look closely, we will see this in the following Rashi, which explains Lot's approach to Tzo'ar.

העיר הזאת קרובה וכו'. (בראשית י"ט:כ')

Behold, this city is near to flee there... (Bereishis 19:20)

קרובה ישיבתה, נתישבה מקרוב, לפיכך לא נתמלאה סאתה עדין (שבת י ע"ב), וכו'. וצוער אחרה ישיבתה אחרי ישיבת סדום וחברותיה שנה אחת, וכו'. והלא עונותיה מועטין ויכול אתה להניחה: (רש"י שם).

Its settlement was "near," i.e., it was settled recently. There-fore, its measure of sin was not yet filled (Shabbos 10b)... Tzo'ar delayed its settlement for one year after Sedom and its companion cities... its sins are less, and You may leave it be. (Rashi, ad loc.)

This is certainly an appropriate place to apply *Chazal*'s teaching that

אל תהי ברכת הדיוט קל בעיניך: (מגילה ט"ו ע"ב)

A plain person's blessing should not be treated lightly. (Megillah 15b)

You never know where the *brachah* will come from! Here was a situation where *Avraham Avinu*'s prayer was incapable of saving a soul, and Lot spared the entire city.

3 When was the Promise Made?

וַיַּעַשׂ ה' לְשָׂרָה כַּאֲשֶׁר דִּבֵּר:

And Hashem did for Sarah as He had spoken. (Bereishis 21:1)

⌒

ashem kept His promise and gave a child to Sarah. Where did Hashem originally promise this?

Rashi explains (*Bereishis* 21:1) that at the *Bris Bein HaBesarim*, Hashem said to Avraham:

לֹא יִירָשְׁךָ זֶה וְכוּ'. (בראשית ט"ו:ד)

"This one (Eliezer) will not inherit you..." (Bereishis 15:4)

This Divine promise was in response to Avraham's expression of his plight: He is childless and his chief servant Eliezer will assumedly inherit him (ibid., v. 2). Following this, the *Bris Bein HaBesarim* took place, in which Hashem made a covenant with Avraham that he would inherit the land of Canaan.

This brings us to the problem: Rashi describes the Divine promise of a son to inherit him as *Bris Bein HaBesarim*. As it appears in the Torah, the promise indeed took place in the context of *Bris Bein HaBesarim*. However, we find *Tosafos* commenting that the Divine promise actually occurred not where it is written (right before the *Bris Bein HaBesarim*) but years later (*Tosafos* s.v. *Lo hayah, Brachos* 7b). It emerges that this promise really took place much later when Avraham was 75, after the war with the four kings. These passages are not written in chronological order, say *Tosafos,* who prove the point by making a calculation.

Avraham was 70 years old at the *Bris Bein HaBesarim*. How do we know? We find that later on the Torah says that the Israelites left Egypt after 430 years. This was 400 years counting from the birth of Yitzchok. Avraham was 100 when Yitzchok was born, as is written expressly in the Torah. Thirty years earlier was the *Bris Bein HaBesarim*, so Avraham must have been 70 at that time.

How old was Avraham when he battled the four kings? *Tosafos* say he was

73 because the entire life-span of the city of Sedom was 52 years. Avraham was 99 when Sedom was destroyed (at that juncture, Avraham was visited by the angels who gave him the good tidings that his son Yitzchok would be born one year later). After further calculations (all detailed by *Tosafos*), it turns out that Avraham was 73 during the war of the four kings against Sedom. Therefore, the Divine promise of a son to inherit Avraham and the *Bris Bein HaBesarim* took place at totally different times.

What shall we say to explain Rashi? It is difficult to state that he disagrees with *Tosafos* and holds that the Divine promise really did take place at the *Bris Bein HaBesarim* since Rashi himself says (v. 15:1) that the above conversation (v. 15:4) occurred *after* the war with the kings, and Rashi, too, agrees that Avraham was 70 at the *Bris Bein HaBesarim*. (See Rashi, *Shemos* 12:40)

Perhaps Rashi disagrees with *Tosafos* and holds that the war with the kings took place when Avraham was 70, which would now allow us to say that the Divine promise really did take place at the *Bris Bein HaBesarim*. (How he will undo *Tosafos'* calculations is beyond the scope of this book.) Alternatively, perhaps Rashi means that the Divine promise was not really a part of the *Bris Bein HaBesarim* at all. So why did Rashi say it was? Because he meant that it is written in the passage of the *Bris Bein HaBesarim,* although chronologically it took place later. Time-wise, it was a separate event, but from the Torah's perspective, it is included under the general heading of the *Bris Bein HaBesarim*.

4

First Aid

וה' פָּקַד אֶת שָׂרָה כַּאֲשֶׁר אָמָר:

And Hashem remembered Sarah as He had said. (Bereishis 21:1)

⌣

The Torah recounts how Avimelech took Sarah and released her, and how Avraham prayed for Avimelech to be healed. Following this episode, Sarah gave birth to Yitzchok. In the order of events, it would appear that Avraham and Sarah were answered by Hashem after Avimelech was healed, not before.

However, Rashi explains that this is not so:

וה' פקד את שרה וגומר... סמך פרשה זו לכאן, ללמדך שכל המבקש רחמים על חברו
והוא צריך לְאותו דבר הוא נענה תחלה,וכו'. שפקדה כבר קודם שרפא את אבימלך
(בבא קמא צ"ב ע"א): (רש"י בראשית כ"א:א')

"And Hashem remembered Sarah..." This passage is connected to here [where Avraham prayed for Avimelech] to teach you that anyone who prays for his friend, and he needs the same thing, he is answered first... For Hashem remembered Sarah before He healed Avimelech (Bava Kamma 92a). (Rashi, Bereishis 21:1)

How do we make sense of the order of events?

It all makes perfect sense if we consider the true causes for these events. Rashi is teaching us that while Avraham was still praying, even before Avimelech was actually healed, the remembrance of Sarah came before the Holy One Blessed be He, and it was decided that she would now give birth to Yitzchok.

That is how we derive the principle that "Anyone who prays for his friend, and he needs the same thing, he is answered first."

Self Improvement — Do It Yourself.

אמר רב יוסף: מצוה בו יותר מבשלוחו: (קידושין מ"א ע"א)

Said Rav Yosef: "It is a greater mitzvah with him than it is with his agent." (Kiddushin 41a)

The mitzvah is greater—and the reward is greater—when you do it yourself.

Do we fathom the difference in reward? Sometimes, people feel it is not so significant of a difference. Perhaps it is not even worth the bother, they think. Ultimately, the mitzvah is done!

Let us take an act of tzedaka, for instance. You can do it yourself, or assign someone else to do it for you. You give the money to the agent and tell him to take care of dispensing the money for you. The person who needs the money ultimately receives it, so what difference does it make who delivers it?

We are making a mistake: There is an enormous difference.

We see from the beginning of *Parshas Vayera* that, ultimately, the factors leading up to *Moshe Rabbeinu* not going into *Eretz Yisrael* began when *Avraham Avinu* gave water to the angels through an agent, rather than bringing the water himself.

יקח נא וכו'. (בראשית י"ח:ד')

Let now a little water be taken...(Bereishis 18:4)

על ידי שליח, והקדוש ברוך הוא שלם לבניו על ידי שליח, שנאמר וירם משה את ידו ויך את הסלע: (רש"י שם)

[The passive form "be taken" implies that it was brought] by an agent. And the Holy One Blessed be He repaid his (Avraham's) children through an agent. As it says: "And Moshe lifted his arm and struck the rock." (Rashi, ad loc.)

Why does Rashi choose to bring a proof from this verse in *Parshas Chukas*? Would it not have made more sense to refer to the original story of the water found in *Parshas B'shalach* when *B'nei Yisrael* were in Refidim (*Shemos* 17:1-7)?

Rashi is hinting an important lesson by emphasizing *Moshe Rabbeinu*'s striking the rock at the incident of *Mei M'riva*. He reveals to us the original cause for *Moshe Rabbeinu* not going into *Eretz Yisrael*! At the end of the forty years, when *Moshe Rabbeinu* was to supply the water "through an agent," i.e., the rock, he was commanded to speak to the rock. Instead, he hit it. That is the famous incident that resulted in Hashem swearing not to let him enter the Land.

If Avraham would have brought the water himself, and *B'nei Yisrael* would have consequently received water in the Wilderness directly from *HaKadosh Boruch Hu*, then this could never have happened.

חיי שרה

CHAYEI SARAH

1 The Other Kohen Gadol

וַתָּמָת שָׂרָה בְּקִרְיַת אַרְבַּע הִוא חֶבְרוֹן בְּאֶרֶץ כְּנָעַן וכו'.

And Sarah died in Kiryas Arba, which is Chevron, in the land of Canaan... *(Bereishis 23:2)*

Why did *Sarah Imeinu* die when she did? Is there any significance to the timing? The truth is that it was extraordinarily significant. All of Jewish history depended on it. To begin with, it was only when Sarah died that Yitzchok was able to marry. It is clear from the order of the Torah's passages that Yitzchok's marriage was contingent on Sarah's death, but the real question is why this is so.

First, let us realize that this was the case with all the *Imahos*, not just with Sarah. Even though the *Avos* overlapped, the *Imahos* never did. Avraham was alive when Yitzchok was developing and growing into his spiritual stature as one of the *Avos*. Yitzchok was alive when Yaakov was developing to be one of the *Avos*. Yet, Sarah had to pass away before Yitzchok could marry Rivkah. Furthermore, Rivkah had to pass away in advance of Yaakov's return to Chevron because Leah could not have assumed her position when Yaakov returned to *Eretz Yisrael* if Rivkah would still have been alive.

Why is it absolutely impossible for the *Imahos* to overlap? I owe the following insight, which provides the answer, to my wife, *shetichya*.

There is a striking correlation between the traditional role of women and that of the *Kohanim*, especially of the *Kohen Gadol*. The comparisons are many. On any day other than Yom Kippur, an ordinary *Kohen* could light the Menorah of the *Bais HaMikdash*. Nevertheless, the very personification of the lighting of the Menorah, the paradigm of the process, was *Aharon haKohen*, the *Kohen Gadol*. Aharon lit the Menorah. While the lighting of the Menorah in the *Bais HaMikdash* was the job of the *Kohen*, the lighting of the Shabbos candles, the menorah of the home, is the job of the woman.

The *Kohen Gadol* presided over the *Bais HaMikdash*, while the traditional role of the woman is to preside over the *mishkan* of the home. This is reflected poignantly in the stories of the *Avos* and the *Imahos*, as the Ramban explains:

וכשבאו אל הר סיני ועשו המשכן ושב הקדוש ברוך הוא והשרה שכינתו ביניהם אז
שבו אל מעלת אבותם, שהיה סוד אלוה עלי אהליהם, והם הם המרכבה (ב"ר מ"ז:ח'),
ואז נחשבו גאולים וכו'. (רמב"ן בהקדמה לספר שמות)

When they came to Mount Sinai and made the Mishkan, and the Holy One Blessed be He returned His Shechinah to rest among them, then they returned to the high level of their fore-fathers. This was in the aspect of G-d being upon their tents, and they (the forefathers) are the very vehicle of G-d's revela-tion. (Ramban, introduction to Sefer Shemos)

The original *mishkan* was actually the home of each of the *Imahos*. That is why we find here in *Parshas Chayei Sarah* that there were three signs of the return of the Shechinah to the home of Rivkah.

שכל זמן ששרה קיימת היה נר דלוק מע"ש לערב שבת וברכה מצויה בעיסה וענן
קשור על האהל ומשמתה פסקו וכשבאת רבקה חזרו: (רש"י בראשית כ"ד:ס"ז)

As long as Sarah was alive:
1. The lamp burnt from Erev Shabbos to Erev Shabbos.
2. There was a blessing in the dough.
3. There was a cloud positioned over the tent. (Rashi, Bereishis 24:67)

The fact that the lamp continued to burn and was not extinguished represents the *ner tamid* of the Menorah, the westernmost lamp that never went out. The constant and miraculously fresh bread (the blessing in the dough) represents the *lechem hapanim* because it would not spoil over the course of the week. The cloud positioned over the tent represents the presence of the Shechinah. These miracles were the signature of Sarah, and, ultimately, the sign that Rivkah had taken over from Sarah. This is the sign of the *Kohen*.

What was the everyday job of the *Kohen*? What did he do all day? He, so to speak, took care of the cooking and the cleaning in the *Bais HaMikdash*. There were no strangers doing this important task. It was the *Kohen* who cut up and prepared the meat. It was the *Kohen* who placed it on the Altar, which is called Hashem's "table." (See *Menachos* 6a, etc.)

Only the *Kohanim* were permitted to enter most of the area of the Temple Courtyard, the floor of which needed cleaning from dirt and refuse. The process of washing and cleaning the floor is described in *Yoma* 58b.

Lest we consider the comparison between the Temple's Altar and the table in a person's home to be overly fanciful, *Chazal* speak clearly on this topic.

המזבח עץ שלש אמות גבוה וארכו שתים אמות ומקצעותיו לו וארכו וקירתיו עץ
וידבר אלי זה השלחן אשר לפני ה': (יחזקאל מ"א:ל"ח)

The wooden Altar was three amos high... and He spoke to me: ("This is the table that is before Hashem." (Yechezkel 41:36

פתח במזבח וסיים בשלחן. רבי יוחנן וריש לקיש דאמרי תרוייהו: בזמן שבית המקדש
קיים מזבח מכפר על אדם, עכשיו — שלחנו של אדם מכפר עליו: (חגיגה כ"ז ע"א)

The verse began with "Altar" and concluded with "table." Rabbi Yochanan and Reish Lakish both said: "When the Temple is standing, the Altar atones for a person. Now, a person's table atones for him." (Chagigah 27a)

Here again, the domain of the *Kohen* paralleled the traditional role of the woman: Serving food to the table.

In fact, if we consider the garments of the *Kohen Gadol*, we will find that one of them resembled an apron! The traditional sign of the time-honored role of the woman, until quite recently, was her apron. There are many "modernized" women who will not wear an apron today for that reason. Yet, once upon a time, it was her distinctive honored mark. The *Kohen Gadol* wore an apron! Rashi calls it the *Eifod* that the royal women wore when they rode on horses. Thus, we see that its design may be understood only by comparison to women's clothing.

It is striking to consider that the *Kohen Gadol* wore a four-cornered garment, the *Me'il*, but he did not wear tzitzis on it. The only ones besides him who are not obligated to wear tzitzis are women! With Hashem's help, we will discuss the reason for this in *Parshas Korach*.

The only significant difference between the role of the *Kohen* in his House and the role of the woman in hers is in the lighting of the lamps. Although they both kindle lamps, the reasons are very different.

Let us consider two well-known verses about lamps from *Mishlei*:

כי נר מצוה ותורה אור: (שם ו':כ"ג)

For a lamp is a mitzvah, and Torah is light. (Mishlei 6:23)

נר ה' נשמת אדם: (משלי כ:כ"ז)

The lamp of Hashem is the soul of a man. (ibid., 2:27)

We see that Torah and mitzvos are called lamps and light, and that a person's *neshamah* is also called a lamp. There is a difference between the two. The woman's role of lighting the lamp is connected to *shalom bayis*. Her lamp's purpose is to give forth light, as the kindling of the Shabbos candles is to produce light, not hide it. Correspondingly, the role of the woman is connected to the light of the *neshamah* and that is why she prays for her family, husband and children at the time of kindling the Shabbos lights. This prayer is one of igniting and of inspiring. It is the heartfelt yearning behind her role as the facilitator of *kedushah*. This is expressed through her role of kindling the Shabbos lights.

In contrast, the role of the *Kohen* is described as:

כי־שפתי כהן ישמרו־דעת ותורה יבקשו מפיהו: (מלאכי ב':ז)

For the lips of the Kohen guard knowledge, and Torah will they seek from his mouth. (Malachi 2:7)

The role of the *Kohen* is to teach the light of Torah. This light shines toward the center as did the light of the Menorah in the *Bais HaMikdash*, whose light was not meant to spread out in its most Divine form. This is because Hashem does not need a lamp to illuminate His House; He is the very essence of light! Rather, this light was primarily to remain in the place of sanctity as a testament to the Oneness of Hashem and His Torah. (See *Shabbos* 22b) That is the purity of Torah, and that is why the Menorah is lit with pure olive oil. It has to be the purest because the Menorah represents the purity of Torah.

Aside from this difference just mentioned, the traditional roles of the *Kohen* and of the woman parallel each other amazingly well.

Let us now return to our question: Why is it impossible for the lives of the *Imahos* to overlap?

The answer is that the Jewish people cannot have two *Kohanim Gedolim* serving simultaneously. Although there existed a deputy *Kohen Gadol*, who stood ready to replace the *Kohen Gadol* for the short-term should the need have arisen, ultimately, there can only be one *Kohen Gadol* at any given time. Thus, the *Imahos*, whose activities represent those of the *Kohen Gadol* in the *Bais HaMikdash*, could not have shared their roles simultaneously. There could only be one *Kohen Gadol* at a time.

Therefore, Sarah died when it was time for Rivkah to take her rightful place serving in the *mishkan* of the *Avos,* which was the tent of their home. When Yaakov returned to *Eretz Yisrael*, Rachel died, and as he was approaching Chevron and it was time for his wife Leah to assume the place of *Eim HaBayis,* the role which Rivkah had held, that was the time that Rivkah died. There could not be any overlap.

This was not the case concerning the *Avos.* They served a different role and it was not problematic for them to serve simultaneously. On the contrary, it was important for them to overlap. Perhaps that is why we find a reference made to *Avraham Avinu* at the beginning of *Parshas Toldos:*

ואלה תולדת יצחק בן־אברהם אברהם הוליד את־יצחק: (בראשית כ"ה:י"ט)

And these are the offspring of Yitzchok the son of Avraham: Avraham fathered Yitzchok. (Bereishis 25:19)

As Rashi points out on the above verse, the Torah is about to tell us about Yaakov and Eisav who are the offspring of Yitzchok, yet, the Torah first saw it important to mention Avraham. In fact, this is the only place where we find all of the *Avos* living in the same place at the same time. This was during the last fifteen years of *Avraham Avinu*'s life. It is, therefore, important for the Torah to note their overlap.

Possibly, the necessity for this overlap is the fact that the *Avos* constitute the world's pillars. They are the tripod upon which the entire universe stands.

עַל שְׁלֹשָׁה דְבָרִים הָעוֹלָם עוֹמֵד, עַל הַתּוֹרָה וְעַל הָעֲבוֹדָה וְעַל גְּמִילוּת חֲסָדִים:

(אבות פרק א:ב)

The world stands on three things: on Torah, on *avodas Hashem* and on deeds of kindness. (*Pirkei Avos* 1:2)

Avraham represents deeds of kindness, Yitzchok represents *avodas Hashem* and Yaakov represents Torah. These components must exist together and, therefore, it was critical that there be a period where, unlike with the *Imahos*, the lives of the *Avos* intersected.

2 The Straw that Broke the Camel's Back

וַיָּבֹא אַבְרָהָם לִסְפֹּד לְשָׂרָה וְלִבְכֹּתָהּ:

And Avraham came to eulogize Sarah and to cry over her.
(*Bereishis* 23:2)

Pirkei Avos speaks of the ten *nisyonos* of *Avraham Avinu*, and, according to the majority of the *Rishonim*, the *Akeidah* was the greatest test of all. It was the last of the ten *nisyonos* that Avraham had to endure. Yet, Rabbeinu Yonah disagrees: He says that the burial of Sarah was the tenth *nisayon*. When Avraham returned from the *Akeidah* after binding Yitzchok on the altar, he now had to go through the difficult purchase of *Me'aras HaMachpelah* from Ephron the Hittite.

There is an obvious problem with Rabbeinu Yonah's explanation. After *Avraham Avinu* had gone through all his previous challenges, how could this relatively minor obstacle compare to the rest? Why was this considered one of the hardest things that Avraham ever had to do? He was cast into the fiery furnace by Nimrod. He encountered a great famine as soon as he arrived in the Promised Land, and faced life-threatening circumstances when he fled as a refugee to Egypt. He passed the tests involved with going to King Avimelech, and, finally, he went through the *Akeidah*. Finding a place to bury Sarah and purchasing it from Ephron seems to pale in comparison to the awesome trials that preceded this. How are we to understand this final test, according to Rabbeinu Yonah?

I believe that the explanation is as follows: Up until *Avraham Avinu*, we see very great people who went through some tremendous challenges and overcame them all. Yet, they ultimately failed in life because after those challenges were over, they let down their guard. They were blinded by the relatively minor tests that came upon them after the great and awesome challenges had dissipated. They were caught off guard, and they were overcome.

Let us take Noach for example. During his entire lifetime, he dealt with the challenges of his wicked and corrupt generation. He underwent a year in the *Teivah* itself, with all of its trials and tribulations, pressures and challenges. When he came out of the *Teivah*, when he was finally at ease and able to relax, the Torah says about him:

ויחל נח איש האדמה ויטע כרם: (בראשית ט':כ')

And Noach, who was a man of the earth, began to plant a vineyard. (Bereishis 9:6)

Noach's guard was down, and he showed himself in an unfavorable light. He failed even the small test of what to plant first.

Let us consider Noach's son, Shem. He could have founded a dynasty of *Kohanim Gedolim*. In fact, he served as the *Kohen Gadol* of his age and greeted *Avraham Avinu* warmly after Avraham's victory over the four kings.

ומלכי צדק מלך שלם הוציא לחם ויין והוא כהן לאל עליון: (בראשית י"ד:י"ח)

And He (Shem) brought out bread and wine, and he was the Kohen of the Almighty G-d. (Bereishis 14:18)

However, the Gemara points out that Shem proceeded to bless Avraham, and only afterwards to bless Hashem. This cost Shem dearly. The priesthood was taken away from his children. Thus, the verse says that "He" was the *Kohen*, implying that his descendants would not be. (*Nedarim* 32b)

Shem, too, went through tremendous tests. He, too, remained righteous in spite of his generation, and spent a year in the *Teivah*. However, much later, after Avraham saved Lot from the four kings, Shem faced his final test and failed. He honored *Avraham Avinu*, the earthly victor, in front of Hashem who controls all events.

This mistake did not have to be made. We see that even Nebuchadnezzar, later to become the evil king of Babylon who destroyed the First Temple, was capable of putting things in proper order. The following Gemara describes a letter written by Merodach Baladan, then King of Babylon, to Chizkiyahu, King of Yehudah. The Gemara mentions Nebuchadnezzar's wise emendation to the letter.

> כתבו ליה: שלמא למלכא חזקיה, שלם לקרתא דירושלם, שלם לאלקא רבא.
> נבוכדנאצר ספריה דבלאדן הוה, ההיא שעתא לא הוה התם. כי אתא אמר להו: היכי
> כתביתו? אמרו ליה: הכי כתבינן. אמר להו: קריתו ליה אלקא רבא וכתביתו ליה
> לבסוף? אמר: אלא הכי כתובו: שלם לאלקא רבא, שלם לקרתא דירושלם, שלם
> למלכא חזקיה: (סנהדרין צ"ו ע"א)

He wrote to him: "Peace be unto you, King Chizkiyahu. Peace to the city of Jerusalem, peace to the great G-d!" Nebuchadnezzar was the scribe of Baladan, but at that time was not there. When he came, he said... "You called Him the great G-d but you wrote Him at the end?" He said: "Rather, write like this: 'Peace to the great G-d, peace to the city of Jerusalem, peace be unto you, King Chizkiyahu!'" (Sanhedrin 96a)

This letter was sent to honor King Chizkiyahu after the sun stopped for him. Nebuchadnezzar realized that the first honor, the first priority, belongs to the Master of the World. Yet, Shem stumbled in setting priorities, and thereby lost the opportunity to be one of the *Avos*. Although he was "*Kohen* of the Almighty G-d," he was unable to reach the level of one of the *Avos*.

Yet, Avraham was different. He went through great trials. He put his life on the line, his wife's life on the line and his child's life on the line. At this point, a lesser person would have sat back and said: "Look what I've accomplished!" Avraham returned from the *Akeidah* and found that his beloved wife Sarah had passed away. It would have been quite human, quite understandable, if we would have found *Avraham Avinu* saying: "On top of all of this, I now have to find a burial place for Sarah? I don't even have a few square feet in this world where I can dig a grave for my wife?" Yet, Avraham *Avinu* remained unquestioning of Hashem's ways. He continued to conduct himself as usual, lovingly accepting the decrees of Heaven, and dealt with this situation as he dealt with all the other challenges of his life.

This, Rabbeinu Yonah is telling us, shows the ultimate greatness of our great forefather Avraham.

3 The Good Life

וַיִּהְיוּ חַיֵּי שָׂרָה מֵאָה שָׁנָה וְעֶשְׂרִים שָׁנָה וְשֶׁבַע שָׁנִים וכו'.

And the life of Sarah was a hundred years and twenty years and seven years... (Bereishis 23:1)

Rashi makes his well-known comment on this verse that all of Sarah's years were the same; they were all good years. Now, this is almost unbelievable. They were all good? We are not told what transpired to Sarah before what is recounted in the Torah, but from where the story starts, we would be hard - pressed to describe her years as good ones.

Sarah was taken by Pharaoh, she reached ninety years old without children, she was taken by Avimelech, she underwent all the trials and tribulations that *Avraham Avinu* had to undergo and her only child was taken to be slaughtered on the altar (and ultimately caused her own death), and all of them were good years? From our perspective, this is a very hard statement to make. We could explain the verse as telling us that she was judged favorably by Heaven regarding all these unpleasant trials and tribulations that made up her life, but, admittedly, this is not the straightforward meaning of the verse with Rashi's commentary.

So what *is* Rashi telling us? He is telling us that the central thread in the tapestry of Sarah's life was "Everything that Hashem does is for the good." *Kol mah de'avid Rachamana, letav avid.* (*Brachos* 60b) Sarah truly experienced the goodness of her life. She actually felt that all her years were good ones. She saw them that way because "Everything that Hashem does is for the good"!

This is a remarkably important point. Just as *Avraham Avinu* had *seivah tovah,* a period when he lived years of goodness in his old age, similarly were all the years of Sarah perceived by her to be full of goodness. Every day was a blessing, and the Torah testifies that her perceptions were, in fact, reality.

4 Human Dignity

What is so special about the body of a human being? Why must we treat it with such respect after death? On first thought it would seem that the physical body is there only to be a vehicle for the *neshamah*, the soul, enabling it to pass through this world. While the *neshamah* is here in this world, it needs the body. Once it leaves and goes to the *olam ha'emes,* then the body loses all importance. According to this line of thinking, perhaps the body just needs to be discarded without further ado.

Yet, we find that honoring the body of the deceased, with proper burial and proper treatment of the body, is something of awesome importance. I believe that by considering the sanctity possessed by *kisvei hakodesh,* Torah scrolls and the like, we can gain insight into the intrinsic value of the body. There is a fundamental difference between a mitzvah object such as esrog or tzitzis, and *kisvei hakodesh.* The former are holy only by virtue of the mitzvah they serve. The latter are considered *kedushah* themselves. *Kisvei hakodesh* have innate holiness. One takes an innocuous piece of animal hide and scratches a few lines onto it. Then one takes some black dye and a quill, draws the shape of the Hebrew letters, and sews the pieces of leather together using sinews.

What made it holy? The *kavanah* of the person who wrote the words transformed these mundane items devoid of all meaning into something that has sanctity beyond comprehension, exceeding any other item of holiness in this world. *Kisvei hakodesh* have such significance that their inherent *kedushah* is indestructible. There is a certain eternity, an inextinguishable everlasting quality, to *kisvei hakodesh*. We see this from the story of Rabbi Chanina ben Teradyon.

מצאוהו לרבי חנינא בן תרדיון שהיה יושב ועוסק בתורה ומקהיל קהלות ברבים וס"ת מונח לו בחיקו. הביאוהו וכרכוהו בס"ת, והקיפוהו בחבילי זמורות והציתו בהן את האור, וכו'. אמרו לו תלמידיו: רבי, מה אתה רואה? אמר להן: גליון נשרפין ואותיות פורחות: (ע"ז י"ח ע"א)

The Romans found Rabbi Chanina ben Teradon sitting and engaging in Torah study and holding public gatherings, with a Sefer Torah resting in his lap. They brought him and wrapped him in a Sefer Torah, surrounded him with bundles of twigs and lit them on fire... His disciples said to him: "Rabbi, what do you see?" He said to them: "The parchment is burning and the letters are flying." (Avodah Zarah 18a)

The letters of Rabbi Chanina's *Sefer Torah* did not burn up. They simply flew away, moving on to a new location. This shows that Torah scrolls, tefillin and mezuzos, once created, can never be destroyed. They are invulnerable and unassailable.

These items are even capable of transmitting their *kedushah* to a secondary object, called *tashmishei kedushah*. If you take an ordinary piece of fabric, which could be thrown in the garbage one day, and you make it into a cover for a *Sefer Torah*, you have transformed it into something that has inherent *kedushah,* albeit less than that of the *Sefer Torah* itself. Now, the fabric must be treated with respect.

Back to the original question: Why is the human body accorded such honor even after the departure of the *neshamah*? The answer is not in the raw materials from which the body is formed, which is mere dirt from the ground, but rather in the fact that the body is the receptacle that houses the *neshamah*. During life, the *neshamah* learns Torah and performs mitzvos. Thus, the body, too, acquires intrinsic holiness. It is transformed into a totally new entity that calls for respect no less than that due to a *Sefer Torah*, and that is why there are clear parallels and comparisons between the *Sefer Torah* and the human body. (See next section, also *Yerushalmi Moed Katan*, ch. 3, *Shulchan Aruch YD* 378:4, *Biur Hagra* 5; *Nefesh Hachim* 4:29)

5   Meritorious Women

The Gemara poses what seems to be a peculiar question, and answers it even more peculiarly.

אמר ליה רב לרבי חייא נשים במאי זכיין? באקרויי בנייהו לבי כנישתא ובאתנויי
גברייהו בי רבנן ונטרין לגברייהו עד דאתו מבי רבנן: (ברכות דף י"ז ע"א)

Rav asked Rabbi Chiya: "Through what do women acquire merit? Through causing their sons to learn Scripture in the synagogue, and through causing their husbands to learn Mishnah in the House of the Scholars, and for waiting for their husbands until they return from the House of the Scholars."
(Brachos 17a)

The Chofetz Chaim (*Chomas HaDas, Maamar Ohr Torah*, ch. 1) is perplexed by the Gemara's opening question. Why do we have to go looking for things that give women merits? Women clearly have many mitzvos! They have all the negative mitzvos, and most of the positive ones as well, being exempt only from time-bound positive mitzvos.

The Gemara's answer is even harder to understand: Women acquire their merit not by what they actually do themselves but by passively waiting for their husbands and children to come home from their places of Torah study.

The Chofetz Chaim elucidates the Gemara by explaining that the matter of *techiyas hameisim,* the resurrection of the dead, is not a simple matter at all. Although it is one of the thirteen principles of faith in which every Jew must believe, it is not necessarily something that will happen to everyone. Only by merit of Torah study will the "dew of light" (*Yeshayahu* 26:19) descend upon a person and bring him back to life. Whereas in terms of reward in *Olam Haba,* it is clear that there is no difference between a woman and a man. Both have mitzvos and will be rewarded in the next world for keeping them. However, there is another level of reward and that is *techiyas hameisim*. For that, you need the merit of Torah study. Nothing else will do. Since women are exempt from the mitzvah of Torah study, they acquire their merit through the study of their sons and husbands. (In addition, the Chofetz Chaim mentions another way for a woman to merit *techiyas hameisim*: by giving money to support a Torah scholar in his studies.)

One way or another, a person needs to be connected to the mitzvah of Torah study in its proper, obligatory form. What process will connect women to an obligation that they do not have? The Gemara answers that through supporting the learning of their husband and children, from the loneliness and pain of waiting for their husband to come home, from the difficulty involved in sending their sons to yeshiva, the women reap their merit and their rewards. (To reiterate, an unmarried woman or one without children would accomplish this by giving money to support a Torah scholar in his studies.) These are all processes by which the women acquire *techiyas hameisim*.

However, now we come to a more fundamental question: Why is Torah learning the only merit in the world that brings a person to *techiyas hameisim*? As we mentioned in the previous section, there is a certain transformation that takes place in a human being, a transformation of his or her material world. This process parallels the *kedushah* of *kisvei hakodesh*. This is what invests an inherent sanctity in the human body. As we explained, this is only through *kisvei hakodesh*, which possess inherent sanctity. An object merely used for a mitzvah does not have this. That is why only Torah study that absorbs into a person's body, *kinyan Torah*, is capable of transforming his flesh and bones into eternity.

The *neshamah* is pure and remains pure. However, the body, which comes from the dust and ashes of materiality, needs to be transformed in a way similar to the parchment and ink of the *Sefer Torah*, which unite to create a most powerful *kedushah* and become an indestructible entity.

So, too, the human body becomes transformed when a person acquires the Torah. This takes place through the forty-eight ways of acquisition of the Torah, as enumerated in *Pirkei Avos* 6:6. This makes it so the human being becomes like *kisvei hakodesh*. He becomes not like the mantle of the *Sefer*

Torah, which is on the level of *tashmishei kedushah,* but like the *Sefer Torah* itself. Therefore, he becomes indestructible like the *Sefer Torah* of Rabbi Chananya ben Teradyon. This indestructibility allows for *techiyas hameisim.* It preserves the body for eternity. Only through acquiring Torah does a person acquire everlasting existence.

Why do we need all the troubles and inconveniences involved with handling the body? Why do we pester the living to go through difficulties to care for the dead? Why was it necessary for *Yaakov Avinu* to request his son Yosef to bear his pall all the way from Egypt to *Eretz Yisrael?*

We now understand why. It is because the body has a continuous life force and significance. It possesses a sanctity that lives on. Thus, we have an extensive process of caring for the body after death in a fashion that gives it due respect. Thus, we find throughout *Tanach* that one of the worst curses that Hashem could give someone is that his body will not be buried but will be thrown in the streets. In a purely physical world, why should a person care about that? Once he is dead, why should it matter to him?

The answer is the everlasting connection between the body and the *neshamah.* Proper placement and treatment of the body after death has at least as much significance as it did when the person was alive. This is because of the time frame involved. We are now speaking of eternity. This is one of the reasons that caring for the deceased is called *chesed shel emes.* It is a *chesed* that remains forever; it is a *chesed* that reflects the fundamental truths of creation. With any other *chesed* we do, it is gone almost immediately. If we donate a meal for a poor person, after a few hours, not much remains of it. However, the *chesed shel emes* that we do for the body of the deceased carries on into *techiyas hameisim.* Perhaps it is of greater significance than any *chesed* we could do for the living!

6 Small Wonders

וַיְהִי יִצְחָק בֶּן אַרְבָּעִים שָׁנָה בְּקַחְתּוֹ אֶת רִבְקָה וכו'. לְאִשָּׁה:

And Yitzchok the son of Avraham was forty years old when he took Rivkah...as a wife. (Bereishis 25:20)

Simply speaking, Rivkah was three years old when she married Yitzchok. (Later in this section we will discuss how this could be in reality.) There is some disagreement over this point, but the general approach is that she was three. The simple meaning of the Torah's verses points in that direction, as we shall see. Avraham was notified of Rivkah's birth right after the *Akeidah,* as Rashi says. Yitzchok was thirty-seven at the time of the *Akeidah,* which occurred right before the death of Sarah. Our verse says that Yitzchok married at forty. Thus, it is logical to conclude that Rivkah was three, and Rashi, therefore, says:

הממתין לה עד שתהא ראויה לביאה שלש שנים (נדה מד ע"ב) ונשאה (סדר עולם פ"א): (רש"י בראשית כ"ה:כ')

Yitzchok waited for her until she would be fitting to live as man and wife, which is at three years old (Niddah 44b), and he married her. (Rashi, Bereishis 25:20, based on Seder Olam, ch. 1)[14]

Another reason to assume that she was three is the fact that when *Avraham Avinu* came to *Eretz Yisrael,* he was seventy-five, and it was not until he was eighty-five that he took Hagar as a *pilegesh.* When he was eighty-six, Yishmael was born. Avraham took Hagar at that point because after Avraham and Sarah had spent ten years in *Eretz Yisrael* without having a child, their only option was for Avraham to take Hagar as a *pilegesh.* All this is stated clearly in the Torah.

However, with Yitzchok and Rivkah there was no option of *pilegesh.* First

---

14   ע"ע סדר הדורות ב' אלפים פ"ח

of all, Yitzchok was considered an *olah temimah,* an unblemished offering to Hashem. He could not compromise this status by taking such a step. Furthermore, Yitzchok understood the significance of his Divinely designated *shidduch.* He realized that Rivkah was chosen to be his wife and thus the mother of *K'lal Yisrael,* as it is written regarding his marriage match with Rivkah:

מה' יצא הדבר: (בראשית כ"ד:נ')

"The matter issued from Hashem." (Bereishis 24:50)

K'lal Yisrael was to originate specifically from Rivkah. Thus, he could not take another woman. Unlike his father Avraham, he prayed that he and his wife should beget children together when he saw that she was not having any.

However, it is clear from the Torah that this was not until Yitzchok was fifty-nine[15], as Yaakov and Eisav were born when Yitzchok was sixty, as the Torah recounts. This means that Yitzchok and Rivkah were married for nineteen years, not just ten, before Yitzchok started davening for offspring. Since Yitzchok married Rivkah at forty, he should have started davening at fifty instead of waiting until he was fifty-nine. Why did he wait?

This is easily understandable if we accept that Rivkah married at the age of three. Thus, Yitzchok starting praying for children ten years after Rivkah turned twelve, the age at which she became capable of childbearing.

When Rivkah turned twenty-two and was still childless, Yitzchok had no other options. He could not take a second wife, and he couldn't divorce Rivkah. Therefore, "Yitzchok entreated Hashem, across from his wife." (ibid., 25:21)

All this supports the premise that Rivkah was three when she married, because if she was older, we are left with the question of why Yitzchok waited nineteen years before he started praying.

Technically, everything works out perfectly. The only problem that exists is the very idea of a girl getting married at the age of three![16] In addition, the

---

15   ע"ע סדר הדורות ב' אלפים ק"ז

16   There may be those who don't find this question problematic. If *Chazal* say that Rivkah was three then that suffices for them and they don't need any explanations. To them I say חילכם לאורייתא. Nevertheless, over the course of many years in *chinuch,* I have encountered many who, while saying אם קבלה היא נקבל, still grapple with trying to understand this approach. It is to them that I direct this answer.

conversation Rivkah conducted with Eliezer, bringing the water, making decisions for herself, sliding off the camel and covering her face due to her recognition of the immense greatness of Yitzchok all seem quite inappropriate for a child of three. It does not fit with our conception of the normal development of a child. Of course, *HaKadosh Baruch Hu* can do anything, but this approach sounds more like an esoteric Midrash than the simple meaning of the text.

However, to help us grasp that this was the simple reality of Yitzchok and Rivkah's lives, let us consider the fact that even in the natural order of the world there is such a thing as great child prodigies. We don't have to go back three thousand years to find such cases. These children exist but are so rare that most of us do not have a chance to see them. Child prodigies can be found in music, science, math, literature and more. There are six-month-old babies who are already reading, talking and expressing thoughts and ideas. At two or three years, they have developed extraordinarily and are able to communicate and deal in an intellectual, mature way with adults. There are children who at the age of nine or ten are in college, or graduating college or going for Master's degrees.

The scientific definition of a prodigy is a child who possesses an extraordinarily high abstract reasoning capability, plus extraordinarily advanced domain-specific skills in a multiplicity of domains. These children perform at adult professional levels in multiple domains and display passionate involvement with numerous domains of prodigious achievement.

There is a documented case of a child who, before he was even three years old, was playing chess, and by age four he was competing in national tournaments against children many years older. By age seven, he was winning those tournaments. Another was reciting poetry at age two and writing complete poems by six. Yet another, Abigail Sin, at ten years old, is Singapore's most celebrated young pianist. Sin started reading at age two.

Maria Gaetana Agnesi (May 16, 1718 – January 9, 1799) was an Italian linguist, mathematician and philosopher. She was recognized as a child prodigy very early on. She could speak both French and Italian at five years of age. By her thirteenth birthday, she had acquired Greek, Hebrew, Spanish, German, Latin and probably a few more languages, as she was referred to as the "Walking Polyglot." She even educated her younger brothers. When she was nine years old, she composed and delivered an hour-long speech in Latin to an academic gathering.

Then there are regular children who are brought up "on the street." Often, these children are mature beyond their years — they have "street smarts" because of the environment they grow up in. Gangs are often made up of these children who are six, seven or eight years old.

Both of these factors existed with Rivkah. Hashem blessed her to be a child prodigy, in the natural order of things, and infused in her all the intellect and understanding needed to be a gifted and intelligent young woman at the age of three. It is not a commonplace phenomenon, but it is also not a miracle. It can exist even today. In addition, Rivka grew up in a "street" house — in the home of Besuel and Lavan Ha'Arami. She was raised like a "street child," in a home of incredible cruelty and craftiness, where it was a constant struggle to stay honorable and decent. Because of her intellectual capacity it did not bother her father and brother to send the little girl out with the flock at the age of three to fend for herself among the male shepherds, even though there was an older brother more than capable of doing the job himself.

In order that the lives of our *Avos* and *Imahos* should follow the Divine plan, Hashem blessed Rivkah with the qualities of intelligence and understanding. He placed her in a home that, under normal circumstances, would have produced a corrupted child, an indecent and negative personality. However, because Rivkah was able to remove herself from this environment by the age of three, she was not adversely impacted by the horrors of her home. It was through her unscathed and vibrant purity that she was able to become part of the home of *Yitzchok Avinu* and bring the Shechinah to rest there. As Rashi points out, the cloud of the Shechinah's presence returned to the tent of Sarah when it became the tent of Rivkah.

Indeed, as Yitzchok understood, "The matter issued from Hashem."

תולדות

TOLDOS

1 The Home in which Eisav Grew Up

O ver the years, I have heard many unfortunate *drashos* on *Parshas Toldos* in which disparaging comments are made about the home of Yitzchok and Rivkah. The speakers equip themselves with warmed-over pop psychology in an attempt to explain the development of Eisav's "personality."

They are often bothered by the fact that Rivkah did not directly confront Yitzchok with what she knew about Eisav. Why did Rivkah have to go through the subterfuge of having Yaakov steal the *brachos* as he did? Does this not point to some sort of marital disharmony, Heaven forbid, and inability to resolve their "personal differences?" Is this not a blatant breakdown of "communication?" Is there not something "dysfunctional" about such a home, they ask?

In these *drashos,* any popular psychological term that the speaker might have in his head is unhesitatingly pinned on Yitzchok and Rivkah.

Perhaps for that very reason, because short-sighted, narrow-minded people could make such an error, the Torah's verses make it quite clear that there is no truth at all to such an approach.

In order to properly appreciate this, let us first consider what the *Ramban* wrote in his introduction to *Parshas Shemos.* He explains the link between *Sefer Bereishis* and *Sefer Shemos.*

והנה הגלות איננו נשלם עד יום שובם אל מקומם ואל מעלת אבותם ישובו. וכשיצאו ממצרים אף על פי שיצאו מבית עבדים עדיין יחשבו גולים כי היו בארץ לא להם נבוכים במדבר:

The exile [in Egypt] is not fully over until the day they return to their place and to the exalted level of their Forefathers. When they went out of Egypt, although they left the state of slavery, they were still considered exiles because they were not in their own land. They were lost in the wilderness.

וכשבאו אל הר סיני ועשו המשכן ושב הקב"ה והשרה שכינתו ביניהם אז שבו אל מעלות אבותם שהיה סוד אלוק עלי אהליהם והם הם המרכבה:

But when they came to Mount Sinai and made the Mishkan, and the Holy One Blessed be He **brought back His Shechinah to dwell among them, then they returned to the exalted level of their Forefathers. This was [a recurrence of] the aspect of G-d's presence being upon their (the Forefathers') tents. They (the Forefathers) were the very vehicle of G-d's presence in the world, [and this was now replicated by the presence of the Shechinah in the Mishkan].**

ואז נחשבו גאולים ולכן נשלם הספר הזה בהשלימו ענין המשכן ובהיות כבוד ה' מלא אותו תמיד: (רמב"ן שמות הקדמה)

Then they were considered redeemed. Therefore, this book [of Shemos] concludes with the completion of the Mishkan and with its being perpetually filled with Hashem's glory. (Ramban, Hakdamas Shemos)

The *Ramban* explains to us that in *Sefer Bereishis*, we find that the presence of the Shechinah was upon the minature *mishkan* that was the homes of the *Avos* and *Imahos*. In Yitzchok and Rivkah's home, the holy Shechinah was a perpetual dweller. Their tent was a *mishkan* in which the Shechinah would reside until the more permanent structures of Moshe's *Mishkan* and, finally, the *Bais HaMikdash* were constructed. This point alone is enough to awaken us to the high level of a personal relationship that existed between Yitzchok and Rivkah, as we know that the Shechinah is present in the home only when there is *shalom* between husband and wife.

תנא משמיה דר' מאיר איש ואשה שכינה ביניהם י"ה, יו"ד באיש, וה"א באשה, זכו שכינה ביניהן ומתברכין, לא זכו שכינה מסתלקת מביניהן ונדבקות שתי האשות ואש אוכלתן: (פסיקתא זוטרתא בראשית ב':כ"ג)

It was taught in the name of Rabbi Meir: With a man and wife, the Shechinah is among them, [which is represented by the Divine Name of] י"ה. The י is in "man," איש. And the ה is in "woman," אשה. If they are meritorious, the Shechinah is among them and they are blessed. If they are not meritorious, the Shechinah leaves them. And the two "fires," אש, [which spells "man" and "woman" without the letters י and ה] become attached to one another, and fire consumes them. (Pesikta Zutarta, Bereishis 2:23)

When there is discord in the home, the Shechinah departs. This forces us to say that there must have been a very high level of unity and harmony between Yitzchok and Rivkah.

Let us start from the beginning of the story.

1. The Torah describes at length the marriage match of Yitzchok and Rivkah. The Torah recounts the astounding Divine providence involved, how Eliezer has miracle upon miracle happen to him in order to show that Hashem is directing him to this extraordinary young girl who will be the perfect match to build the perfect home and thereby become the mother of *K'lal Yisrael*. As the Torah states, "The matter issued from Hashem." (*Bereishis* 24:50)

2. Let us not forget that the beginning of *Parshas Toldos*, with the story of Eisav, is adjacent to the end of *Parshas Chayei Sarah*. There, Yitzchok brings Rivkah into his mother's tent, and, as Rashi says, sees the embodiment of his righteous mother Sarah. He is comforted over the loss of his mother.

והרי היא שרה אמו, שכל זמן ששרה קימת היה נר דלוק מערב שבת לערב שבת וברכה מצויה בעסה וענן קשור על האהל, ומשמתה פסקו, וכשבאת רבקה חזרו:
(בראשית כ"ד:ס"ז)

She (Rivkah) was just like his mother Sarah. As long as Sarah was alive, the lamp would burn from Erev Shabbos to Erev Shabbos, there was a blessing in the dough and there was a cloud positioned above the tent. When she died, they ceased. And when Rivkah came, they returned. (Rashi, Bereishis 24:67)

These incredible symbols of the holy *mishkan,* of the tent of Sarah, reemerge when Rivkah enters the tent. These were direct parallels to the *ner tamid* of the Temple's Menorah that never went out, the *Lechem HaPanim* of the Temple's golden table that remained fresh from week to week, and the clouds of glory that hovered over the *Mishkan* of Moshe. All of these were in the home of *Rivkah Imeinu*!

3. We could not hope for the Torah to describe a relationship of husband and wife more clearly and openly than it does with Yitzchok and Rivkah:

ויבאה יצחק האהלה שרה אמו ויקח את רבקה ותהי־לו לאשה ויאהבה

(בראשית כ"ד:ס"ז)

And Yitzchok brought her into the tent of his mother Sarah, and he took Rivkah and she became his wife, and he loved her. (Bereishis 24:67)

The above description of their marital relationship is the testimony of the *Borei Olam* Himself.

4. Equally compelling is the Torah's description of their relationship later on, when they reside in Gerar, the city of Avimelech.

ויהי כי־ארכו־לו שם הימים וישקף אבימלך מלך פלשתים בעד החלון וירא והנה יצחק

מצחק את רבקה אשתו: (בראשית כ"ו:ח')

And it happened when he (Yitzchok) spent a long time there (in Gerar) that Avimelech, King of the Philistines, looked at the window and realized that Yitzchok is laughing with his wife Rivkah. (ibid., 26:8)

The relationship of Yitzchok and Rivkah is revealed to us in so many ways! Perhaps it is for this very reason. The Torah wants to reinforce the point that Yitzchok and Rivkah were extraordinarily close to each other, and actually saw eye to eye on everything.

5. We find that there is unanimity even in their approach to some of Eisav's actions.

ויהי עשו בן־ארבעים שנה ויקח אשה את־יהודית בת־באֵרי החתי ואת־בשמת בת־

אילן החתי ותהיין מרת רוח ליצחק ולרבקה: (בראשית כ"ו:ל"ד-ל"ה)

And when Eisav was forty years old, he took as a wife Yehudis the daughter of Beeri the Hittite, and Bosmas the daughter of

Eilon the Hittite, and they caused bitterness of spirit to Yitz-chok and to Rivkah. (ibid., 26:34–35)

Nevertheless, there are some questions that need to be answered. Why did Yitzchok not know what Eisav was really like? Why did Rivkah not tell Yitz-chok what she knew?

Let us consider a similar situation that appears a little later in *Sefer Bere-ishis*. When Yosef is sold into slavery, and the brothers return to Yaakov and inform him that Yosef is "dead," the Torah tells us that Yaakov could not be consoled.

ויקרע יעקב שמלתיו וכו'. ויתאבל על־בנו ימים רבים. ויקמו כל־בניו וכל־בנתיו לנחמו וימאן להתנחם ויאמר כי־ארד אל־בני אבל שאלה ויבך אתו אביו: (בראשית ל"ז:ל"ד-ל"ה)

And Yaakov tore his garments… and mourned over his son for many days. And all his sons and daughters arose to console him, but he refused to be consoled. He said: "For I will descend in mourning to my son, to She'ol." And his (Yaakov's) father cried for him. (ibid., 37:34–35)

Yitzchok, who was Yaakov's father, cries for Yaakov because he knows that Yosef is still alive (*Bereishis Rabba* 84:21), and he sees how Yaakov is suffering greatly. If Yitzchok knows, why does he not tell his son Yaakov and spare him the pain? *Chazal* answer that Yitzchok knows only because Hashem revealed it to him. Yitzchok says to himself: My son is also a prophet like I am. If Hashem wanted him to know, He would tell him, too. Hashem is not telling him for a reason. Thus, it is my responsibility to remain silent. It is the Divine Will that this be hidden from Yaakov.

This helps us understand what happened in *Parshas Toldos* with Eisav. When Eisav left Yitzchok to go hunt for venison, Rivkah seizes this opportunity. Obviously, she knows what is happening due to her prophetic vision.[17] Thus, she instructs Yaakov to go immediately to his father Yitzchok to receive the *brachos*. Yet, Yaakov is reluctant. He is concerned that he might end up with a curse in place of a blessing, but his mother Rivkah convinces him to go.

---

17   Although Rivkah is not listed as one of the seven prophetesses, she clearly was bestowed a level of spiritual awareness called *ruach hakodesh*.

ותאמר לו אמו עלי קללתך בני: (בראשית כ"ז:י"ג)

And she says to him: "My son, your curse is upon me." (Bereishis 27:13)

This is a very strange thing for someone to say. How does it help Yaakov if she says she will take the curse upon herself? How is this supposed to work? If Yitzchok curses Yaakov, what makes the curse jump to Rivkah? The *Targum* on this verse puts everything into perspective.

ואמרת ליה אמיה עלי אתאמר בנבואה דלא ייתון לוטיא עלך ברי: (תרגום שם)

His mother said to him: "My son, it was said to me in prophesy[18] that curses will not come upon you." (Targum Onkelos, ad loc.)

We understand from this *Targum* that, indeed, Hashem revealed to Rivkah that the *brachos* would go to Yaakov and that he would be safe from any curse. We see that Rivkah knew crucial matters that were revealed only to her. She knew that Eisav had left to fetch venison, she knew all about the *brachos* and who it was that Heaven meant to receive them and she knew that Yaakov would come out unharmed. Why didn't she say anything to Yitzchok?

The answer is as before. Rivkah knew that Yitzchok, too, was a prophet. If Hashem had wanted Yitzchok to know, He would have told him — just as He revealed to Rivkah what was going on. She understood that the *brachos* needed to go to Yaakov, and realized that it needed to take place in this manner, without Yitzchok realizing to whom he was giving the *brachos*. Thus, she realized that she was not to reveal anything to Yitzchok.

This answers another puzzling episode that occurred many years earlier. When Rivkah was pregnant with Yaakov and Eisav, and she received a prophecy that she was carrying two different nations within her, why did she not report it immediately to her husband? This surely cannot be attributed to Yaakov's attachment to Eisav, who was not yet born! Rather, she understood that if Hashem had wanted Yitzchok to know, He would have told him directly. That is how great Yitzchok was. She understood it was a prophecy directed to

---

18   Again, this prophesy was probably on the level of *ruach hakodesh*.

her, and she could not share it. In the words of the *Ramban*:

שאמרה אין אנכי צריכה להגיד נבואה לנביא כי הוא גדול מן המגיד לי:

(רמב"ן בראשית כ"ז:ד' וע"ע שם איך שהסביר הענין)

She said: "I do not need to tell a prophecy to a prophet who is greater than the one (Shem ben Noach) who told it to me." (Ramban, Bereishis 27:4, see additional explanation there.)[19]

For this same reason, Rivkah was prevented later on from telling Yitzchok that Eisav wanted to kill Yaakov. She did not share this information, but sent Yaakov away.

Let us take note how Rivkah comes to speak to Yitzchok at the end of *Parshas Toldos*. Here, she openly shares her concerns with her husband in a most straightforward fashion, since Hashem permits her to speak.

ותאמר רבקה אל יצחק קצתי בחיי מפני בנות חת אם לקח יעקב אשה מבנות חת כאלה מבנות הארץ למה לי חיים: (בראשית כ"ז:מ"ו)

And Rivkah said to Yitzchok: "I am unable to bear my life, due to the Hittite women. If Yaakov takes a wife from Hittite women like these, from the women of the land, of what worth is my life?" (Bereishis 27:46)

Yitzchok listens to Rivkah and sends Yaakov away to Lavan. We manifestly and unambiguously see that the claim that there was no communication between Rivkah and Yitzchok is patently false and blatantly libelous. The notion that she did not express her feelings to him is so obviously erroneous that the need to even broach the issue is unfortunate. By just opening up a *Chumash*, it jumps out at us from every verse that such an approach is ill-informed.

Lacking support from the verses themselves, these speakers are wont to cite the commentary of the *Ha'amek Davar,* written by the *Netziv*, on *Bereishis* 24:64–65. They think that here, at last, they have found proof of the negative quality of the relationship between Yitzchok and Rivkah. Commenting

---

19   ע"ע דרשות הר"ן — הדרוש השני וז"ל אמנם זאת הנבואה לא ידעה יצחק, כי המתנבאים בימים ההם מן הנראה שלא היה
להם רשות לפרסם נבואתן וכו'. עכ"ל

on when Rivkah first saw her future husband Yitzchok, this is what the *Netziv* says, in full.

ותשא רבקה וגו' ותרא את יצחק בעודו עומד ומתפלל והי' אז כמלאך אלהים נורא מאד. וכמבואר ברבה שראתה ידיו שטוחות בתפלה ע"כ נבעתה מאד:

"And Rivkah lifted up her eyes" and she saw Yitzchok while he was standing in prayer and was then like an angel of G-d, very awesome. As it says in Bereishis Rabba, she saw his arms outstretched in prayer and therefore she was very frightened.

מי האיש הלזה. אשר אני מתפעל ומתפחד ממנו. וכמבואר בב"ר בלשון הלזה משמעו אדם מאוים ונורא. ע"כ כששמעה שהוא אישה. ותקח הצעיף ותתכס. מרוב פחד ובושה כמו שמבינה שאינה ראויה להיות לו לאשה ומאז והלאה נקבע בלבה פחד. ולא היתה עם יצחק כמו שרה עם אברהם. ורחל עם יעקב. אשר בהיות להם איזה קפידא עליהם לא בושו לדבר רחת לפניהם. משא"כ רבקה:

"Who is this (halazeh) man" that I am shocked by and scared of? As explained in Bereishis Rabba, the word halazeh implies a person who is terrible and fearsome. Therefore, when she heard that he is her husband, "she took the scarf and covered her face" out of fear and embarrassment, since she understood that she is not fitting to be his wife. And from then on, fear was fixed in her heart. She was not with Yitzchok the way that Sarah was with Avraham, and Rachel with Yaakov. If there was something that bothered them, they were not embarrassed to speak heatedly about it with their husbands. But Rivkah was not this way.

וכ"ז הקדמה להסיפור שיבוא בפ' תולדות שהיו יצחק ורבקה מחולקים בדעות. ומכ"מ לא מצאה רבקה לב להעמיד את יצחק על דעתה בדברים נכוחים כי היא יודעת האמת כי עשו רק ציד בפיו. וכן בשעת הברכות:

And all this is an introduction to the story that will come in Parshas Toldos, where Yitzchok and Rivkah had differing opinions. But nonetheless, Rivkah did not have the heart to win over Yitzchok to her opinion through convincing argument, because she knew the truth that Eisav was being verbally deceptive.

And similarly at the time of the brachos, [she refrained from convincing her husband].

וכ"ז הי' סיבה מהקב"ה שיגיעו הברכות ליעקב דוקא באופן כזה וכאשר יבואר במקומו. ואלו היתה רבקה עם אישה כמו שרה ורחל אם אנשיהן לא הי' מגיע בזה האופן. והכל בהשגחה פרטית מראש שתגיע רבקה ליצחק בשעה שתבהל ממנו ויצא אחרית דבר כפי רצונו ית':

All this was set up by Hashem so that the brachos would come to Yaakov just in the way they did, as will be explained there. For if Rivkah would have related to her husband as Sarah and Rachel did to their husbands, the brachos would not have come in this way. Everything was directed in advance by Divine Providence so that Rivkah would meet Yitzchok at a time when she would be frightened by him, and later events would take place according to His Will, may He be blessed. (Ha'amek Davar, Bereishis 24:64–65)

Far from proving the premise that these speakers cite him for, the *Netziv* is actually describing a remarkably positive relationship. When Yitzchok would pray, he would be enveloped by a tremendous and awe-inspiring *kedushah*. He was a perfect and unblemished offering to Hashem. Rivkah, on her way from Lavan's house, was granted by Heaven the opportunity to witness this moving sight and thereby appreciate the true spiritual greatness of her husband-to-be. She was able to gaze at this angelic being speaking to his Creator and was extraordinarily moved and impressed by the sight. Rivkah, therefore, developed a solid, reality-based respect for who her husband was.

The *Netziv* explains that this created an environment in which Rivkah would not contradict Yitzchok's opinions or talk back to him. Occasionally, we find Sarah talking strongly and perhaps tenaciously to Avraham, or Rachel speaking heatedly to Yaakov, but Rivkah always had a certain awe and deference toward her husband. Says the *Netziv*, this was carefully planned in advance by Divine Providence. It was Hashem's will that she should comprehend the absolutely, great reality of who Yitzchok truly was and the greatness of his prophecy, so that when she did wrestle with ideas that conflicted with his, she dealt with him with the reverence that he correctly deserved, not underestimating who her husband was. Sometimes, in a personal relationship, we act with less respect than our partner is worthy of due to familiarity. Rivkah, however, put her husband on a pedestal and kept him there.

This wasn't wrong, inappropriate or inaccurate. *Yitzchok Avinu* amply deserved this high esteem from his wife. Even though in the normal course of events a tzaddik might hide his true level, even from his own wife, Hashem did not wish this to be the case here.

In my humble opinion, it is possible to reconcile the explanation of the *Netziv* with my explanation in the following manner: It was because of Rivkah's reality based awe and true reverence for her husband that led her to realize his close relationship to *HaKadosh Boruch Hu,* which in turn led her to realize that if Hashem wanted him to know what she knew He would inform Yitzchok Himself.

Nevertheless, even were one to understand the *Netziv* as explaining the events in a different manner, it would in no way give any credibility, whatsoever, to those who wish to project conflict, discord and disharmony Heaven forbid, into their holy relationship. Rather, in the words of the *Netziv,* "All this was set up by Hashem so that the *brachos* would come to Yaakov just in the way they did." By Hashem, whose name is peace and whose seal is peace.

---

2 Did Eisav Really Fool Yitzchok?

It is commonly assumed that Yitzchok had no idea who Eisav really was. Implicit in this approach is that Eisav was able to fool his father into thinking that he was some sort of righteous person. There are strong arguments that this was not the case at all. *Yitzchok Avinu* knew very well who Eisav was, as we can see from the following:

1. Eisav never had a *bris milah*. As explained by *Daas Zekeinim MiBaalei HaTosafos, Bereishis* 25:25, at the age of eight days, Eisav was judged as ill because of the ruddy color of his skin. Thus, he was not permitted to have a *bris* on the eighth day. Since before the Torah was given there were no *tashlumin* for a missed *bris,* Eisav was not able to have a *bris* until he turned thirteen. (See *Kli Chemdah, Parshas Toldos* 2)

At the age of thirteen, Eisav refused to undergo a *bris milah,* as explained in the above-mentioned *Daas Zekeinim*. Thus, Yitzchok knew very well that Eisav remained uncircumcised willingly. Yitzchok had to know that there was something seriously wrong with him.

2. *Chazal* say that the Shechinah would leave whenever Eisav would appear. Within the very story of the *brachos*, we see that Yitzchok took a very sober approach to Eisav. Yitzchok knew he had to bolster up Eisav with a powerful merit just to keep the Shechinah there long enough to deliver the *brachos*. It was for this reason that Yitzchok asked Eisav to bring him the delicacies so that the merit of *kibbud av va'eim* would induce the Shechinah to remain. It was clear to Yitzchok that Eisav was not a worthy individual in his own right.

At the very end of the *Parsha*, when Yitzchok gave *brachos* to Yaakov before Yaakov left to *Charan*, there was no need for Yaakov to bring Yitzchok any food. This was because Yaakov was a fitting receptacle of blessing. However, Eisav, who was a cracked receptacle, needed to be properly prepared. He needed to be sent out to do something worthwhile for a change.

3. When Eisav married, it caused "bitterness of spirit to Yitzchok and to Rivkah" (*Bereishis* 26:35). Rashi (ad loc.) explains that the smoke of the idolatrous worship that Eisav's wives engaged in caused an odor that was extraordinarily distasteful to Yitzchok and Rivkah. Here, too, is evidence that well before the story of the *brachos*, Yitzchok was aware of Eisav's lowly spiritual level. Yitzchok understood that Eisav was far from being a tzaddik.

4. The instructions given by Yitzchok to Eisav reveal Yitzchok's true perspective on him. As Rashi explains in *Bereishis* 27:3, Yitzchok told Eisav to make sure that the meat was from kosher slaughter and not *neveilah*, and he reminded him not to bring anything that was stolen property!

This is truly a bizarre set of instructions. If a parent sends his child to the butcher to buy meat, and warns the child to make sure to go to the kosher butcher, not to the *treif* butcher, to not buy the ham, to not rob anyone leaving the store and to pay for the food, it would be obvious that the parent has major concerns about his child. Yitzchok was well aware who Eisav was.

5. As Rashi comments (ibid., v. 21), Yitzchok's suspicions were aroused by Yaakov's mention of Hashem. Yitzchok picked up on the fact that such speech would be out of character for Eisav. If Eisav was known to studiously avoid mentioning Hashem, he surely did not have much of a reputation as a tzad-

dik.

If all this is true, why was Yitzchok giving Eisav the *brachos* in the first place? The answer is quite simple. "Yitzchok loved Eisav because *tzayid* was in his mouth" (*Bereishis* 25:28). *Tzayid* means something trapped, and Rashi explains this to mean that Eisav "trapped" Yitzchok with the words in his mouth.

As the Midrash brought by Rashi explains, Eisav would come to his father and ask, "How do you give *ma'aser* from straw? How do you give *ma'aser* from salt?" These seem to be rather elementary questions that every child knows the answer to. Of course, one only gives *ma'aser* from food, and only food that grows from the earth—not salt and straw. If an adult student today would ask such a question, would his rabbi consider it a profound question? Clearly, it is an ignorant question that only a person lacking proper background in Torah would ask.

Consequently, it had to be abundantly clear to Yitzchok that Eisav was just trying to impress him. Yet as little as he knew, as little as he progressed in his learning, there still remained one major advantage, one extraordinarily positive quality that Eisav had. That was his performance of *kibbud av va'eim.* Yitzchok, in order to keep Eisav close to him, reinforced his observance of that mitzvah. Yitzchok recognized that Eisav's pitiful efforts to fool and impress him stemmed from Eisav's inner desire for his approval and respect. That was the only power that Yitzchok had over Eisav to hold onto him. It was with this in mind that Yitzchok showed Eisav extra attention and affection.

It is notable that this was not artificial attention or feigned love. There was a true bond of love between father and son, even knowing who Eisav was. The Torah speaks of their relationship unambiguously. Hashem writes in His Torah that "Yitzchok loved Eisav." If the Torah says he loved him, it must have been real love.

Rivkah did not see the value in this approach. Either due to the prophecies she had received before the birth of her twin children or because of her pragmatic nature, Rivkah felt that it was more important to give full support to and elevate Yaakov, who was the *"the man of perfection, dwelling in the tents* [of Torah]" (ibid., 25:27).

We now come back to the big question: Why did Yitzchok want to give the *brachos* to Eisav?

To be sure, the blessings of spirituality and *Eretz Yisrael* had only one deserving address — Yaakov. No one dreamed of granting such matters to Eisav. As we will see, Yitzchok will *later* give to Yaakov the inheritance of *Eretz Yisrael* that originated with Avraham, the future receiving of the Torah and the entire spectrum of spirituality. However, that is not what is transpiring now when Yaakov comes in to take Eisav's *brachos*.

Just after Yaakov exits upon receiving the *brachos,* Eisav comes in and asks, "Don't you have a blessing left for me?" Yitzchok answers, "I have no more blessing, your brother took it." What is this supposed to mean? Later, when Yaakov leaves to go to the house of Lavan, Yitzchok, indeed, has a very important blessing left: the blessing of Avraham to inherit *Eretz Yisrael*!

Obviously, Yitzchok never intended that for Eisav. That was never part of the package of *brachos* that Yaakov and Eisav vied over. The blessing that Yitzchok had intended to bestow upon Eisav, which was no longer available when Eisav came in a little too late, was the blessing of *gashmiyus*, blessings of the physical world. As the commentators explain, Eisav and Yaakov were supposed to be partners in the development of *K'lal Yisrael*. Eisav would take care of the *gashmiyus*, while Yaakov would be involved in the *ruchniyus*. Eisav would support Torah. He would be the "Zevulun" for the "Yissachar" who was Yaakov.

Rivkah felt that this was a gamble not worth taking. In her opinion, putting Yaakov's entire support system in the hands of Eisav was asking for disaster. It would appear that *HaKadosh Boruch Hu* agreed with her approach.

In the end, Yitzchok's valiant attempts to keep Eisav within the fold did not succeed. Ultimately Yitzchok concluded by saying: "Also blessed shall he (Yaakov) be" (ibid., 27:33). Here, Yitzchok admitted that the blessings of *gashmiyus* should stay where he had put them, with Yaakov. However, this does not imply that Yitzchok did not understand the character of Eisav previously. Everything was conscious and thought out. It was just a difference of opinion over what was the correct approach when dealing with Eisav.

3   Yitzchok on his Own

Throughout his life, *Avraham Avinu* experienced situations and circumstances that were unique to him and not shared by the other *Avos*. The same is true of *Yaakov Avinu*. The latter part of *Sefer Bereishis* speaks of the various hardships, travels and difficulties of Yaakov. It is interesting to note that we do not seem to find circumstances unique to Yitzchok in the same way as an independent individual standing by himself. The Torah is replete with stories of Yitzchok either connected to his father Avraham or to his children Yaakov and Eisav. None appear to be identified solely as his own.

Everything that happens to Yitzchok, it appears, already has happened to Avraham. Even when Yitzchok seems to be acting independently, it is just a repeat of what Avraham has already done. It is a reflection of the *avodah* of Avraham. Avraham goes to Gerar; Yitzchok goes to Gerar. Avraham finds his wife in danger and says "she is my sister"; Yitzchok finds his wife in danger and says "she is my sister." Avraham digs wells; Yitzchok redigs the very same wells and names them with the very same names.

Where do we find something that is unique to Yitzchok? Is there any event that can be said to represent or embody the special *avodah* of *Yitzchok Avinu*? As we examine the Torah, we find a solitary instance that sets Yitzchok apart from Avraham and Yaakov, expressed so briefly that we hardly notice it.

ויצו אבימלך את־כל־העם לאמר הנגע באיש הזה ובאשתו מות יומת: ויזרע יצחק בארץ ההוא וימצא בשנה ההוא מאה שערים ויברכהו ה': (בראשית כ"ו:י"א-י"ב)

And Avimelech commanded all the people, saying: "Whoever harms this man and his wife shall surely die." And Yitzchok sowed in that land and he found in that year a hundred times [more produce than estimated], and Hashem blessed him. (Bereishis 26:11–12)

Yitzchok is in Gerar and there is a famine in the entire area. He does not go down to Egypt for food, but deals with the problem where he is, in *Eretz Yisrael*. *"And Yitzchok sowed in that land."* Yitzchok plows; Yitzchok plants in that arid dry land without rain. *"And he found in that year a hundred times [more produce than estimated], and Hashem blessed him."*

This short segment in the life of Yitzchok, ostensibly lacking deep significance, actually defines the nature of his very being. This account of the "hundred times" appears to be the only *avodah*, the only incident, that is uniquely Yitzchok. It does not involve Avraham and the *Akeidah*. It has nothing to do with the births of Yaakov and Eisav or the incident of the *brachos*. It is exclusively Yitzchok. What is the significance of this incident?

There is a fascinating commentary of the *Netziv* that sheds light on this, found in the *Harcheiv Davar* (further elucidations of the *Ha'amek Davar*) on *Parshas Vayishlach* 34:1, article 2. The *Netziv* cites a Midrash saying that Avraham was called Yisrael, and Yitzchok was called Yisrael. Thus, he raises the question: If so, why is Yisrael considered especially to be the name of Yaakov?

The *Netziv* answers by explaining the significance of the title "Yisrael." It signifies acting on a level that is above the laws of nature, which can express itself in various areas. As the *Netziv* explains, every person needs to attain three things in his life: defense from his enemies, *parnassah* and peace. Without peace, nothing good will last.

There is support for this last statement of the *Netziv* from Rashi in *Parshas Bechukosai*.

שמא תאמרו, הרי מאכל והרי משתה אם אין שלום אין כלום, תלמוד לומר אחר כל
זאת "ונתתי שלום בארץ", מכאן שהשלום שקול כנגד הכל: (רש"י ויקרא כ"ו:ו')

Perhaps you will say: "We have food, we have drink, but if there is no peace, then there is nothing." Therefore, the Torah says after all these [blessings], *"And I will place peace."* From here [we learn] that peace is equal to all. (Rashi, *Vayikra* 26:6)

Let us return to the commentary of the *Netziv*. When it comes to defense from one's enemies, *Avraham Avinu* achieved a level that was above the laws of nature. We see this when he was thrown into the fiery furnace by Nimrod. Again he is protected when he goes down to Egypt, and again he emerges unscathed from the war he waged against the four powerful kings of Mesopotamia. Thus, he earned the title of "Yisrael" in this respect.

Yitzchok also earned the title of Yisrael in a certain area, says the *Netziv*.

However, only when Yaakov earned it in the area of peace (by miraculously maintaining good relations with Lavan and Eisav) was the aspect of "Yisrael" completed. That is why Yisrael is a name that belongs especially to Yaakov.

In what area did Yitzchok earn the title of "Yisrael," indicating action on a level above the laws of nature? The *Netziv* says it was in the area of *parnassah*. Yitzchok perfected the *avodah* of *parnassah*. *"And he found in that year a hundred times [more produce than estimated], and Hashem blessed him."*

Now we understand how the incident of the "hundred times" expresses the unique achievement of *Yitzchok Avinu*. It is his effectuation of a life above the laws of nature and the acquisition of the name "Yisrael."

However, it is bewildering that Yitzchok fulfilled specifically this role. He is the personality we would least expect to excel in the field of *parnassah*. The image we have of *Yitzchok Avinu* is that of *Avodah* and *Midas HaDin*. We see him as supremely strict and pious, having as much to do with this world as does the pile of ashes from the *Akeidah* that he represents. He is occupied with prayer and sacrifices — how can he be earning a living?

This is because we picture someone dedicated to Divine service as a person whose head is in the stars, someone totally disconnected from normal life. Yet, the Torah tells us that just the opposite is true. Yitzchok represents *parnassah*!

This seeming contradiction in the character of *Yitzchok Avinu* is paralleled by a teaching of *Chazal* in *Shabbos* 89b that records a discussion that will take place in the future between Hashem and the *Avos*. Hashem approaches the *Avos* and says, "Your children sinned to Me," awaiting a convincing reply. Avraham and Yaakov both disappoint Hashem by saying that the people who sinned should be wiped out in sanctification of Hashem's Name. However, Yitzchok pleases his Maker by standing up to protect *K'lal Yisrael*.

Although *Yitzchok Avinu* represents the stringency of judgement, only he comes to protect those who sinned. He meticulously calculates the maximum amount that a person could sin during the course of his life, ascertains his figures and makes an offer to Hashem: "You take half; I'll take half." In this way, Yitzchok saves *K'lal Yisrael*.

Yitzchok, while retaining the quality of *Din* which was his essence, ultimately saves all of Creation. What does *Din* mean? We find the answer at the beginning of Creation: *"In the beginning, Elokim created the heavens and the earth."* The Divine Name of *Elokim*, which represents *Din,* brought this world into existence and, ultimately, it will be *Din* that will bring it to its true fulfillment. The purpose of Creation was to infuse material reality with spirituality, with *kedushah,* and recognize that in truth, everything is for spirituality. Material reality exists only here in this world, which is a mere corridor leading to the World to Come.

We are constantly enjoined to take from the mundane and add it onto the holy. For instance, there is a mitzvah to accept Shabbos upon ourselves some time before sunset and not to conclude Shabbos until some time after dark because Shabbos is *mei'ein Olam Haba.* It represents the World to Come. Thus, we add onto its sanctity. We take from the mundane moments of the weekdays and add them to Shabbos, thereby sanctifying them. The underlying concept is that everything that exists is only for the sake of serving Hashem.

The greatest manifestation of this concept was Yitzchok himself. He represented the fact that a person's *parnassah,* his materially oriented activities, are all part of the service of Hashem. It's all together. There are no two aspects. There is no such thing as secular and holy. We cannot divorce the mundane aspects of life from spirituality. Therefore, *Yitzchok Avinu* represents and typifies the proper approach to *parnassah.* He stands for the fact that *K'lal Yisrael* is here only to serve Hashem.

It is from *Yitzchok Avinu,* and him alone, that *K'lal Yisrael* has as an inheritance — the Divinely inspired ability to make sure that every aspect of life is elevated and sanctified.

What does *Din* signify? The existence of *Din* in this world was part of the original thought that G-d had regarding the creation of the world: *"In the beginning, Elokim created."* Let us not forget that the purpose of the world's creation was only for *K'lal Yisrael.* Thus, the end result is that the Jewish people is preserved, *K'lal Yisrael* is saved, *K'lal Yisrael* is redeemed — all through the same trait, the trait of Yitzchok, which produced the "hundred times."

ויצא

VAYEITZEI

1 Understanding Reality

וַיֵּצֵא יַעֲקֹב מִבְּאֵר שָׁבַע וַיֵּלֶךְ חָרָנָה:

Yaakov left Beer Sheva and went to Charan. (Bereishis 28:10)

Yaakov leaves Beer Sheva in southern *Eretz Yisrael* and travels north, passing by Har HaMoriah and Yerushalayim. He continues north through Syria to the region called *Padan Aram,* where the town of Charan is located. It would appear that his travels take about 700-800 miles until he reaches his destination. Thus, it is peculiar that Rashi comments, based on the Gemara in *Chulin* 91b, that when Yaakov reaches Charan he suddenly exclaims:

אפשר שעברתי על מקום שהתפללו אבותיו ולא התפללתי בו. יהב דעתיה למהדר,

וחזר עד בית אל: (רש"י בראשית כ"ח:י"ז)

"How could I have passed by the place where my fathers prayed (Mount Moriah in Jerusalem) and I did not pray there?" He decided to return, and came back until Bais El. (Rashi, Bereishis 28:17)

Interestingly enough, Yaakov merits *kefitzas haderech,* as the above Gemara goes on to say. Hashem moves the world, so to speak, and brings it toward Yaakov so that he does not have such a long journey to get back to Yerushalayim. However, the whole story seems very strange. *Yaakov Avinu* passed Yerushalayim relatively soon after leaving Beer Sheva, perhaps after a day or two's journey. Yerushalayim is only about 50 miles from Beer Sheva. Yaakov then travels another 400-500 miles, and only when he gets to Charan does it suddenly strike him that he missed Yerushalayim! What took him so long? If anything, one would have expected Hashem to be upset with him: "It took you so long to remind yourself, to realize that you missed Yerushalayim and now you suddenly turn around to come back?" How are we to understand this puzzling event?

We could answer by considering how extensively *Yaakov Avinu* prepared himself for this trip to Charan. He spent fourteen years in the *bais midrash* of Shem and Ever,[20] which followed sixty-three years in the home of Yitzchok and Rivkah where he was "*the man of perfection, dwelling in the tents* [of Torah]" (ibid., 25:27). He was incredibly immersed in constant Torah study and never spent a moment away from Hashem and His will.

Yaakov Avinu was a man capable of working with honesty and integrity for Lavan, exerting himself for his "employer" in the admirable way described in the Gemara in *perek Hasocher es hapoalim.* (Bava Metzia 93b) We can be quite sure that he put in at least that much effort during the sixty-three years he spent learning Torah in the home of Yitzchok and Rivkah. Even his fourteen years spent in the *bais midrash* of Shem and Ever were characterized by incredible constancy of Torah learning. *Yaakov Avinu* never lay down to sleep; he only dozed off where he was sitting and then returned to his Torah study. (Rashi, *Bereishis* 28:11) This totals seventy-seven years of putting in tremendous effort, to prepare to go to the home of Lavan.

At this point, we may ask what motivated *Yaakov Avinu* to go to the *bais midrash* of Shem and Ever instead of heading directly to Charan? There is a certain explanation offered by some, which is flawed as far as the facts are concerned but is still worth mentioning because of the idea it contains: Yaakov went to Shem and Ever because he wanted to hear from Shem what people were like before the *Mabul.* He wanted a firsthand report about the mindset of the wicked people who perished in the Great Flood in order to prepare himself properly for what awaited him in Charan. The flaw in this explanation is that

---

20 Although Shem and Ever actually had different *batei midrash* (See 'מדרש רבה בראשית פרשה ס"ג פסקה ה'), this is the generic term we find used by the אחרונים (See פרי צדיק פר' החודש אות ט' ומגלה עמוקות עה"ת) (פרשת ויצא ועוד).

Yaakov came to the *bais midrash* of Shem and Ever after Shem had already passed away, but the idea may be true in so far as his learning from Shem's grandson Ever. Perhaps Ever had a tradition from his grandfather what life was like before the Flood.

However, the idea behind this explanation bears more then a grain of truth. The idea is that there is a difference between the sixty-three years of theoretical, "pure" learning in which Yaakov engaged in the tent of Yitzchok and the fourteen years of practical application that he underwent in the *bais midrash* of Shem and Ever. Yaakov was ensuring that when he would finally arrive in Charan and be ushered into the home of the wicked Lavan, he would be able to stay there as long as it takes and still come out unmarred. As we find later, this was, in fact, what he ultimately accomplished.

עם לבן הרשע גרתי ותרי"ג מצוות שמרתי ולא למדתי ממעשיו הרעים:

(רש"י בראשית ל"ב:ה')

"With Lavan I lived (גרתי), and I kept the 613 (תרי"ג) mitzvos — I did not learn from his evil deeds." (Rashi, Bereishis 32:5)

Similarly, Yaakov's mother Rivkah was an invaluable source of information regarding life in the house of Lavan. Although the time she spent there was relatively short, she was capable of impressing upon him the seriousness of the situation and teaching him much of what he needed to know. With all of that preparation, Yaakov felt secure. He felt he was totally equipped. Thus he left the *bais midrash* of Shem and Ever to go to Charan.

In spite of all this preparation, Yaakov's arrival in Charan can be compared to a rural farmer from heartland America who makes his big trip to NYC. He has heard about the great metropolis and seen pictures of the skyscrapers. He knows "all about it" from television and the movies. Now, he gets on a bus and travels to New York. He comes into the bus terminal, goes down into the subway and gets off at Broadway and 42nd Street to see Times Square. In spite of his carefully collected knowledge and preparation, he emerges from the subway into those brilliant, glaring lights, looks up at those mammoth, towering buildings and is simply overwhelmed. There is no way to really prepare for such an experience. Someone who has never been there is perforce awestruck when he arrives.

Lehavdil, Yaakov Avinu readies himself for the forces of impurity that fill

Charan. He knows of the evilness of the place, of the *charon af* of Charan (i.e., Hashem's anger against the place). He believes himself to be spiritually prepared for whatever he will meet there.

Finally, he arrives. *"Yaakov left Beer Sheva and went to Charan."* With all of his preparation, Yaakov finds it to be nothing he could ever have imagined. He realizes that there is one piece missing from the equation: his prayer for special help from Hashem to handle this massive challenge. He suddenly realizes that he had had an opportunity to daven at the place of the *Akeidah*, at Mount Moriah, where his grandfather Avraham had bound his father Yitzchok on the altar and thereby opened up the "gate of Heaven."

However, Yaakov had no way of knowing that something was lacking in him until he arrived in Charan and experienced the unimaginable. That is why he suddenly turns around and goes back, and that is why there is no criticism made about his behavior. Hashem is not displeased by his actions; on the contrary, Hashem is proud of his realization and He miraculously brings Yerushalayim toward Yaakov so he will not have to walk all the way back. Yaakov has *kefitzas haderech* and is returned to Yerushalayim to daven for special *siyata dishmaya*. He thereby institutes the *Maariv* prayer, which is the prayer of night, of exile, the prayer for the strength to withstand the trials of Charan.

What is "Padan Aram?"

The previous explanation of Yaakov's journey to Charan sheds light on another issue. My rebbe, HaRav HaGaon Dovid Feinstein, *shlita,* has noted in his *chiddushim* how the Torah switches between various names in describing the place where *Yaakov Avinu* went to. Throughout *Parshas Toldos*, until the end, it is called only *Padan Aram*. It is never called Charan. For instance, when that *Parsha* introduces Rivkah, it refers to her as "the daughter of Besuel from *Padan Aram*." When Eliezer goes to Charan in the beginning of *Parshas Chayei Sarah*, it is not called Charan, but rather *Padan Aram*.

Yet Rashi (*Bereishis* 25:20, s.v. *mipadan*) points out that the name of this place was not really *Padan Aram* at all but rather Aram Naharayim. It went by the name of *Padan* because there were two "Arams": Aram Naharayim ("Aram of the two rivers") and Aram Tzovah.

Padan means an ox-yoke. This expression is used to refer to things that come in a pair, since the yoke pairs the two oxen to each other. This expression applies to Aram Naharayim due to its two rivers. Nowadays, we might have described *Padan Aram* as the "twin cities" of Aram. Thus, the name *Padan Aram* was in use as the common term for that area.

When Eliezer goes there, there is nothing special about the name of the place to which he is being sent. All *Avraham Avinu* tells him is:

כי אל ארצי ואל מולדתי תלך ולקחת אשה לבני ליצחק: (בראשית כ"ד:ד')

To my country and to my homeland shall you go. And you shall take a wife for my son, for Yitzchok. (Bereishis 24:4)

Avraham does not even give the place a name. Why here, in our *Parsha*, does the Torah switch from the place's normal designation and call it Charan?

At the end of *Parshas Noach*, we find Terach leaving Ur Kasdim and traveling west to the land of Canaan, bringing along with him his entire family including Avraham and Sarah.

Here, the place is called Charan. We are told:

ויהיו ימי תרח חמש שנים ומאתים שנה וימת תרח בחרן: (שם ל"ב)

And the days of Terach were two hundred and five years, and Terach died in Charan. (ibid., 11:32)

Rashi takes note of the word "Charan" and comments:

בחרן. הנו"ן הפוכה, לומר לך עד אברם חרון אף של מקום בעולם: (רש"י שם)

חרן. *The letter* ן *[of the word Charan] is backwards. This tells you that until Avram, Hashem had anger (*חרון אף*) toward the world. (Rashi, ad loc.)*

Thus, we learn from Rashi that the very name "Charan" alludes to Hashem's anger. This is because Charan was a place that was the antithesis of G-dliness, of spirituality.

This gives us the key we need. When Eliezer went to bring Rivkah, it was not relevant to tell us that this place was anti-spiritual. It was more than sufficient for the Torah to tell us that Rivkah was from the home of Lavan and Besuel, and we knew it all. Whereas here in *Parshas Vayeitzei,* Yaakov is going there and has to take on this new spiritual challenge. Thus, it is important for the Torah to inform us of the form of this challenge: It is going to take place in Charan. Yaakov is going to confront an area that is characterized by the fact that it incites Hashem's anger. Here, he is going to confront the cause of G-d's wrath against the world.

Let us conclude by noting that after *Yaakov Avinu* saw the vision of the ladder leading from earth to Heaven and received the promise from Hashem that He would be with him wherever he goes, we find that *"Yaakov lifted up his feet"* to go (ibid., 29:1). As Rashi explains there, the feet of Yaakov carried themselves. When Yaakov heard the good news that Hashem would guard him, he avidly trusted in this promise and his steps were made light and easy. As Rashi explains, *"his heart carried his feet."* Where was he able to go easily? Where did he feel he was going with a Divine promise of success? The Torah continues, *"...and he went to the country of the people of the east (קדם)."* Here it is not called even Charan, rather קדם. As we explained in *Parshas Lech Lecha* in the section *Go West*, the term קדם refers to being farther away from the Shechinah, since the Shechinah is in the west. Yaakov was going to "the people of קדם," to people who are distant from Hashem and His will. Nevertheless, Yaakov felt that at this juncture, after having davened to Hashem and receiving the good news of Hashem's protection and help, he was able to go meet the challenge.

3   Hishtadlus

The concept of *hishtadlus* is commonly understood as the obligation to engage in an action that appears to be accomplishing a certain result according to the natural order of things, while one knows full well that the result is ultimately attained thanks to Hashem Himself. Thus, a person goes to work to earn money, but Hashem provides the *parnassah.* So, too, in many other areas. Doing something that is clearly not going to accomplish the desired result should not be considered *hishtadlus* at all. If a person jumps up in the air and says he is going to fly, obviously nothing is going to happen. That would not be called *hishtadlus*.

Yet, we see in *Parshas Vayeitzei* that this approach is not totally correct. There is an aspect of *hishtadlus* that exists even if, according to the natural order of things, the action should not really accomplish anything. *Yaakov Avinu* goes to sleep and puts rocks around his head. We have a tradition that there were twelve rocks, and we are aware of many of the deeper meanings and innuendoes connected with this event.

Simply speaking, Yaakov took a group of rocks and put them around his head. As Rashi explains the simple meaning of this event (*Bereishis* 28:11), he put them there in order to protect himself from attack by wild animals. Anyone can realize that this would appear to make no sense. A bunch of rocks around a person's head will not protect him from any animal. Even the smallest animal can climb over the rocks to reach his head or attack him from his legs or from his arms. So what is gained if his head is "protected" in this way? It is not shielded from above, only from the side. Clearly, the rocks represented a futile attempt.

Yet, Yaakov *Avinu* had no other recourse; that was all he could do in the situation. He must have trusted that *HaKadosh Boruch Hu* would miraculously provide his protection while he slept at night. Even within this context, in order to minimize his relying on miracles as much as possible, Yaakov did some sort of *hishtadlus*. To the objective observer it appeared to be a meaningless and worthless action, but Yaakov felt that since it did something that pointed in the direction of providing protection, it was necessary to do.

We find Dovid HaMelech acting likewise in a similar situation. Most people are prejudiced because they know the end of the story, but let us put our hindsight aside for a moment and think objectively about Dovid's decision to enter into single combat with Golyas. What difference would it have made if he had gone with his bare hands or with his slingshot? The likelihood of success in his mission would not have been much less even if his intent was to crush Golyas with his bare hands. Golyas himself found it downright hilarious that some young man without any armor would come out against him. Thus, if Dovid would have gone out with only his bare hands, it would have been the same. Nevertheless, he took his slingshot along: This was his *hishtadlus*.

Dovid's *hishtadlus* was to use whatever he had. If you have nothing, you go with nothing. If you have a rock or a pebble, you go out with the rock or pebble. If you have a rock or a pebble and a slingshot, you go with the slingshot, too. Whatever you have, that is the *hishtadlus* called for in order to minimize reliance on miracles, an *avodah* that Hashem requires of us. And so it was. From time immemorial, "Dovid and the slingshot" is engraved in the consciousness of even the non-Jewish world, although objectively speaking, it was absolutely meaningless. It was as futile as *Yaakov Avinu* putting rocks around his head.

Thus, we learn that even an insignificant amount of *hishtadlus* is necessary in a situation where everything seems to be helpless. If a person is on the level to be connected to Hashem and trust in Him totally that He will protect, then whatever the person does as *hishtadlus* will suffice.

4 Tefillin and Rocks

We find a *machlokes* between the *Magen Avraham* and other *Acharonim* about what to do if the strap of the *tefillin shel yad* rips all the way at the top, next to the *yud*-shaped knot that touches the *tefillin*. This *machlokes* is found in *Orach Chayim,* ch. 42, and the *Ba'er Heteiv* (ad loc., s.v. *Mayhem*) discusses whether it is permissible to switch the strap around and use the other end of it to tie the *yud*-shaped knot. This will cause the part of the strap that was previously close to the *tefillin* to now be further away from it, possibly contradicting the prohibition on lowering an object from a higher level to a lower level of *kedushah,* a prohibition that is called *ma'alin bekodesh v'ein moridin.*

The *Magen Avraham* holds that it is forbidden to switch around the strap, whereas the *Eliyahu Rabba* brings in the name of his grandfather, the *Gaon Maharash,* that it is, indeed, permitted. The *Gaon Maharash* proves it is permitted from the fact that in *Parshas Vayeitzei,* we find that *Yaakov Avinu* puts rocks around his head — and afterwards, as Rashi says, he takes the stone that was under his head and makes it into a *matzeivah* (a one-stone altar). As Rashi explains, the rocks were fighting with each other since each one wanted the tzaddik to rest his head on it, and in the end, the rocks miraculously joined into one big stone. The *Gaon Maharash* asks what was accomplished by merging the rocks. In the end, Yaakov's head was only on one spot and he did not lay his head on the rest. Yet, it seemed to be a satisfactory solution to the problem.

From this, the *Gaon Maharash* proves that the whole unit is considered the same. It did not matter which side of the large stone Yaakov actually put his head on; the *kedushah* the stone received spread out equally and was the same everywhere. The same applies to the broken *tefillin* strap. It does not matter if the end that was once close to the *tefillin* is now further away, since the *kedushah* of the strap is the same everywhere.

Counters the *Sha'arei Teshuvah* (ibid.): This proof is unconvincing, as the miracle might have occurred differently. It is possible that the rocks were not just bonded with one another but actually mixed homogeneously like a liquid, such that no one rock was further away from the tzaddik's head than any other rock.

It would seem to me that the *Gaon Maharash* was correct, if we take it as an actual proof and not just as a supportive idea from the *Chumash*. Let us take another look at the argument against him, and we will see the flaw in it. It was suggested by the *Sha'arei Teshuvah* that the original rocks were reworked into a new, homogeneous stone. Why, though, would this solve the problem? According to this view, all parts of a unit do *not* have the same *kedushah*. This being so, the various parts of the newly created stone should have complained just as the original rocks did: The head of the tzaddik is only on one part of the stone, not on the whole stone! The bottom of the rock should be the top, and the side should also want to be on top...

Thus, we must agree that the *kedushah* of a unit is equally spread throughout.

5   Yaakov's Laws

וַיֹּאמַר נָקְבָה שְׂכָרְךָ עָלַי וְאֶתֵּנָה:

And he said: "Specify your wage to me, and I will give it."
(Bereishis 30:28)

After Yaakov expresses his intention to return to *Eretz Yisrael*, Lavan makes an offer. He asks Yaakov to state his price for staying on in Charan to tend the flocks, and Lavan will "honor" the agreement. Thus Yaakov made up with Lavan to remove the speckled and the dappled sheep, the brownish sheep and the dappled and speckled among the goats. The agreement was that all future sheep and goats that had such an appearance would belong to Yaakov. This would be his wages.

We know that a miracle occurred, and the sheep and goats bore speckled and dappled offspring for Yaakov's sake. However, according to the natural way of things without resorting to miracles, it was possible for Yaakov to follow the course of action described in the *Parsha* and still earn the tremendous amounts of sheep eventually born. It is not necessary to understand this episode as solely based on a *nes*. We may also assume that Lavan happily accepted this arrangement because he did not think it was possible for Yaakov to actually get the sheep that were to be his wage. However, Yaakov knew otherwise.

Lavan went and removed all the animals that had any sort of white in them – ringed, dappled, He did the same with the goats.

The original agreement was that Yaakov would get only the offspring that had black speckles and dapples. Lavan even took out the black goats that had any white spots whatsoever. Here, the verse says:

כל אשר־לבן בו: (בראשית ל׳:ל״ה)

Any that there is white in it. (Bereishis 30:35)

Simply speaking, the above verse means that Lavan took out even the goats that were completely white. This was because Lavan assumed that from black goats come only black goats and that from white and black goats together come speckled goats. Thus, he removed all of the white goats so that according to the natural course of things, as he understood it, Yaakov would not have any goats bearing the right coloring. Yaakov was going to get absolutely none — no wages at all because the agreement was that he would receive only the multicolored ones. How could multicolored offspring be born to a unicolored flock?

Unaware of the laws of genetics, Lavan's goal was thwarted by his own actions.

Without going into technical genetic formulas for goats and sheep, there are three possibilities that we can expect to see in the first generation of animals. Given that black is dominant and the different forms of white are recessive, the first possibility arises when homozygous black mate with homozygous black. (In other words, we are referring to black animals that carry only black genes.) One hundred percent of the animals bred this way will reproduce homozygous black.

The second possibility is when a homozygous black mates with a heterozygous black, a black animal that carries a recessive white gene. Fifty percent of the animals will be homozygous black, and fifty percent will be heterozygous black. Yet, we still have a phenotype of only black animals. (In other words, the animals all look black although they might carry a recessive white gene.)

The third possibility is when a heterozygous black mates with a heterozygous black. The simple statistical probability is that twenty-five percent will be black and homozygous, and fifty percent will be black and heterozygous. The result will be a seventy-five percent phenotype of black. However, and most important for us, statistics say that twenty-five percent of the animals born will bear the various whitish colorings: spotted, speckled and dappled. It is in this scenario that Yaakov has non-black animals.

The total probability, adding them all up, gives us the following percentages in the first generation: 58.33% possibility for all black homozygous and 33.33% possibility for all black heterozygous. This assumes that we start at the beginning of the process with even amounts of all in the entire group. Given that we have equal amounts throughout the entire mating process, there will be only an 8.33% possibility for non-black sheep in that first generation.

All the same, as we know, statistical probabilities do not determine what actually happens in the real world. Even though there is a 50/50 probability before any given birth that the child will be either a boy or a girl, one family could have ten boys while their neighbor has ten girls. The same applies here. Although statistically speaking most of the births of group number three will be black, it is still possible for one hundred percent to be spotted, speckled and dappled. Similarly, it is within the realm of possibility for group number two to produce one hundred percent heterozygous animals. Furthermore, there is no absolute requirement that any homozygous sheep mate with another of its kind. If things worked out right, in the first generation alone, one third of the animals born would go immediately to *Yaakov Avinu*.

In addition to this, Yaakov segregated the recessives once they were born. (This refers to the animals with non-black coloring.)

וישת לו עדרים לבדו ולא שתם על־צאן לבן: (שם מ')

He formed separate droves of his own and did not mix them with Lavan's flock. (ibid., v. 40)

When those recessives mated, one hundred percent of the offspring would be Yaakov's. Whereas if they would be allowed to mate with animals carrying black genes, the percentage of non-black offspring would be statistically much less. Yaakov continued in this way. Every time he had a recessive animal, he would segregate it so that his group would always produce animals that would belong to him.

From the group belonging to Lavan, we can assume that in the first generation, Lavan would receive at least fifty percent of the animals born. If against all odds, "miraculously," the homozygous mated only with heterozygous and the remaining heterozygous mated with each other, the result would still be one hundred percent black animals from the former group. However, in such a case, all the offspring would be heterozygous and capable of producing non-black animals in the next generation.

Thus, let us say that after the first generation, fifty percent of the animals belonged to Yaakov and fifty percent belonged to Lavan. As Yaakov continued to segregate out his recessives, he received a higher and higher percentage of the later animals. This creates the possibility, according to natural law, that all of the next generation, which was produced from heterozygous mating with heterozygous, would belong to Yaakov. Lavan, on the other hand, would only receive a consistent result from the mating of the homozygous sheep. This process would make Yaakov fabulously wealthy. All this is entirely possible even according to the laws of nature, since what actually happens is not dictated by statistical probability, as we all know.

Let us conclude by noting that Yaakov's acquisition of sheep and goats as recounted in this *Parsha* was more then just acquisition of wealth. Rather, the entire episode is indicative of the essence of Yaakov. Rashi comments on Yaakov's sheep in the passages dealing with the offerings of the *Mishkan*:

כבש אחד. כנגד יעקב, "והכשבים הפריד יעקב:" (רש"י במדבר ז':כ"א, כ"ח:י"ט)

One sheep. This represents Yaakov, as it is written, "And Yaakov separated the sheep." (Rashi, Bamidbar 7:21 and 28:19)

6 Lamb Sticks

וַיִּקַּח לוֹ יַעֲקֹב מַקַּל לִבְנֶה לַח וְלוּז וְעַרְמוֹן וַיְפַצֵּל בָּהֵן פְּצָלוֹת לְבָנוֹת...

Yaakov took for himself fresh sticks of poplar and hazel and chestnut, laying bare the white of the sticks... (Bereishis 30:37)

How are we to understand this seemingly obtuse passage describing how *Yaakov Avinu* prepared sticks of wood and set them up in the watering troughs of the flock? He went through this procedure so the animals would see the white sticks and afterwards mate, thus, somehow influencing the color of the offspring. We can understand this episode as follows:

When the animals mated, Yaakov would pray that he should get the maximum possible number of speckled and dappled animals. He was praying for his *parnassah*. We know that physical stimuli impact a person's davening and ability to properly concentrate. This fact is reflected in the war that *Moshe Rabbeinu* led against Amalek. Moshe stood on the mountain and raised his hands in prayer. When he raised his hands, the Israelites overcame the Amalekites, and when he lowered his hands, the Amalekites overcame the Israelites. (*Shemos* 17:11) *Chazal* comment on this:

וכי ידיו של משה עושות מלחמה או שוברות מלחמה. אלא לומר לך, כל זמן שהיו ישראל מסתכלים כלפי מעלה ומשעבדין את לבם לאביהם שבשמים היו מתגברים. ואם לאו, היו נופלין: (ר"ה פ"ג מ"ח)

And did the hands of Moshe make the war or break the war? Rather, it is to tell you that as long as Israel looked upwards and subjugated their hearts to their Father in Heaven, they overcame. And if not, they would fall. (Mishnah, Rosh HaShanah 3:8)

Chazal are telling us that when *Moshe Rabbeinu* raised his hands high, *K'lal Yisrael* would pray and direct their hearts to their Father in Heaven. As the same statement of *Chazal* goes on to say, this was the secret of the *Nechash HaNechoshes* as well. This bronze serpent constructed by *Moshe Rabbeinu* had miraculous "healing powers" because it caused people to look upwards, to their Father in Heaven. It was the visual stimulus of seeing Moshe's hands raised in prayer, or the *Nechash HaNechoshes* raised on a pole, that caused them to direct their hearts to Hashem.

As the *Shulchan Aruch* tells us in *Orach Chayim*, ch. 90, a person who is unable to pray with a minyan should nevertheless go to pray in a shul, although he will be praying there alone. Why? The *Mishnah Berurah* (ibid., s.v. 33) explains that a shul is a place of *kedushah* and a prayer is more acceptable to Heaven when prayed there.

Besides the enhanced *kedushah* that exists in a shul, it is undeniable that the physical stimuli of such an atmosphere enhance one's concentration and intention while davening. Perhaps, this is even what the commentators are referring to when they emphasize the *kedushah* of the shul in this context.

Let us now return to *Yaakov Avinu* and his peeled sticks. When Yaakov would pray for his *parnassah* by visualizing the spotted, speckled and dappled sticks, his intention would be heightened and his prayer would become more intense.

Although the simple meaning of the passage implies that there were some physical factors involved with the peeled sticks that we do not quite understand, nevertheless, it is also recounted there that Yaakov saw in his dream how the angels were directing the animals so that the right ones would mate with each other, producing the desired advantage over Lavan — in spite of Lavan's valiant efforts to trick Yaakov out of what was due him. This dream reflects the *kedushah*, the *ruchniyus*, that is behind the whole story. This clearly supports our explanation in the previous section that the miracle of Yaakov's flock increasing was not a supernatural event, but rather one that operated within the bounds of the laws of nature. We will explain this point:

It is not plausible that the angels that Yaakov saw in his dream actually took animals from Lavan's flock and brought them to Yaakov's. This would be totally unnecessary if we are talking about a supernatural event. Furthermore, it would seem to be a form of theft, as this was contrary to their agreement. The agreement was that Yaakov would receive those animals that would be born in a natural fashion. This was to be his wages. The agreement surely did not include angels coming surreptitiously at night to bring Lavan's spotted animals to mate with Yaakov's black ones. No one in their right mind would have agreed to such a clause! The animals that were the preexisting property of Lavan had nothing to do with this arrangement.

Furthermore, such an idea is in opposition to how Hashem runs the world.

ואמר רבי יוחנן משום רבי שמעון בן יוחי: מאי דכתיב (ישעיהו ס"א) כי ה' אהב משפט
שנא גזל בעולה:

Said Rabbi Yochanan in the name of Rabbi Shimon ben Yochai: "What is the meaning of that which is written, 'For Hashem loves justice; He hates theft in a burnt offering'?" (Yeshayahu 61)

משל למלך בשר ודם שהיה עובר על בית המכס, אמר לעבדיו: תנו מכס למוכסים.
אמרו לו: והלא כל המכס כולו שלך הוא אמר להם: ממני ילמדו כל עוברי דרכים, ולא
יבריחו עצמן מן המכס:

It may be compared to a human king passing by the toll house. He said to his servants: "Pay tolls to the tolls officials." They said to him: "But all the tolls are yours alone!" He said to them: "Let all the travelers learn from me not to run away from the toll."

אף הקדוש ברוך הוא אמר: אני ה' שנא גזל בעולה, ממני ילמדו בני ויבריחו עצמן מן

הגזול: (סוכה ל' ע"א)

Thus, the Holy One Blessed be He said: "I, Hashem, hate theft in a burnt offering. Let My children learn from me to run away from theft." (Sukkah 30a)

If Hashem hates theft to such an extent, it would be absurd for us to think that He had the angels "steal" the sheep of Lavan in order for them to mate with Yaakov's sheep. Besides, if we are explaining this episode as a pure miracle, why would Heaven go through the laborious process of sending angels to transport sheep to and fro in the middle of the night?

Therefore, we are compelled to understand the angels bringing the male animals of Lavan into the mating process in light of the recessive genes approach we put forth in the previous section. Those genes had been inherited from animals that were presently found among the flock of Lavan, i.e., the earlier generations of animals. Yet, those genes were still quite active in the mating process. It was those inherited recessive traits that aligned to produce the new, spotted flock that was to belong to Yaakov. With this approach, we can understand the whole passage according to its straightforward meaning.

7 Yaakov's Empty Hands

Yaakov cried when he met Rachel by the well in Charan (*Bereishis* 29:11). Why? Because he came empty-handed, unlike his father's servant Eliezer who had appeared in the same place on a similar mission, but laden with gold and precious items. As Rashi (ad loc.) explains, Elifaz son of Eisav overtook Yaakov before Yaakov reached Charan. Elifaz, contrary to his father's order to kill Yaakov, made do with merely depriving him of his property, based on Yaakov's argument that "a poor person is considered as dead."

This story is often cited in praise of Elifaz, who did not obey Eisav's order to kill *Yaakov Avinu*. I believe the opposite is true. The wrong interpretation of the story is being presented by those who cite it this way. Rather, let us take into account the fact that Elifaz knew who Yaakov was. Elifaz realized that if he had contended with Yaakov, he may very well have ended up the loser. Therefore, he had to figure out how to circumvent what his father had told him *in order to save his own life*. So he confronted Yaakov with this perplexing issue: How may I honor my father's request while leaving you alive? Yaakov responded: "Take my property, because 'a poor person is considered as dead.'"

Are we to really believe that Elifaz didn't want to lie to his father? Are we to really believe that Elifaz had a surge of conscience when his father ordered him to kill Yaakov. What was Elifaz afraid of? Was he really so concerned about the mitzvah of *kibbud av va'eim*? If so, what did he do in the end? He lied brazenly, claiming that he had murdered his uncle Yaakov, in order to fulfill the mitzvah of *kibbud av va'eim*. This explanation is patently ridiculous. Rather, we must say that Elifaz was essentially a murderer who pulled out at the last minute only to avoid becoming the victim. Can we really believe that his concern was over the sin of *retzichah,* albeit honoring his father in the process? Only to the Mafia would such an act be considered honoring one's elders! We must view Elifaz not as a *shaliach mitzvah* but as a cowardly hit man.

Elifaz was interested in extricating himself from the situation in the way that was best for Elifaz. Let us not forget that Elifaz was the father of Amalek. Elifaz married his own *mamzeres* daughter, from whom Amalek was born. Elifaz is worthy of contempt, not of pity for his "moral quandary" and emotional plight when meeting Yaakov.

Yaakov declares, "With my staff I crossed this Jordan" (*Bereishis* 32:11). As Rashi (ad loc.) explains, his staff was all he had after Elifaz left. I think we can safely assume that, given the opportunity, Elifaz would have taken that, too. Elifaz, the father of Amalek.

וישלח

VAYISHLACH

1 Survival Skills

וְהָיָה הַמַּחֲנֶה הַנִּשְׁאָר לִפְלֵיטָה:

And the remaining camp will survive. (Bereishis 32:9)

Yaakov *Avinu* prepared for battle and split his camp into two. If one of his camps would be severely attacked, at least the second camp would survive. The way Rashi explains the scenario, Eisav was already on the way ready for battle and the war was expected to take place right where they were. Yaakov foresaw a vicious war, and wanted to ensure that at least one group would be spared destruction.

והיה המחנה הנשאר לפליטה. על כרחו, כי אלחם עמו: (רש"י בראשית ל"ב:ט')

"And the remaining camp will survive" against his (Eisav's) will, since I will battle with him. (Rashi, Bereishis 32:9)

If this really was Yaakov's plan, the course of events is mystifying. Who was in this other camp — the one granted highest chances of survival?

We might assume that he would have split his family and his property equally between the two camps. Yet, we must admit that the most important thing to save was the family members themselves. The common notion is that he had half of his family in one camp and the other half with him in the other camp. However, if this is true, how are we to explain the fact that everyone was together in one place? Yaakov lifted up his eyes and saw Eisav coming (32:1), and they *all bowed* down to Eisav. There was not a single family member in any other camp. All of the wives and children were there bowing down on the ground and graciously greeting their mortal enemy Eisav. If everyone was together with Yaakov, then what or whom was Yaakov hoping to save through the other camp — his sheep and goats?

In order to solve this enigma, we could say that a great change occurred after Yaakov had the nighttime battle with Eisav's guardian angel and triumphed over him. Let us posit that right away in the morning, when he no longer feared a war with Eisav, he brought everyone back together and that is why we find everyone in one place.

However, this easy explanation cannot be reconciled with the verses.

ויקם בלילה הוא ויקח את שתי נשיו ואת שתי שפחתיו ואת אחד עשר ילדיו ויעבר את מעבר יבק וכו'. (שם ל"ב:כ"ג)

And he arose that night and took his two wives and his two handmaidens and his eleven children and he passed over the Yabbok crossing... (ibid., 32:23)

Long before there was any inkling of a coming confrontation with an angel, we find *Yaakov Avinu* together with the entire family crossing the Yabbok stream. It is clear, then, that even before meeting the angel, the entire family had remained together. Then we find:

ויזרח לו השמש כאשר עבר את פנואל וכו'. וישא יעקב עיניו וירא והנה עשו בא וכו'. (שם ל"ב:ל"ב, ל"ג:א')

And the sun rose for him as he passed Penuel... and Yaakov raised his eyes and saw, and behold, Eisav is coming... (ibid., 32:32, 31:1)

Almost immediately after Yaakov parted with the angel, Eisav was upon him. So when did *Yaakov Avinu* split up everybody and then gather them back together? Except for when Yaakov was alone with the angel, they were all together at all times. So if the entire family was continuously together, who did Yaakov place in the other camp?

Simply speaking, we could answer as follows: Yaakov had originally planned to have two camps. One camp was to consist of the whole family with the sole exception of himself. Of course, he would have wanted to save the entire family. Yaakov was going to fight Eisav alone and allow them to escape and be saved. That is what Rashi meant when he said: *"'And the remaining camp will survive'* against his (Eisav's) will, since I will battle with him."

At that point, Eisav was looking to kill just Yaakov. He came looking for him alone, not for anyone else. Eisav probably did not even know about Yaakov's family, as we find later that he asks who all of these people are: *"Who are these to you?"* (ibid., 33:4).

It is clear that it would have been in everyone's best interest to keep the family away from Yaakov in another camp. Yaakov would be alone, perhaps with servants, to face Eisav. However, once he emerged victorious over Eisav's guardian angel, he then went back without fear and rejoined his family to greet Eisav.

② Eisav's Merit

וַיָּשָׁב בַּיּוֹם הַהוּא עֵשָׂו לְדַרְכּוֹ שֵׂעִירָה:

And Eisav started back that day on his way to Seir. (*Bereishis* 33:16)

When Eisav returned to his home in Seir, Rashi (ad loc.) points out that he returned there alone. The four hundred men who had accompanied him on the mission to fight Yaakov were no longer around. What happened to them? They slipped away one by one, and were rewarded in the days of *Dovid HaMelech* for their present abandonment of Eisav.

Rashi refers us to a story at the end of *Shmuel* I. Dovid and his men had left their families and possessions in the camp to go on a mission and returned to find the camp destroyed, their wives and children taken captive by Amalek. Dovid then took his six hundred men to wage a war of revenge against Amalek. Ultimately, four hundred went with him while two hundred stayed back to guard the remaining provisions. The army of Dovid fought day and night and proceeded to wipe out a giant army of Amalekites, descendants of Eisav. Dovid was victorious, and almost none of the enemy escaped.

Rashi cites a verse describing Dovid's war against Amalek:

ולא נמלט מהם איש כי אם ארבע מאות איש נער אשר רכבו על הגמלים וינסו: (שמואל א' ל':י"ז)

Not a man of them survived, except four hundred youths who were riding camels, who fled. (Shmuel I, 30:17)

This verse links the story back up with Eisav's four hundred fleeing men.

There are several obvious questions to be asked. First of all, who is being rewarded here? The reward should have gone to the four hundred men who abandoned Eisav, so what does this have to do with Eisav's descendants who were saved from Dovid? The four hundred men who had accompanied Eisav were not Eisav's own descendants; they were his warriors. How can they be rewarded by Eisav's future descendants being saved from the sword of Dovid?

We are forced to conclude that their act of leaving Eisav was somehow connected with something commendable that Eisav did himself, and therefore he was rewarded. By the time that Eisav had caught up with Yaakov, he had begun to feel that the warriors were unnecessary. Perhaps he even encouraged them to go home. That would explain why Eisav's descendants were later saved.

This incident with *Dovid HaMelech*, an amazing episode in itself, leads us to a much more difficult issue. We know that *Shaul HaMelech* was punished because he did not kill Agag and all the animals of Amalek. Yet, who did he actually kill?

והמתה מאיש עד־אשה מעלל ועד־יונק וכו'. (שמואל א' ט"ו:ג')

And you shall kill from man to woman, from suckling to child...
(Shmuel I, 15:3)

This part of the command he fulfilled. Only one person did he leave alive: Agag, King of Amalek. We know that Haman came from Agag, who was kept alive. Agag was visited by a female slave the last night of his life, before the

Prophet Shmuel slayed him the next day, and she had a child. Haman is descended from that child. It is because of this event that the entire story of Purim unfolds.

However, if it is true that Shaul had wiped out all of Amalek as he was supposed to, then how did a formidable Amalekite contingent of four hundred men escape Dovid so shortly afterwards? The entire reign of Shaul was two years, and the story of Dovid with the four hundred escaping men took place while Shaul was fighting his last battle with the Philistines, in which Shaul died. If the beginning of the reign of Shaul to the end of his reign was two years, where did all these thousands and thousands of Amalekites slain by Dovid come from? They certainly did not come from that one child who was the ancestor of Haman.

From this incident, we see that it never was Hashem's intention for Shaul to wipe out every single Amalekite, just as it was not Hashem's intention that Yehoshua completely wipe out Amalek shortly after the Exodus from Egypt, when the Israelites had their first encounter with Amalek. That great event is to be saved for the Final Redemption, when Amalek will be totally destroyed. It is for then, and then alone, that we are commanded:

זכור את אשר עשה לך עמלק וכו'. תמחה את זכר עמלק: (דברים כ"ה:י"ז)

Remember what Amalek did to you... obliterate the memory of Amalek. (Devarim 25:17)

This command was never meant to be totally fulfilled in the days of Yehoshua, nor in the days of Shaul or Dovid. There would always be some people left over.

The entire episode of Shaul and Agag must now be understood quite differently. We can assume that there were either different camps of Amalekites or even different tribes of Amalekites. Agag was the king of only one of those tribes. The responsibility of Shaul was not to wipe out Amalek totally. Rather Shaul was tested regarding his ability to follow through on the command of Hashem as communicated to him by a prophet. It was never meant to be a complete and total destruction of Amalek.

This understanding is reflected in our *Parsha* as well. It is written, *"And Eisav started back that day on his way to Seir"* (*Bereishis* 33:16). This takes place when Eisav requests to travel along with Yaakov, and Yaakov politely turns down the request. When, asks Rashi, do Yaakov and Eisav eventually meet up as Yaakov promised? That is only in the time of the *Mashiach*.

For the sake of this ultimate confrontation, there has to be a continuation of Eisav. This confrontation requires not just some distant descendants of Eisav, but people who represent Eisav's very essence, the worst of Eisav: None other than the people of Amalek.

Thus, when Eisav returns to Seir, he does so by himself. As a reward for the fact that Eisav did not lead his four hundred men at this juncture into what would have been the final war, but rather came and left peacefully, he merited that there would always be remnants of his descendents who would be able to escape the Jews. Now we understand why Amalek has continued, why Edom has continued. However, eventually, when *HaKadosh Boruch Hu* sees it fit, they will all be wiped out thoroughly and completely, never to return.

3 Rivka Cries for her Children

R*achel Imeinu* had a special merit that enabled her to pray for *K'lal Yisrael*: She brought a co-wife into her household through the act of giving the *simanim* over to Leah, and she thereby relinquished being the sole wife of Yaakov and the mother of all of *K'lal Yisrael*. She shared everything with Leah, and, in the end, mothered only three of the twelve tribes (Ephraim, Menashe and Binyamin). Due to this tremendous act of sacrifice on her part, *K'lal Yisrael* was saved after the destruction of the First Temple: *"And the children will return to their borders"* (*Yirmiyahu* 31:16), thanks to her prayers.

We should wonder why Rivkah did not have a similar merit because her burial was truly disgraceful to her honor, and this was only because of the personal sacrifices she made. From Midrash Tanchuma (*Ki Teitzei* 4), we learn the circumstances of Rivkah's funeral. This Midrash is cited by Ramban (*Bereishis* 35:8) and hinted to by Rashi as well (ad loc.).

The Midrash describes how there was no one to attend to Rivkah upon her death. Her father-in-law Avraham had already passed away, her aged husband Yitzchok was blind and could not take care of matters and her righteous son Yaakov was abroad, first returning from Lavan's home. Who was left? Only her other son, Eisav. The Ramban (ad loc.) maintains that Eisav, too, would not have attended to her because he actually hated her! At this juncture, he blamed her for the loss of the *brachos*. It was a real disgrace.

Before the episode of Yaakov taking the *brachos* it is clear that Eisav had tremendous respect for his mother. He left his special garments with her; he trusted her and not his wives. However, because Rivkah looked out for *K'lal Yisrael* and saw to it that Yaakov would receive the *brachos,* Rivkah incurred Eisav's wrath and ultimately was to be buried in disgrace. In the end, her pall was taken out secretly at night lest people curse the womb that gave birth to Eisav, who was hated in the whole area. For this same reason, the Torah does not explicitly mention her burial or its date.

What brought this dishonorable and disgraceful burial upon Rivkah? It was only her sacrifice for *K'lal Yisrael*!

Where do we find that Rivkah was ever repaid for this?

As we previously noted in Parshas Toldos, in the section *Yitzchok on his Own*, the Gemara (*Shabbos* 89b) describes a discussion that will take place in the future between Hashem and the *Avos*. Hashem approaches the *Avos* and says, "Your children sinned to Me," awaiting a convincing reply. Avraham and Yaakov both disappoint Hashem by saying that the people who sinned should be wiped out in sanctification of Hashem's Name. However, Yitzchok pleases his Maker by standing up to protect *K'lal Yisrael*. He meticulously calculates the maximum amount that a person could sin during the course of his life, ascertains his figures and makes an offer to Hashem: "You take half; I'll take half." In this way, Yitzchok stands up to save *K'lal Yisrael*.

While we find no such story about Rivkah, we may assume that Yitzchok and Rivkah form one entity in their protection of *K'lal Yisrael*. Perhaps Rivkah, too, will utilize her powerful merit, as Rachel used hers after the destruction of the First Temple, and she will stand up to claim repayment for the disgrace she incurred in bringing about the Final Redemption for *K'lal Yisrael*.

This could explain the following enigma. Rivkah sends off Yaakov to Lavan with the following stipulation:

וישבת עמו ימים אחדים עד אשר תשוב חמת אחיך: עד־שוב אף־אחיך ממך ושכח את אשר־עשית לו ושלחתי ולקחתיך משם: (בראשית כ"ד:מ"ד-מ"ה)

And you shall dwell with him for a few days until the rage of your brother subsides. Until the anger of your brother subsides from you, and he forgets what you did to him. And I will send and take you from there. (Bereishis 24:44–45)

Rivkah promises to send for Yaakov after Eisav calms down. When did this really happen?

When Devorah, Rivkah's wet nurse, was sent to *Alon Bachus* (ibid., 35:8) to meet up with Yaakov upon his return from Lavan, can we really say, at that point, that Eisav's anger had turned aside from Yaakov? Certainly not! Eisav and his descendants have continued to bitterly persecute the Jews since then until now. This will not happen until *Rivkah Imeinu's* ultimate call, when sinners will cease from the earth and the wicked will be no more (*Tehillim* 104:35).

4 The Missing Prayer of Avraham

When Avraham and Yitzchok require *parnassah* or confront their enemies, we do not have any record, in the Torah[21], of them davening to Hashem. When Yaakov needs *parnassah* or confronts an enemy, a major component of the story is his prayer to Hashem. Why is this? When Avraham is thrown by Nimrod into the fiery furnace, when he goes down to Egypt due to famine or when he goes to war against the four kings, we do not find any record of him first praying. When Yaakov confronts a possible war with Eisav, the Torah elaborates on his davening. At Mount Moriah before setting off to Charan, Yaakov prays for *parnassah*.

Furthermore, when Avraham and Yitzchok are confronted by danger, we

---

21   אע"פ שפשוט שהתפללו ע"ע פיוט לתפלת גשם: זהר גם הוא לשפך לב כמים

do not find them expressing fear over their lack of worthiness to be saved. Yet, *Yaakov Avinu* does. *"And Yaakov was very afraid..."* (*Bereishis* 32:11), and Rashi (ad loc.) explains his worries: Perhaps due to his sins, he will not be protected by Hashem.

An answer to this can be seen in what the *Netziv* says in the *Harcheiv Davar* (*Bereishis* 34:1, article 2; see our discussion of this *Netziv* in *Parshas Toldos* in the section titled *Yitzchok on his Own*.)

The *Netziv* cites a Midrash saying that Avraham was called Yisrael, and Yitzchok was called Yisrael. Thus, he raises the question: Why is Yisrael considered especially the name of Yaakov?

The *Netziv* answers by explaining the significance of the title "Yisrael." It signifies acting on a level that is above the laws of nature, which can express itself in various areas. As the *Netziv* explains, every person needs to attain three things in his life: defense from his enemies, *parnassah* and peace. Without peace, nothing good will last.

When it comes to defense from one's enemies, *Avraham Avinu* achieved a level that was above the laws of nature. We see this when he was thrown into the fiery furnace by Nimrod. Again he is protected when he goes down to Egypt and again he emerges unscathed from the war he waged against the four powerful kings of Mesopotamia. Thus, he earned the title of "Yisrael" in this respect. Yitzchok also earned the title of "Yisrael," in the area of *parnassah*.(as explained in *Parshas Toldos*).

However, only when Yaakov earned it in the area of peace, by miraculously maintaining good relations with Lavan and Eisav, was the aspect of "Yisrael" completed. That is why Yisrael is a name that belongs especially to Yaakov.

The supernatural way that *Avraham Avinu* handled protection from his enemies was an integral part of what was transmitted to him. It was part of his essence. So, too, was Yitzchok's way of handling *parnassah*. *Yaakov Avinu*'s area to handle things supernaturally was that of peace. So when it came to *parnassah* or protection from his enemies, the supernatural quality did not come to Yaakov automatically at all. It required a constant effort of prayer in order for him to be protected from Eisav or have his material needs provided. However, when he finally achieved peace with Lavan and Eisav, it was through miraculous means.

ויבא יעקב שלם עיר שכם: (בראשית ל"ג:י"ח).

And Yaakov came in a state of wholeness (shalem) to the city of Shechem. (Bereishis 33:18)

The wholeness called *shalem*, i.e., *shalom*, was the special trait of *Yaakov Avinu*. This is in contrast to protection from enemies and *parnassah*, which were not his special traits. It is possible, therefore, that in these areas, Yaakov needed an enhanced level of prayer, while the same efforts were not needed by Avraham and Yitzchok.

5   When Wealth is a Blessing

We all know that Hashem does not always give wealth and prosperity to a person as a blessing. Occasionally, a person is given exactly what is bad and dangerous for him; Heaven gives him what we would call "enough rope to hang himself with." This idea is expressed by *Shlomo HaMelech*:

עשר שמור לבעליו לרעתו: (קהלת ה':י"ב)

Wealth that is kept for its owner for his detriment. (Koheles 5:12)

On the other hand, *Birkas Kohanim* is the paramount blessing to the Jewish people, and it begins with "May Hashem bless you and keep you." As Rashi, quoting *Chazal*, explains (*Bamidbar* 6:24), this speaks of Hashem giving us and guarding for us material wealth. Rashi emphasizes the importance of "and keep you": If the goodness is not guarded, if it does not continue, it is of no significance.

Therefore, it is puzzling that we find *Yaakov Avinu* saying to Hashem before his encounter with Eisav:

קטנתי מכל החסדים וכו'. (בראשית ל"ב:י"א)

I have become small due to all the kindnesses... (Bereishis 32:11)

As Rashi explains (ad loc.), Yaakov was concerned that his merits had been diminished by all the kindnesses showered upon him by Hashem, and he therefore lacked Divine protection. Yet, this is hard to understand. If Hashem had indeed done a kindness to Yaakov by granting him his wealth, then the kindness would have had significance only if it would have continued: If Yaakov would have been saved from Eisav and something worthwhile would have eventually been accomplished with it. Heaping upon Yaakov a multitude of kindnesses, giving him wives, children and wealth just to have them destroyed immediately upon his return home, would not have appeared to fit *Chazal*'s definition of a blessing at all. What, then, was Yaakov's concern of "I have become small [in merit] due to all the kindnesses?"

If Hashem indeed had done a kindness to him, by definition it must have been a lasting one — and Yaakov had nothing to fear. Eisav would not have been able to take away any of the kindness that Hashem had given. If it had not been a true kindness, if Yaakov had received nothing of lasting value, then his merits had not been decreased!

If the Torah had used any term other than "kindness," *chesed*, perhaps the contradiction would not be so strong. Yet, the Torah called it *chesed*. Thus, the dilemma stands: If it was a *chesed*, Yaakov would perforce survive unharmed. If it was not a *chesed*, if he received nothing of lasting value, his merits were not diminished.

This issue requires further thought. *Tzarich iyun.*

---

6   True Love

What is *Chazal*'s example of a false and fickle love?

כל אהבה שהיא תלויה בדבר, בטל דבר, בטלה אהבה. ושאינה תלויה בדבר, אינה בטלה
לעולם. איזו היא אהבה התלויה בדבר, זו אהבת אמנון ותמר וכו'. (אבות פרק ה':ט"ז)

Any love that is dependent on an external factor, when that factor ceases, the love ceases. And that which is not dependent on an external factor, it never ceases. What is a love that is dependent on an external factor? This is the love of Amnon for Tamar... (Pirkei Avos 5:16)

Here, *Chazal* skipped over Shechem and Dinah and instead spoke of the love of Amnon for Tamar, an incident not from the Torah but from *Nevi'im*. Why? How would *Pirkei Avos* have defined the love of Shechem for Dinah? Wouldn't we say that it was also a love dependent on external factors?

Although it is reasonable to assume that after an extended period of marriage with Dinah, if it would have taken place, Shechem would have come to hate her (as Amnon did with Tamar), the Torah's account does not reflect this in any way. First it says "Shechem saw her," then it says "he took her..." and after that it says "and his soul cleaved to Dinah." Then it says "he loved the maiden" (*Bereishis* 34:3). We see that he still loved her even after having fulfilled his initial desires, unlike the case of Amnon and Tamar where he immediately hated her.

How would *Chazal* define this relationship of Shechem and Dinah? Perhaps the external factor on which Shechem's love was dependent was Dinah's beauty. In fact, subsequently, HaRav Yisrael HaCohen Chesir, *shlita,* pointed out to me that this is the opinion of Ramban.

> והחשק הגדול לשכם כי היתה הנערה יפת תאר מאד, אבל לא סיפר הכתוב ביפיה
> כאשר עשה בשרה וברבקה וברחל, כי לא ירצה להזכיר יפיה בהיותו אליה למכשול
> עון, ובשבח הצדיקות דבר הכתוב וכו'. (רמב"ן שם פסוק י"ב)

> *The great desire of Shechem was because she was a maiden who was very beautiful. But Scripture did not tell of her beauty as it did with Sarah, Rivkah and Rachel, because it did not wish to mention her beauty since it was a cause of sin for her. And Scripture speaks in praise of the righteous women.* (Ramban, ibid., v.12)

With this in mind and in order to resolve our difficulty, R' Shmuel Globus suggested the following: Shechem's love was, indeed, dependent on an external factor. However, the beauty of the righteous women (such as Sarah, Rivkah, Rachel or, in this case, Dinah) was a reflection of their inner spiritual perfection. As such, a love dependent on it would not so quickly cease. Therefore, Shechem's love for Dinah was not chosen by *Chazal* as a classic example of a love that ceases.

Eisav's Destiny

Let us understand Eisav's role and destiny by posing a simple question: Why did Yaakov go to Lavan? The Torah says because Yaakov needed to escape Eisav's wrath.

ויאמר אלקים אל יעקב וכו'. ועשה־שם מזבח לקל הנראה אליך בברחך מפני עשו אחיך: (בראשית ל"ה:א')

And G-d said to Yaakov... make there an altar to the G-d who appeared to you when you fled from Eisav your brother. (Bereishis 35:1)

Thus, we have Hashem's testimony that the real factor motivating Yaakov to leave was Eisav's wrath. The whole idea of going to Lavan to find a wife was actually just a subterfuge. It was not the motivating factor.

This leads us to the real question: What would otherwise have motivated Yaakov to go and get married? What was the plan going to be? Yaakov was sixty-three when he left Beer Sheva, and when he arrived in Charan (after the fourteen years he spent in the yeshiva of Ever) he was seventy-seven. When were Rivkah and Yitzchok thinking that Yaakov should get married? Why did they wait so long?

It appears that if it had not been for Eisav, Yaakov would not have married at this time and *K'lal Yisrael* would never have been *K'lal Yisrael*. This leads us to the surprising conclusion that only because Eisav sought to kill Yaakov did *K'lal Yisrael* come into being!

Thinking further along these lines, let us consider a Midrash (*Shemos Rabba* 1:32) that comments on Moshe Rabbeinu's arrival in Midian, when he helped Yisro's daughters at the well. Moshe had fled from Egypt to escape punishment for killing the Egyptian whom he found smiting a Hebrew slave.

The Midrash compares the situation with Moshe and Yisro's daughters to that of a man bitten by a poisonous lizard who goes to soak his foot in the river, only to see a child drowning there. He stretches out his arm and saves the child, who says, "If not for you, I would be dead!" The man replies, "I did not save you, rather it was the lizard that bit me and that I fled from that saved you." Similarly, when Yisro's daughters thanked Moshe for saving them from the shepherds, Moshe attributed it to the Egyptian that he had killed. That is why the daughters reported to Yisro, *"An Egyptian saved us from the shepherds" (Shemos* 2:19), because thanks to the Egyptian that Moshe had killed, Moshe came to Midian.

We learn from this Midrash to attribute a result to its ultimate cause.

Now let us consider the declaration made by someone who brings *bikkurim* to the Temple. (This declaration is also a fundamental part of the Haggadah of Pesach.) It is written there:

ארמי אבד אבי וירד מצרימה וכו'. (דברים כ"ו:ה')

> *An Aramean sought to destroy my father, and he descended to Egypt... (Devarim 26:5)*

Simply, the verse is telling us that there is a connection between Yaakov's stay with Lavan for twenty-two years and Yaakov's subsequent exile in Egypt. There are many commentaries to explain this connection. However, if we would go back and identify the true source of this chain of events, we would have to place the "blame" for Yaakov's descent to Egypt on Eisav. As we mentioned, it was Eisav's anger and the threat this posed to Yaakov's life that brought Yaakov to Lavan in the first place.

Thus, we must conclude that, ultimately, it was Eisav who brought us to the *kur habarzel (Devarim* 4:20), the iron crucible that was Egypt. This is what forged us into a nation capable of receiving the Torah and inheriting *Eretz Yisrael.*

We could say that this is the meaning of the prophecy that *Rivkah Imeinu* received:

שני גיים בבטנך ושני לאמים ממעיך יפרדו ולאם מלאם יאמץ ורב יעבד צעיר:
(בראשית כ"ה:כ"ג)

> *There are two peoples in your womb, and two nations will separate from your innards. And one nation will overpower the other nation, **and the older will serve the younger.***
> *(Bereishis 25:23)*

The older, Eisav, will always be serving the younger, Yaakov. Even when it appears that Eisav is predominant, he will be serving Yaakov. He will never be able to escape this destiny.

Similarly, when Eisav receives the *brachos* that Yitzchok has left over for him after blessing Yaakov, it is only to keep Yaakov "on the straight and narrow." Should Yaakov veer off the track, Eisav will be waiting to set him back. This is what is written there regarding Eisav:

ואת אחיך תעבד והיה כאשר תריד ופרקת עלו מעל צוארך: (בראשית פרק כ"ז:מ')

And you shall serve your brother; and it will be that when you will be aggrieved, you will break his yoke from upon your neck. (ibid., 27:40)

Yitzchok says to Eisav: "You will always be serving your brother, even when you break the yoke from your neck." The more Eisav oppresses Yaakov and drives him into suffering and *galus,* the more Yaakov is purified and readied to receive the eternal good that is awaiting him.

Eisav's destiny will always remain "his brother's keeper."

This illustrates a most basic lesson: Even when circumstances appear to be very destructive and threatening, whether on a national level or a personal one, Hashem's will is guiding these events for our ultimate benefit.

אמר רב הונא אמר רב משום רבי מאיר וכן תנא משמיה דרבי עקיבא לעולם יהא אדם
רגיל לומר כל דעביד רחמנא לטב עביד: (ברכות ס' ע:ב)

Said Rav Huna, said Rav, in the name of Rabbi Meir, and so was it taught in the name of Rabbi Akiva: A person should always be in the habit of saying, "Whatever the Merciful One does, He does it for the good." (*Brachos* 60b)

8   Going and Coming

When Yaakov originally left *Eretz Yisrael* to go to Charan he left from Beer Sheva. When he returned, why did he return to Chevron? How did he know to go to Chevron and not to Beer Sheva? Why was his family not still in Beer Sheva?

One possible answer is that, in fact, Yaakov did not go to Chevron because he knew Yitzchok was there. Rather, when Yaakov was in Alon Bachus, he discovered that his mother had passed away. Hashem came to him there for the mitzvah of *nichum aveilim*. Regarding the time Yaakov was in Alon Bachus, it is written that Hashem blessed him (*Bereishis* 35:9). Rashi explains that this blessing was actually *birkas aveilim,* since Yaakov was in *aveilus* over his mother Rivkah.

Perhaps Yaakov, indeed, had intentions to return to Beer Sheva, where he had departed from many years ago. However, it is reasonable to assume that he took a detour to Chevron first to visit his mother's *kever*. When he got there, he discovered that his father was also there.

As we know, Yitzchok was blind. When Rivkah was finally buried in Chevron (after having been snuck out in the middle of the night, as explained in the section above titled "*Rivkah Cries for her Children*"), we may assume that Yitzchok came there for the *kevurah*. Since he was blind and, assumedly, it was hard for him to take care of himself alone, we can postulate that he moved his residence to Chevron and never returned to Beer Sheva, and that is why Yaakov found him there.

וישב

VAYEISHEV

1   "Pastural" Counseling

וַיֵּלְכוּ אֶחָיו לִרְעוֹת אֶת צֹאן אֲבִיהֶם בִּשְׁכֶם:

And his brothers went to pasture their father's flock [or: to pasture themselves] in Shechem. (Bereishis 37:12)

Our verse describes the intentions of Yosef's brothers on two levels. Why did they go to Shechem? Ostensibly to pasture their father's flock. Yet, Rashi (ad loc.) notes that in the *Sefer Torah*, there are dots on top of the word אֶת. These dots point to another meaning: The brothers' intention in going to Shechem was to "pasture themselves."

This explanation is bewildering. How does a person "pasture himself," and was this really their intention?

The *Rosh's* commentary on the Torah sheds light on this. He explains that when Yosef's brothers cast him into the pit in Shechem, this set in motion a sequence of events that resulted in the brothers being provided with sustenance in Egypt during the years of famine, as it is written, "Yosef leads them like a flock" (*Tehillim* 80:2). When our verse says, "their father's flock," this refers figuratively to "their father's children," i.e., themselves. Thus, the ultimate result of their actions was that they benefited and "pastured" themselves when they went down to Egypt. So explains the *Rosh,* and a similar explanation is found in *Sefer Oheiv Yisrael.*

Thus, when they thought they were going to pasture their father's flock, they ended up taking care of themselves and supporting themselves during the years of famine.

However, in *Tanach*, we find that the term לרעות את עצמן, "to pasture themselves," is quite a negative description. In *Sefer Yechezkel*, we find the leaders (the "shepherds") of the people accused of doing this.

הוי רועי ישראל אשר היו רעים אותם וכו'. (יחזקאל ל"ד:א')

Woe, O shepherds of Israel, who would pasture themselves...
(Yechezkel 34:1)

היו מענגין ממעון חבריהם אשר תחתיהם וכו'. הלא משפט הרועים לרעות את הצאן
ולא לרעות את עצמן: (רש"י שם)

They would pamper themselves with the money of their fellows who were under them... whereas the role of the "shepherds" is to pasture the flock and not to pasture themselves. (Rashi, ad loc.)

This passage makes quite a strident criticism of the leaders, the *Metzudas Dovid* (ad loc.) adding that these leaders were pasturing themselves "to fatten their flesh." Thus, we may conclude that such a term is a very negative one in the lexicon of *Tanach*.

Perhaps this term was chosen to describe Yosef's brothers in our *Parsha* in order to emphasize that which was to befall *K'lal Yisrael* due to their unfortunate actions. The *machlokes* that developed between Yosef and his brothers planted the seed from which grew all the future instances of *machlokes* in the people of Israel, leading to the *cheit hameraglim,* and later to the *sinas chinam* that destroyed the Second Temple. This was the ultimate source of all *machlokes* among Jews.

The Torah thus hints to us that the actions of Yosef's brothers ultimately led to the leaders of the Jewish people pasturing themselves and "fattening their flesh" at the expense of their brethren whom they were supposed to be caring for, in the days of *Yechezkel.* Yosef's brothers themselves did not act in such a way, but the end result was such.

We could offer another explanation of Yosef's brothers pasturing themselves.

Simply put, the brothers originally went to Shechem in order to serve their father by tending to his flock. However, when it came to the crucial decision of what to do with their troublesome younger brother, Yosef, who showed up just then and there, they acted in a self-serving fashion. They surely did not have their father Yaakov's best interests in mind when they decided to sell Yosef. They thought only of themselves, seeking to solve their personal quandary in a way that seemed right and appropriate to them. As *Tanach* puts it, they "pastured themselves."

2   Worlds Apart

וַיֵּשֶׁב יַעֲקֹב בְּאֶרֶץ מְגוּרֵי אָבִיו...

And Yaakov dwelled in the land of his father's sojournings...
(Bereishis 37:1)

Rashi on our verse discusses how *Yaakov Avinu* sought to dwell in a state of tranquility, and presents it as a criticism: Is it not enough for a tzaddik to receive the tremendous reward that awaits him in the World to Come? Does he have to seek a life of tranquility also in this world? Therefore, the calamity of Yosef sprang upon him.

It sounds like Yaakov was asking for too much. Yet, we find in *Chazal* that this is quite an acceptable approach for tzaddikim:

אמר רבא: אטו צדיקי אי אכלי תרי עולמי מי סני להו? (הוריות י' ע"א)

Said Rava: If the tzaddikim eat in two worlds, is this displeasing for them?
(*Horiyos* 10a)

Furthermore, we find the following written about *Avraham Avinu:*

וה' ברך את אברהם בכל: (בראשית כ"ד:א')

And Hashem blessed Avraham with everything. (Bereishis 24:1)

Avraham left this world satiated and "in the goodness of old age" (ibid., 25:8). In other words, the end of his life was characterized by a state of tranquility. Yitzchok's life was not marked by a lack of tranquility either. Yitzchok knew the truth that Yosef was alive. Although he shared in his son Yaakov's suffering over Yosef's "demise," Yitzchok knew what Yaakov did not. Torah and *Chazal* do not speak of Yitzchok's life as one of suffering in the way they do of Yaakov's life.

Yaakov himself, who surely carried a heavy burden of suffering for so long, spent the last seventeen years of his life in Egypt in a state of marked tranquility. These were years that he was able to spend in peace and calm with all of his children and grandchildren. How are we to understand this, in light of the criticism earlier leveled at him for seeking to dwell in tranquility?

When we begin to investigate this issue it becomes even more problematic because the rights to a good life in this world were the very point of conflict between Yaakov and Eisav while they were still in their mother's womb. Rashi's criticism of Yaakov is thus most enigmatic when viewed in this light as it makes it sound as if Hashem agreed with Eisav's argument that Yaakov had no real place in this world and no rights to a normal life. Yet, this cannot be so.

Let us consider how Eisav viewed Yaakov's accomplishments in this world.

וכשבא יעקב מבית לבן וראה לו עשו בנים ובנות עבדים ושפחות א"ל יעקב אחי לא
כך אמרת לי שתטול אתה העולם הבא ואני אטול העולם הזה מנין לך כל הממון הזה
שתתשמח:

When Yaakov came from the house of Lavan and Eisav saw that he had sons and daughters, servants and handmaidens, he said to him: "Yaakov, my brother! This is not what you told me, that you will take the World to Come and I will take this world. Why do you have all this wealth, to rejoice in it?"

הרהר עשו בדעתו ומה העולם הזה שאינו חלקו נתן לו הקדוש ברוך הוא שכרו העולם
הבא שהוא חלקו על אחת כמה וכמה: (ילקוט שמעוני בראשית פרק כ:ה רמז קי"א)

Eisav thought to himself: "If Hashem gave him reward in this world, which is not his portion, all the more so regarding the World to Come, which is his portion!" (Yalkut Shimoni Bereishis, ch. 25:111)

The *Maharal* has some interesting comments on this Midrash. After explaining how Yaakov's nature was appropriate for spiritual matters and for the World to Come, and how Eisav's nature was appropriate for the physical matters of this world, he raises a question: What were they fighting over in their mother's womb? They would seem to have no conflict, no point of contention, since each had his own interests and his own "world" in which to pursue them. The *Maharal* then goes on to explain why the opposite is true.

דודאי כל אחד היה רוצה בכל, שהרי עולם הזה ועולם הבא שניהם נבראו לאדם. ואם לא היה עשו, היה ליעקב עולם הזה וגם עולם הבא, כי לא היה נמצא ההיפך שהוא ראוי אל עולם הזה. ומפני כי יעקב ועשו הפכים, לכך לפי מדריגת יעקב – אין מציאות לעשו, וכן לפי מדריגת עשו – אין מציאות ליעקב כלל. ולכך היו מריבים בנחלת שני עולמות:

Surely, each one wanted it all. For this world and the World to Come were both created for man. And if not for Eisav, then Yaakov would have this world and also the World to Come, since there would not be someone of opposite nature who was fitting for this world. And since Yaakov and Eisav are opposites, it comes out that according to Yaakov's perspective, Eisav has no existence. And according to Eisav's perspective, Yaakov has no existence at all. Therefore they were fighting over the inheritance of two worlds.

כי יעקב היה רוצה בעולם הזה והעולם הבא, כאילו אין כאן עשו: (נצח ישראל פרק ט"ו)

For Yaakov wanted this world and the World to Come, as if Eisav did not exist. (Maharal, Netzach Yisrael, ch. 15)

According to the above Midrash with the *Maharal*'s explanation, and several other statements of *Chazal* (for instance *Midrash Yelamdeinu, Vayishlach* 71), we see clearly that Yaakov sought both worlds — and Hashem gave them to him. Hashem granted *Yaakov Avinu* a right to *Olam Hazeh*. Why then should Rashi raise an objection to Yaakov's living in tranquility?

My son Akiva Yosef, נ״י, asked an enlightening and instructive question. Why do we find in the beginning of *Parshas Toldos* that when Yaakov and Eisav are fighting over their worlds, Yaakov responds to Eisav's claims? Let Eisav say whatever he wishes. Let him argue his heart out. What Hashem wants to do, He will do! Hashem is the Master of all worlds. If *Yaakov Avinu* needs *Olam Hazeh* and *Olam Haba,* Hashem will surely give it to him. And if *Yaakov Avinu* does not need it, of what value is it? For what purpose is Yaakov fighting with Eisav and angering him so? Let Eisav think whatever he wants, and leave it be.

This question forces us to re-analyze the whole episode. First, we are brought to the conclusion that the "debate" between Yaakov and Eisav constituted a most singular and fateful event. That which Yaakov and Eisav wanted and chose for themselves is that which Hashem would ultimately grant them, for Hashem's initial intent was for them both to receive both worlds. As the *Maharal* points out, that was what they wanted. They apparently had the free choice to decide what they were going to have.

However, Eisav became dissatisfied and said, "I don't want the original deal. I'm not interested in being a partner with you, Yaakov, in your *Olam Haba.* I don't want to supply you with your material needs that are required for your pursuit of *Olam Haba.* I'll take the *gashmiyus* all for myself and have it here, and you can have the *ruchniyus.*"

This was exactly what concerned Rivkah later on. She knew that the material blessings that Eisav was to receive from his father Yitzchok were meant to be shared. Yaakov and Eisav were meant to have a partnership in *Olam Hazeh* **and** *Olam Haba.* However, Rivkah realized that Eisav was not really interested in the partnership because he did not want the *Olam Haba* part. He wanted only the *Olam Hazeh,* and all of it. He sought to cut Yaakov out of this world altogether: to kill him.

When Yaakov expressed his desire for both worlds, it thus came out that he would also receive the material world that was originally to be Eisav's. Yet, while both this world and the next were to be exclusively Yaakov's, the whole concept of *gashmiyus* now must be understood in the context of its ultimate purpose.

This world was never meant to be related to in the way of *vayeishev,* "dwelling," but in the way of *vayagar,* "sojourning." The former implies permanence; the latter, temporality. Here lies Rashi's criticism: Yaakov sought to live in this world in the way of *vayeishev.* That was the problem.

My rebbe, HaRav HaGaon Dovid Feinstein, *shlita,* comments on the approach of *Yitzchok Avinu* on this matter. Although Yitzchok was so-to-speak imprisoned in *Eretz Yisrael* and could not leave, he always retained the approach of *vayagar*. It is written of Yaakov that he dwelled in "the land of the sojournings of his father" (*Bereishis* 37:1), implying that his father Yitzchok was always a sojourner. *Yitzchok Avinu* had the greatest excuse of all to be a "dweller." He was told by Hashem that this was where he had to stay. It was as if Hashem Himself had told him to be a "dweller." Yet, he constantly moved around; he did not settle down in one place in *Eretz Yisrael*. He lived as a sojourner because it was still the land of Canaan; it was not yet *Eretz Yisrael*. So it was with *Avraham Avinu* before him, who understood that his presence in the land was only as a *ger*, a "stranger."

If so, why did Yaakov depart from the way of his forefathers? Let us understand Yaakov's situation. After his victory over Lavan and Eisav, he contemplated the thought that he could now take on the way of a permanent dweller in the *Olam Hazeh* of *Eretz Yisrael*. He had fathered the Tribes and was ready to build the permanent House of Israel.

However, the time was premature. *HaKadosh Boruch Hu* had decreed that soon would come a great exile of four hundred years. That deep *galus* was to be the crucible that would create *K'lal Yisrael,* and if Yaakov would already now become a permanent dweller in the land, it would detract from this essential process. It would stand in the way of his children's ultimate perfection and refinement, which was to be attained only in the "iron crucible" (*Devarim* 4:20) of Egypt.

In addition, the *Avos* were given the role of showing their future descendants how to live in *Olam Hazeh* — how to live and function in this world with all its material aspects, but only as a sojourner!

This brings us to the next point: Understanding the deeper meaning of *galus*. In what way is *galus* a fitting punishment, in the sense of *middah kenegged middah*? Why is it that when *K'lal Yisrael* is not deserving of the *Bais HaMikdash*, it is destroyed and they are driven into *galus*? What does it accomplish to undergo *galus*? I answered the following at the *shalom zachor* of my son R' Shimon Meir, הי"ו, and I later repeated it after the *bris* to our great Rosh Yeshiva, Maran HaRav HaGaon Moshe Feinstein, *ztzvk"l*.

Galus comes when a person lives with the attitude that this world is the ultimate place where he really belongs, that the world belongs to him and that by living in this world he fulfills the purpose of his creation. Even if one lives in *Eretz Yisrael, Eretz HaKodesh* — but in the way of "*vayeishev*" — this seriously flawed approach carries with it the punishment of *galus*.

If we make the mistake, *chas veshalom*, of thinking like Eisav, Hashem does us the favor of setting us straight. He says to us, "You are confusing the everlasting with the transitory. You are exchanging *chayei olam* for *chayei sha'ah*," (See *Beitzah* 15b.) At this point, Hashem sees that the best, in fact the only, cure for our diseased way of thinking is to go into *galus* — to move. In this way, we are brought to realize that this world is not our true residence.

Thus, we wake up to the fact that *Olam Hazeh* is only a corridor (Avos 4:16), a stage to pass through in order to reach our rightful place: *Olam Haba*. In this world we are only sojourners. This whole world is no more than a *sukkah*, whereas the house is the World to Come. (We will explain this point more in depth in *Parshas Shemos*.)

All this is represented by Yaakov's descent into *galus*, which was the outcome of the calamity of Yosef that sprang upon him right when he sought to dwell in tranquility, as Rashi explains on our verse. This calamity was not some kind of cruel turn of fate for a trouble-stricken soul; rather, it was the beginning of *K'lal Yisrael*'s exile in Egypt. If living in *Eretz Yisrael* causes even a spiritual giant like *Yaakov Avinu* to entertain thoughts of living in the way of *vayeishev*, even in its most lofty formulation, then the only place for us is in the Egyptian house of slavery. This was the beginning of all the persecutions and servitude, as this world is not a world of *vayeishev*. It is a world of *vayagar*.

Rashi's criticism is not against living in tranquility nor is it against material wealth and prestige that come with the *brachos* originally intended for Eisav. Rashi is focusing on the point of *vayeishev*. Yaakov, in truth, was right. Yaakov won against Eisav and gained rights to life in this world. However, *Olam Hazeh* comes with a condition: It is subservient to *Olam Haba*, and cannot be treated in the way of *vayeishev*. We can be only sojourners in this world.

3   Musings on the Brothers

אלה תלדות יעקב יוסף וכו'. (בראשית ל"ז:ב')

These are the offspring of Yaakov: Yosef...(Bereishis 37:2)

Rashi brings a Midrash to explain why our verse makes it sound as if Yaakov's descendants were primarily Yosef, in spite of the fact that Yaakov had thirteen children.

This Midrash states that the primary purpose for which Yaakov worked for Lavan all those years was to receive Rachel, from whom was born Yosef. Rashi continues with more reasons from the Midrash as to why Yosef is Yaakov's primary descendant:

...ושהי' זיו איקונין של יוסף דומה לו. וכל מה שאירע ליעקב אירע ליוסף זה נשטם וזה
נשטם, זה אחיו מבקש להרגו וזה אחיו מבקשים להרגו, וכן הרבה: (רש"י בראשית ל"ז:ב'
מבראשית רבה שם ו').

...And Yosef's face was similar to his. And all that happened to Yaakov happened to Yosef. This one was hated, and that one was hated. This one had a brother who sought to kill him, and that one had brothers who sought to kill him. And there are many more [similarities]. (Rashi, Bereishis 37:2, based on Bereishis Rabba, ad loc. 6)

It turns out that the most significant individual in Yaakov's life after the death of Rachel was Yosef. Eventually, Yaakov was to spend twenty-two years mourning Yosef. From the perspective of Yaakov, Yosef had the preeminent position among his sons. Yaakov came to Lavan's house with the intention to build a whole *K'lal Yisrael,* yet, Rashi tells us that all revolved around Yosef. If it was not for Yaakov working for Rachel who gave birth to Yosef, Yaakov would not have had any children. There would have been no *K'lal Yisrael.*

In light of this, we would expect to see Yosef in a leadership position in the continued history of *K'lal Yisrael.* Yet, Yosef's unique contributions to Jewish history are only sparsely present. It would almost appear as if Yosef is remembered more for the wicked Yerovam ben Nevat than for the righteous Yehoshua bin Nun. It is true that we bless our children to be like Efraim and Menasheh, placing Efraim before Menasheh because of Yehoshua who descended from Efraim. Still, when we discuss Yehoshua conquering *Eretz Yisrael,* the emphasis is not on the fact that Yehoshua represents Yosef.

From our perspective, the most significant individual identified with Yosef was Yerovam ben Nevat of the ten northern tribes, who represented the kingdom of Yosef. It was Yerovam ben Nevat who began the downward spiral of idolatry that caused the ten tribes to vanish. Thus, the reality of *K'lal Yisrael* today is totally severed from Yosef. He disappeared from the map altogether. If Yosef is the primary descendant of Yaakov, why does he disappear, so totally, from the picture? This issue requires further thought. *Tzarich iyun.*

Similarly, and equally perplexing, is the strange progression of events connected to Reuven. Due to all of his "errors," the Torah severely criticizes him. However, behind these errors is Reuven's attempt to act as the bechor, the firstborn son and natural leader, and act with responsibility. His objective is to act for the honor of his mother Leah. His objective is to act to save Yosef and his objective is to earnestly assure the safety of Binyamin. Yet, not once but twice, his efforts are rebuffed. Each time he is rejected.

Here he is, the oldest son, asserting his position and pursuing his obligations, yet, he stumbles terribly each time. The first time he tries to save Yosef from the pit, the credit is given to Yehudah. The second time he tries to guarantee the safety of Binyamin, when he promises his father to take responsibility for the return trip to Egypt, he is again superseded by Yehudah. He can't seem to get it right at all. This is virtually inexplicable.

Apparently, Shimon and Levi are twin partners in all activities, but one becomes the unrivaled leader in matters of spirituality. The Temple's service is in the hands of Levi alone. This tribe is called "The King's legion," as Rashi points out in the beginning of *Sefer Bamidbar* (1:49). The destiny of Shimon is to be dispersed among *K'lal Yisrael,* in a position of overwhelming insignificance relative to every other tribe. This is a very strange phenomenon and a troubling one to reflect upon.

We could almost apply here the verse of "The stone that the builders despised has become the corner stone" (*Tehillim* 118:22). We witness here individuals who did not start out with much importance, both in terms of their activities and their parents' expectations, who became prominent. There must be some underlying rationale to the fact that Yehudah took the predominant position as king and Levi took the preeminent position in the *Bais HaMikdash*, while those individuals who seemed to have the greatest potential fell by the wayside.

In order to resolve Reuven's fall from greatness, we need to understand Yaakov's critique of him: "*pachaz kamayim*" (*Bereishis* 49:4). Reuven was impetuous and consistently acted with undue haste. When Reuven volunteered to take responsibility for Binyamin on the return trip to Egypt, we see that Yaakov immediately dismissed his proposal as inappropriate. Rashi describes Yaakov's harsh dismissal of Reuven's proposal:

אמר בכור שוטה הוא זה, הוא אמר להמית בניו, וכי בניו הם ולא בני:

(רש"י בראשית מ"ב:ל"ח)

He said: "This is a foolish firstborn. He says to kill his sons—
and are they his sons and not mine?" (Rashi, Bereishis 42:38)

This was when Reuven offered his two sons as security for taking care of Binyamin on the way and bringing him back safely. We know that a person will risk his life to protect his children. Naturally, he cares for them more than for his own self. So why was Reuven's offer deemed inadequate by Yaakov? Yet, Yaakov considered the offer ludicrous.

Later, Yehudah made a very similar offer. He did not use his children as security, rather himself. Here, Yaakov should have said: "This is a foolish child. What gain do I have from saving one son at the expense of another?" Yet, Yaakov accepted the offer. Why? Because Yehudah knew the secret of proper timing. He did not speak up impulsively but waited until the food was gone. Reuven, however, volunteered to lead the dangerous mission when the pressure did not yet warrant it. They still had food left. At that time, Yaakov recognized that the offer was not an acceptable one. Rashi states clearly that this was Yehudah's wisdom.

יהודה אמר להם, המתינו לזקן עד שתכלה פת מן הבית: (רש"י בראשית מ"ג:ב')

Yehudah said to them: "Wait for the elder (Yaakov) until bread
ceases from the house." (Rashi, Bereishis 43:2)

It emerges that Reuven's foolishness was not in what he said but in when he said it. Even though Reuven's sincerity was deserving of admiration, he went about his mission without proper deliberation. Such a person cannot serve as king of the people of Israel. Yehudah's way of doing things was calculated and thought out. That was the difference.

Let us now consider the enigma that the fate of Shimon and Levi differed so radically although they always acted in tandem. Why did Levi become the spiritual leader while Shimon was dissipated throughout the land?

In truth, both Shimon and Levi stand out in their extreme actions as we first see in their response to their sister Dinah's kidnapping. But what was it that produced this substantial difference between the zealousness of Levi and that of Shimon?

Rashi (ibid., 42:24) points out that on the brothers' first trip to Egypt, when Yosef imprisoned one of them, he chose Shimon because he sought to separate him from Levi. This was because the whole idea of attacking Yosef in the first place originated with Shimon. Rashi says that Shimon was the one who spoke to Levi and created the idea. He was the instigator. Even though Reuven came up with the plan of placing Yosef into the pit (rather than killing him), it was Shimon who actually implemented the plan and threw him in.

It is one thing to come up with an idea, to agree to a plan. However, it is something else altogether to practically implement a violent and extreme course of action, especially where it was not properly thought out.

Lehavdil, let us consider what happened when Doeg Ha'Adomi reported to King Shaul that Dovid had escaped, and had been assisted by the Kohen Gadol in Nov (where the *Mishkan* was then located). Doeg came up with the idea of killing all of the kohanim of Nov, but no one was willing to actually do it. The others stood around and watched while only Doeg actually slaughtered the innocent kohanim, and it was Doeg, and Doeg alone, who lost his portion in *Olam Haba.* This shows that actually implementing an ill-advised course of action is much worse than merely agreeing to it. That is why Shimon was held primarily responsible for the ill-advised activities that he and Levi participated in, and he paid a much greater price.

Another factor that explains why Levi's fate was so utterly different from

Shimon's can be found in *Parshas Mikeitz* in connection with the *teshuvah* that Yosef's brothers began to do.

ויאמרו איש אל אחיו אבל אשמים אנחנו: (בראשית מ"ב:כ"א).

And one man said to his brother: "Indeed, we are guilty." (ibid., 42:21)

The Torah does not reveal who said to whom. However, Rashi (ibid., 49:5) states that since Shimon and Levi are called "brothers" by the Torah, we may conclude that the earlier statement of "And one man said to his brother" (*ibid* 37:19), in connection with the initial attack on Yosef, was Shimon speaking to Levi. Although there it was Shimon who was the speaker, we can speculate and it stands to reason that here, regarding their *teshuvah,* it was Levi who spoke to Shimon. If we are correct in this assumption, it is quite plausible and reasonable to posit that this interaction between Levi and Shimon was what prompted Yosef to imprison Shimon rather then Levi. Yosef realized that Levi, while bearing serious guilt for attacking him, was having serious doubts about the part that he played.

There is another good reason to assume that it was Levi who started the *teshuvah* process by saying *"Indeed, we are guilty,"* since the Torah later recounts how *"**the one** opened his sack to give fodder to his donkey"* (ibid., 42:27), and Rashi (ad loc.) says that the expression *"**the one**"* refers to Levi, who was left as a single individual without his partner Shimon. Clearly, this situation of opening their sacks and finding their money inside was an impetus from Heaven prompting them to do *teshuvah* for selling Yosef to Egypt. Their response was appropriate:

ויצא לבם ויחרדו איש אל אחיו לאמר מה זאת עשה אלקים לנו: (בראשית שם כ"ז)

And their hearts went out, and they trembled each to his brother, saying, "What is this, that G-d has done to us?" (ibid., 42:27)

We see that Levi was chosen by Heaven to be the one to discover that their money had been returned to them, that something was seriously wrong. He was chosen by Heaven to lead the *teshuvah* process. This supports our assumption that Levi was playing this role previously and was the one who exclaimed: *"Indeed, we are guilty."* He motivated and galvanized the others to do *teshuvah,* awakening in them a sense of true regret over the sale of their brother Yosef. This propensity for *teshuvah* made the tribe of Levi a leading one, and the tribe most fitting to perform the Temple service that attains atonement for Israel's sins.

Furthermore, we cannot properly understand the diverging fates of Shimon and Levi if we ignore a key incident in which their fervently intense and passionate way of handling matters pitted these traditional partners one against the other. Pinchas is considered to be a paragon of the Levites' holy zealousness, while the example of zealousness for Shimon remains Zimri! (See further elaboration on this theme in *Parshas Vayechi* in the section *Parallel Lives*.)

In the incident with the licentious Moabite women, we find Zimri, a leader of the tribe of Shimon, taking action in a most unfortunate way, causing the loss of his own life and that of twenty-four thousand others at Ba'al Peor in Shittim. Zimri did not hesitate or hide, but went straight to *Moshe Rabbeinu,* arguing that these foreign women were permitted to them. Who was Zimri's antagonist? Pinchas of the tribe of Levi. Pinchas was the only one to go ahead, take the law into his own hands and spear Zimri. His stand against Zimri thereby personified the zealousness of the tribe of Levi who, years earlier, had all rallied around *Moshe Rabbeinu* at the time of the Golden Calf.

It is truly an enigma that Shimon's great energy did not express itself as an overpowering positive force. Rashi tells us that Shimon married Dinah (ibid., 46:10). Thus, he had the power of two of Yaakov's children.

(According to one explanation in Rashi, while all of Yaakov's sons married twin sisters who were born with them [ibid., 37:32], these sisters are not counted among the seventy souls who formed the kernel of the Jewish people and who went down to Egypt with Yaakov. However, Dinah *is* counted among them. Therefore, we must conclude that these other sisters did not bear the spiritual power of *K'lal Yisrael*.)

Chazal say that Dinah was also representative of the qualities of Yosef. Even so, these dynamic and potent qualities did not develop in the future history of the *shevet* of Shimon as it did in that of Levi's. (See further on this topic in *Parshas Va'yechi, Least Likely to Succeed?*)

4 The Elderly Woman Named Tamar

How old was Tamar when she married Yehudah's son, Er?

Rashi (*Bereishis* 38:24) says that Tamar was the daughter of Shem ben Noach, "Kohen to the Most High G-d" (*Bereishis* 14:18, Rashi ad loc.). That is why she was initially sentenced to burning, since that is the form of punishment appropriate to a Kohen's daughter who commits adultery.

When Shem died, *Yaakov Avinu* was fifty years old. When Yaakov received the blessings from Yitzchok, he was sixty-three, as it was thirteen years later. After learning for fourteen years, he went to Charan, and fourteen years afterwards, Yosef was born. Seventeen years after that, Yosef was sold to Egypt. Thus, it comes out that Yosef was sold into slavery fifty-eight years after the death of Shem.

Rashi tells us (*Bereishis* 14:1) that Yehudah married Bas Shua (from whom Er and Onan were born) shortly after Yosef's sale to Egypt.[22]

Based on the details of what happened with them, we can also assume that Er was at least thirteen years old[23] when he married Tamar, which would add another fourteen years to our calculation.[24] This would mean that even if Tamar was born when her father Shem died, she would still be at least seventy-two years old.[25]

How old was Yehudah? At Er's marriage to Tamar, he could not have been more than thirty-six. All of Yaakov's children (except for Binyamin) were born within a seven-year period, ending with the birth of Yosef. If Reuven was seven months old at the birth of Shimon, fourteen months old at the birth of Levi

---

22 Midrash *Shochar Tov* (38:5) states that Er was born when Yosef was fifteen years old.

23 *Yalkut Shimoni* (*Bereishis* 35:145) states that Er was eight years old.

24 Nine years according to *Yalkut Shimoni*.

25 Sixty-five years old according to the Midrashim.

and twenty-one months old at the birth of Yehudah, it comes out that Yehudah could be at most slightly more than five years older than Yosef. So when Yosef was seventeen, Yehudah was no more than twenty-two.

If Yehudah was twenty-two when Yosef was sold, that would mean that fourteen years later, Yehudah was thirty-six. So when Tamar married Er, assuming that Er was thirteen, Tamar was at least seventy-two[26] and Yehudah was thirty-six.

5 The Benefits of Old Age

וְיִשְׂרָאֵל אָהַב אֶת יוֹסֵף מִכָּל בָּנָיו כִּי בֶן זְקֻנִים הוּא לוֹ...

And Israel loved Yosef because he was a son of old age to him (or: for [the sake of] him)... (Bereishis 37:3)

R ashi states in numerous places that the words לִי, לוֹ, לְךָ, וּלְכֶם, commonly translated as "to me," "to him," etc., depending on their context, will have other meanings.

Whenever we find these words used together with speech they will mean on behalf of.

ודבר הוא לך. בשבילך ידבר אל העם. וזה יוכיח על כל לך ולי ולו ולכם ולהם הסמוכים לדבור, שכלם לשון "על" הם: (רש"י שמות ד':ט"ז)

He shall speak for you: This means he will speak to the people on your behalf. This will prove that any time [the words] ולי לך וֹלוּ ולכם and להם are said in context with speaking, they will have the meaning "on [behalf]."(Rashi, Shemos 4:16)

If nothing is actually being spoken or transferred they mean "for me," "for

---

26   Or Er was eight and Tamar was at least sixty-five! My son, R' Avraham Eliyahu, הי"ו pointed out that Peretz had two sons, Chetzron and Chamul by the time K'lal Yisrael went down to Eygpt.

him," etc. In other words, they indicate "for the sake of."

אשר ינחלו לכם. בשבילכם, וכו'. ולא יתכן לפרש "לכם" זה ככל "לכם" שבמקרא,
שאם כן היה לו לכתוב "יַנְחִילוּ" לכם. "יִנְחֲלוּ" משמע שהם נוחלים לכם בשבילכם
ובמקומכם, וכו'. (רש"י במדבר ל"ד:י"ז)

[These are the men] who will take possession of the land for you: ...It would not be correct to explain this "לכם" as all other "לכם" which occur in scripture. If this was so, it (the Torah) should have written יַנְחִילוּ לכם [in the Hiphil form], i.e., they will give the possession to you. Rather, יִנְחֲלוּ לכם [the Kal form] implies that they themselves take possession on your behalf and in your place... (Rashi, Bamidbar 34:17)

The following are other examples of this:

· ילחם לכם. בשבילכם. (רש"י שמות י"ד:י"ד)

· המקנא אתה לי. וכו'. לי. כמו בשבילי. (רש"י במדבר י"א:כ"ט)

· שלח לךָ. לדעתך, (רש"י שם י"ג:ב')

· לו. הקריאה היתה שלו ולהנאתו (רש"י שם כ"ב:ה')

· ילחם לכם. בשבילכם: (רש"י דברים א':ל')

Now we come to our verse. What does it mean that Yosef was a son of old age "for [the sake of] him," i.e., his father Yaakov? How could Yosef be a son of old age for his father's sake? Either he was a son of old age or he was not a son of old age. HaRav Yisrael HaCohen Chesir, *shlita*, suggested that the *Kli Yakar*'s commentary on our verse answers this question.

The *Kli Yakar* says that Yosef, indeed, was not the same for everyone. He behaved with his father as a mature person of old age, whereas with his siblings, the sons of Bilhah and Zilpah, he behaved as an immature lad (See Rashi, *Bereishis* 37:2). This inconsistent behavior was actually a sign of Yosef's wisdom and good manners, says the *Kli Yakar*. Yosef knew how to adjust himself to his company and behave appropriately.

We could, therefore, say that Yosef's actions reflecting "old age" were done for the sake of his father Yaakov. They were intended as a benefit and a *nachas* for him.

This approach, explaining the word לוֹ, fits well with another key verse in our *Parsha*:

וְעָשָׂה לוֹ כְּתֹנֶת פַּסִּים: (בראשית ל"ז:ג').

And he made for him a tunic of fine material. (Bereishis 37:3)

Yaakov made the *kesones pasim* for Yosef's sake, for his benefit.

מקץ

MIKEITZ

1 The Nile River Valley

וּפַרְעֹה חֹלֵם וְהִנֵּה עֹמֵד עַל הַיְאֹר:

And Pharaoh is dreaming, and behold, he is standing by the Nile. (Bereishis 41:1)

⌣

The Nile River, the longest river in the world, was unique because there was a very extensive system of irrigation canals (*ye'orim*) that extended out from it to water the fields, as Rashi explains on our verse. This system developed because Egypt does not have much rain. Thus, Egypt's fields drank from the Nile.

The Nile is quite a peculiar river, one of the few that travels from south to north. It flows from the rain forests of central Africa where it rains all the time and, under normal circumstances, there is never a water shortage. Thus, the Nile always has water.

Due to this unique situation, Egypt is not dependent on the fluctuating rainy seasons like other countries are. Sedom is described in the Torah as *"Like the garden of Hashem, like the land of Egypt"* (*Bereishis* 13:10). Since Egypt was always rich and fertile due to the special blessings that the Nile produced, the great city of Sedom in its prime, and the entire fertile crescent, were secondary to Egypt in this regard.

The emphasis that our *Parsha* places on the Nile River, though, is puzzling.

This is underscored by Rashi's extensive explanation on the first verse of the Egyptian irrigation system and how it compares to that of other lands. True, Rashi is explaining to us why the Nile is called *ye'or,* "irrigation canal." But why do we need such a detailed philological explanation of the origin of the Nile's name? If we would be devoted to the study of geography, economics or ancient history, the role of the Nile River in ancient Egyptian society would surely be a matter of significance. However, *Parshas Mikeitz* does not come to teach us these subjects. It comes to tell us of the dream of Pharaoh and the ensuing course of events that brought Yosef out of prison. For our purposes, we need just the basic facts relevant to the dreams and their interpretation, and how they foretold the years of plenty and then the years of famine.

Why do we need a lesson about the Nile delta and its distributaries?

The answer is that we can learn a lot from it by juxtaposing this opening verse, *"and behold, he is standing by the Nile,"* to the statement of Rashi that concluded the previous *Parsha,* which tells us of Yosef's shortcoming by placing his hopes on the *sar hamashkim.* Yosef, unjustly imprisoned in the royal dungeon, hoped that the *sar hamashkim* would mention his plight to Pharaoh and bring about his release. Because Yosef trusted in this cursed Egyptian officer rather than relying solely on Hashem, he had to spend an extra two years in the dungeon.

Furthermore, there is this "Great Divide" that separates *K'lal Yisrael* from the Egyptians? The verse quoted by Rashi says:

אשרי הגבר אשר שם ה' מבטחו ולא פנה אל רהבים: (תהלים מ:ה)

Fortunate is the man who places Hashem as his trust and does not turn to the arrogant. (Tehillim 40:5)

Who is the man who "places Hashem as his trust?" It is Yosef. And who are these arrogant people? Rashi explains that they are the Egyptians. The opening verse of our *Parsha,* with Rashi's explanation of it, teaches us about the nature of the Nile River in order to reveal what distinguishes *K'lal Yisrael* from the Egyptians.

According to the natural conditions that existed, Egypt needed no one. They were fully self-reliant. Therefore, they were the furthest from *bitachon.* All their material needs came to them "automatically" as they did not need to answer to anyone or anything, not Above nor on earth. This led them to the heights of arrogance.

K'lal Yisrael and, by extension, *Eretz Yisrael* are totally dependent on Hashem. When it rains, we understand Hashem that is pleased with us. If it doesn't rain, we understand that He wants us to improve our ways. That is the meaning of "Fortunate is the man who places Hashem as his trust." *Eretz Yisrael,* in contradistinction to Egypt, is a land of mountains, valleys and streams. It relies on the rain of Heaven for its water (*Devarim* 11:11). This means that the survival of its inhabitants depends on the mercy of the One who brings the rain. Hashem watches over the Land. His eyes are on it from the beginning of the year until the end (ibid., v.12). Praying to Hashem and requesting rain — *vesein tal umatar livrachah* — is the very foundation of *emunah* and *bitachon* in Hashem.

As Jews, we know that if we listen to Hashem's mitzvos, He will give us the rain we need as it states in the second paragraph of the Shema. If not, Hashem stops the heavens and there is no rain. In fact, this latter possibility is also part of the blessing. In this way, Hashem does not allow us to lose sight of our purpose and task in this world. He does not allow us to become arrogant and forget that we depend upon Him always.

That is why the Torah saw it necessary to tell us that Pharaoh made himself into a god. The source of his arrogance was because "he is standing by the Nile." That was the trait of the land over which he ruled, and that is the type of person he became.

Parenthetically, this same trait seems to have been responsible for the undoing of Sedom and its sister cities as well. The Torah describes Sedom as follows:

כל־ככר הירדן כי כלה משקה לפני שחת ה' את־סדם ואת־עמרה כגן־ה' כארץ מצרים באכה צער: (בראשית י"ג:י')

The whole plain of the Yarden was all well watered, before Hashem destroyed Sedom and Amorah. Like the garden of Hashem, like the land of Egypt as approaching Tzoar. (Bereishis 13:10)

Before Sedom's destruction, there was no Dead Sea. Instead, the Jordan River flowed directly into the area without stop, creating lush farmland that was similar to the automatically irrigated fields of Egypt. This meant that the peoples of this area were not dependent on the rains the way the rest of *Eretz Yisrael* was.

2 Dreams

וַיַּעַן יוֹסֵף אֶת פַּרְעֹה לֵאמֹר בִּלְעָדָי אֱלֹקִים יַעֲנֶה אֶת שְׁלוֹם פַּרְעֹה:

Yosef answered Pharaoh, saying: "It is without me. G-d will provide an answer for Pharaoh's welfare." (Bereishis 41:16)

I n *Parshas Vayeishev,* when Yosef interpreted the dreams of the imprisoned *sar hamashkim* and *sar ha'ofim,* he was careful to preface his remarks by mentioning that interpretations belong to Hashem. Yosef gives the credit to Hashem. He does the same here when he is introduced to Pharaoh in *Parshas Mikeitz.* Pharaoh says: "I hear that you are a capable person." Then he tells him the dream. However, Yosef attributes his wisdom to Hashem, saying, "It is without me. G-d will provide an answer..."

We all understand that Hashem is "The One who gives you the strength to do valiantly" (*Devarim* 8:18). We should never ever think that we have the ability to do anything without Hashem's help. It is not "my strength and the power of my hand" (ibid., v. 17) that grants us success in our endeavors.

However, while Yosef has tremendous success throughout his career in Egypt, he does not regularly present himself as someone whose abilities are dependent on Hashem.[26a] When he speaks to Potifar, we do not find him saying, "By the way, the success I have brought you actually comes from Hashem." When Potifar asks him to do something, we do not find him saying, "I'll take care of that, but don't forget that the success will come from Hashem, not from me." Rather the posuk makes the point of informing us that it is Potifar who realizes, on his own, "*that Hashem was with him and that Hashem made all that he did prosper...*" (ibid., 39:4).

Why when it comes to interpreting dreams is this extra piety and recognition of Heaven's role required? Why is it necessary to preface the discussion by saying that "G-d will provide an answer for Pharaoh's welfare?"

26a   עיין רש"י בראשית לט:ג אע"פכ לא הדגישה התורה זה

Yosef, through these elaborate prefaces, is explaining something about dreams. He is saying that in order to understand the dreams properly, you must realize where they emanate from. A common dream is the fabrication of one's own mind and imagination. It does not have to mean anything at all. If someone has a terrible nightmare, it is probably because he was thinking about terrible things during the day. If a person is lying in the dungeon wondering about his fate, his unconscious mind wanders to eerie and bizarre images. Why should the dreams of the imprisoned *sarim* have to mean anything at all?

Thus, Yosef's prefatory remarks are actually part of the interpretation. He is telling them that what they experienced was not the nocturnal product of a troubled mind but a sort of prophetic sense. Something is going to happen to them in the future. But without understanding that Hashem is speaking to them, the dream can bear no meaning. It would be frivolous to attempt to interpret it.

Yosef says to them: "Hashem is talking to you! He is trying to tell you what is going to happen, and there is a reason why He is revealing it to you. It is His will that you should know, and thus I will advise you what you should do about it."

In our *Parsha* Yosef states this quite clearly:

ויאמר יוסף אל־פרעה וכו' את אשר האלקים עשה הגיד לפרעה: (בראשית מ"א:כ"ה)

And Yosef said to Pharaoh: "...That which G-d is doing, He has told to Pharaoh." (Bereishis 41:25)

This is stated before the interpretation in order to explain where the interpretation is coming from. It is more than just Yosef's innate sense of reliance on Hashem; it is a prerequisite to understanding the dream itself. "There is a reason why Hashem is trying to tell you this. Therefore, I have to give you advice as to what you should do about it." The guidance is part and parcel of the interpretation.

3   Good Turns

וַיֹּאמֶר פַּרְעֹה אֶל יוֹסֵף אֲנִי פַרְעֹה וּבִלְעָדֶיךָ לֹא יָרִים אִישׁ אֶת יָדוֹ וְאֶת רַגְלוֹ
בְּכָל אֶרֶץ מִצְרָיִם:

*And Pharaoh said to Yosef: "I am Pharaoh. And without you,
no man shall raise his hand or foot in all the land of Egypt."*
(Bereishis 41:44)

W hen we see in the Torah the repeated use of a certain word in close
proximity, and it is a relatively rare word, we may assume that there
is a connection. As we discussed above, it is written:

ויען יוסף את־פרעה לאמר בלעדי אלקים יענה את שלום פרעה: (בראשית מ"א:ט"ז)

*Yosef answered Pharaoh, saying: "It is without me (bil'adai). G-d
will provide an answer for Pharaoh's welfare." (Bereishis 41:16)*

Targum Onkelos explains the word *bil'adai* as meaning "without my
wisdom." Yosef is saying that this is not from my power or abilities, rather it is
totally from Hashem.

Then we find Pharaoh answering him:

ויאמר פרעה אל יוסף אני פרעה ובלעדיך לא־ירים איש את־ידו ואת־רגלו בכל־ארץ
מצרים (שם מ"ד)

*And Pharaoh said to Yosef: "I am Pharaoh. And without you
(bil'adecha), no man shall raise his hand or foot in all the land
of Egypt." (ibid. v. 44)*

This must be connected to what Yosef had said. It implies that Yosef's
reward for saying *bil'adai* is that Pharaoh says back to him, "And *bil'adecha*,
no man shall raise ..."

HaRav Yisrael HaCohen Chesir, *shlita,* subsequently pointed out that this
thought is found in the *Tur al HaTorah* commentary.

Baruch shekivanti.

4 Health and Beauty

Rivkah is described as follows in *Parshas Chayei Sarah*:

והנה רבקה יצאת וכו' והנער(ה) טבת מראה מאד: (בראשית כ"ד:ט"ו-ט"ז)

And behold, Rivkah is going out... and the maiden is very fair of appearance. (Bereishis 24:15–16)

This seems to describe a person of great beauty. Yet, Rachel, who was also beautiful, is described quite differently.

ורחל היתה יפת־תאר ויפת מראה: (שם כ"ט:י"ז)

And Rachel was beautiful of form and beautiful of appearance. (ibid., 29:17)

Rashi (ad loc.) explains that "*toar*" refers to the shape of the face, while "*mar'eh*" refers to the shine of the face, "*ziv k'lastar.*" Thus, we see that the Torah limits its praise of Rivkah to her appearance, while Rachel is praised for both her form and appearance.

Now we come to our *Parsha*. Yosef in Potifar's house is described as follows:

ויהי יוסף יפה־תאר ויפה מראה: (שם ל"ט:ו')

And Yosef was beautiful of form and beautiful of appearance. (ibid., 39:6)

Rashi (ad loc.) comments that Yosef's good looks came from the fact that he took extra care in his personal grooming and health. Upon assuming a position of authority in Potifar's estate, he started to eat and drink well and curl his hair.

In short, all the people we have discussed had a beautiful appearance, "*mar'eh*." However, not all of them had a beautiful form, "*toar*." Yosef did, and we know that he took good care of himself. Thus, we may surmise that a beautiful "appearance" is something that a person has naturally that is enhanced with healthy eating. As Rashi puts it, this is the shine of a person's face. On the other hand, a beautiful "form" is something that can be acquired through grooming. It can result from a wealthier, healthier environment, in which one takes good care of oneself.

Based on this approach, let us consider what Pharaoh saw in his dream. First, it says:

והנה מן־היאר עלת שבע פרות יפות מראה ובריאת בשר: (שם מ"א:ב')

And behold, seven cows with beautiful appearance and healthy flesh are coming up from the Nile. (ibid., 41:2)

These are healthy looking cows. Similar to what Rashi explained concerning Yosef, this is beauty that comes from healthy food and good conditions. This verse describes what Pharaoh actually saw in his dream. However, when Pharaoh speaks of the dream, he reports his vision of the cows with a certain variation.

והנה מן־היאר עלת שבע פרות בריאות בשר ויפת תאר: (שם י"ח)

And behold, coming up from the Nile are seven cows of healthy flesh and beautiful shape. (ibid., v. 18)

Pharaoh fails to describe them as having a beautiful appearance. If he saw cows that were beautiful of appearance, why did he report them as beautiful of shape? This could leave one to mistakenly attribute their appearance to something artificial. If Pharaoh wants to get an accurate interpretation of his dream shouldn't he report it accurately?

In answer to this question, HaRav Yisrael Chesir directed me to the *Midrash Tanchuma*, which explains that Pharaoh changed some of the details when he related his dream in order to check out Yosef's interpretative abilities.

אמר פרעה חלום חלמתי כשבא לומר לו את החלום בקש לבודקו והיה מהפך לו את החלום אמר ליה והנה מן היאור עולות שבע פרות. אמר ליה יוסף לא כך ראית אלא יפות מראה ובריאות בשר וכו'.: (מדרש תנחומא מקץ פרק ג')

Pharaoh said: "I dreamed a dream." And when he came to tell him the dream, he wished to test him and switched the dream around for him. He said to him: "And behold, coming up from the Nile are seven cows..." Yosef said to him: "That is not what you saw. Rather, they were 'with beautiful appearance and healthy flesh...'" (Midrash Tanchuma, Mikeitz, ch. 3)

5 Rings of Influence

וַיָּסַר פַּרְעֹה אֶת טַבַּעְתּוֹ מֵעַל יָדוֹ וַיִּתֵּן אֹתָהּ עַל יַד יוֹסֵף וכו'

And Pharaoh removed his ring from his hand and placed it on the hand of Yosef... (Bereishis 41:42)

There are three individuals mentioned in *Tanach* who were given rings to make them viceroy, and each one of them is associated with the war against Amalek.

The first is Yosef, as mentioned in our verse. Yehoshua, a descendent of Yosef, is later chosen to wage war against Amalek.

This Midrash (*Bereishis Rabati, Vayeitzei* 30:25) also makes some interesting comparisons between Yosef and Amalek. Due to these comparisons, Yosef is the most fitting candidate to defeat Amalek, the leading scion of Eisav, and visit upon him his punishment from Hashem. Some of these comparisons are as follows:

1. Yosef said, *"I fear G-d"* (*Bereishis* 42:18), whereas about Amalek it is written, *"And he did not fear G-d"* (*Devarim* 25:18).

2. Yosef was small among his brothers, as it is written, *"For he was a son of old age"* (*Bereishis* 37:3), and about Amalek it is written, *"Behold, I have placed you small among the nations"* (*Ovadiah* 1:2).

3. Eisav lost his rights as a firstborn through his evil deeds, whereas Yosef was not originally a firstborn but acquired these rights through his good deeds.

4. Yosef expressed faith in *Techiyas HaMeisim*, as it is written, *"G-d will surely remember you"* (*Shemos* 13:19), whereas Eisav denied *Techiyas HaMeisim*, as it is written, *"Behold, I am going to die"* (*Bereishis* 25:32).

5. Yosef grew up among two wicked people, Potifar and his wife, but did not learn from their deeds. Eisav grew up among two tzaddikim, but did not learn from their deeds.

The second individual who became viceroy through receiving the king's ring was Haman, who was a descendant of Agag, king of Amalek. About Haman is written:

ויסר המלך את־טבעתו מעל ידו ויתנה להמן: (אסתר ג:י)

And the King removed the ring from his hand and gave it to Haman. (Esther 3:10)

The third individual was Mordechai. After Haman is executed, thanks to Mordechai's efforts and prayers, it is written:

ויסר המלך את־טבעתו אשר העביר מהמן ויתנה למרדכי: (אסתר ח:ב)

And the King removed his ring which he had taken away from Haman, and gave it to Mordechai. (ibid., 8:2)

Yosef and Mordechai, who descends from Binyamin, are the children of Rachel. (Mordechai was actually a scion of King Shaul.) The Midrash we cited above says that Yosef's descendant Yehoshua, a descendant of Efraim ben Yosef, was chosen to lead the first battle against Amalek because Yosef was the son of Rachel.

Why are Rachel's children chosen to receive royal rings, become viceroys and fight Amalek?

The Gemara (*Bava Basra* 123a) tells us that Rachel's children were fitting to have the rights of the firstborn, as it is written, *"These are the offspring of Yaakov: Yosef..."* (*Bereishis* 37:2). This verse implies that Yaakov's primary offspring was Yosef. However, Leah's children received the firstborn rights instead through the merit of Leah's great prayers. Hashem partially returned the birthrights to Rachel in reward for her modesty in giving the *simanim* to her sister. Yosef capitalized on these rights when he split into two tribes and thus received two portions in *Eretz Yisrael*. As we know, the firstborn takes a double portion.

From this Gemara we see that it is because of Rachel that her children are fitting to have the rights of the firstborn, i.e., to take the leadership of *K'lal Yisrael*.

There is also a Midrash that accords the leadership specifically to the children of Rachel:

כיון שמלך שאול אמר הקדוש ברוך הוא אין זרעו של עמלק נופל אלא ביד בנה של
רחל כן אתה מוצא ברפידים נפל ביד יהושע שנאמר ויחלוש יהושע את עמלק (שמות
י"ג) אמר הקב"ה לעולם השבט הזה מוכן להיפרע מן עמלק מניין ממה שהשלים
בנביא מני אפרים שרשם בעמלק אחריך בנימן וכו'. (פסיקתא רבתי פרשה יג)

*When Shaul began to rule as king, the Holy One Blessed be He
said: "The offspring of Amalek will only fall into the hand of
Rachel's son." You find that in Refidim, he (Amalek) fell into
the hand of Yehoshua, as it is written, "And Yehoshua weakened Amalek" (Shemos 17:13). Said the Holy One Blessed be
He: "This tribe is always ready to extract punishment from
Amalek..." (Pesikta Rabbasi, ch. 13)*

Yet, all this is enigmatic. Yehudah should be the warrior who challenges
Eisav/Amalek, since the kingship belongs to the tribe of Yehudah. We find
many places where the Torah speaks of Yehudah's valor in war.

HaRav Yonasan Eibeshitz, in his famous work *Yaaros HaDevash* (part 1,
derush 3), takes note of this incongruity. He answers that as far as conquering Eisav himself is concerned, Yehudah plays the leading role. It is written
about Yehudah, *"Your hand is on the neck of your enemy"* (Bereishis 49:8),
and the Midrash (*Shocher Tov*, ch. 18) comments on this verse that victorious
war is led only by Yehudah. Fighting Amalek is a different story altogether.
Amalek has a mother with great merits, and it takes a mother with even greater
merits—*Rachel Imeinu*—to overcome him.

Who was Amalek's mother, and what great thing did she do in her life? The
Torah says, *"And the sister of Lotan was Timna"* (Bereishis 36:22). Rashi comments (ibid., v. 12) that this verse was written to tell us that Timna was a princess. Nevertheless, she left it all to cleave to Avraham by becoming a concubine
to one of his descendants, namely, Elifaz the father of Amalek. Thus, we see that
Amalek's mother had great *mesirus nefesh* for spirituality.

Who can counteract such *mesirus nefesh*? Rachel can, since she performed
a parallel act of *mesirus nefesh*, but one that was even greater. Let us compare
the acts of these two women: Timna had no choice but to become a concubine if
she was to marry Elifaz since he already had a number of wives before she came
along. Rachel, on the other hand, had the chance to be Yaakov's primary wife,
but she sacrificed it when she gave the *simanim* to Leah. As a result, she became

"wife number two." In other words, she had the status of a concubine.

It emerges that only Rachel's children have a merit great enough to overcome the merit that Amalek inherited from his mother.

Based on this amazing insight of the *Yaaros HaDevash*, we can explain not only why the children of Rachel led the war against Amalek but also why they received royal rings and become viceroys. It is written regarding Bilaam's prophecy:

וירא את עמלק וישא משלו ויאמר ראשית גוים עמלק ואחריתו עדי אבד:

(במדבר כ"ד:כ')

And he saw Amalek and he took up his parable and said: "The first among nations is Amalek. But his end is to be eternally destroyed." (Bamidbar 24:20)

Throughout the course of history, Amalek will exist. At times, he will seem to be disappearing, but this is only temporary. The true and final defeat of Amalek will occur only at the end of days when Dovid of the tribe of Yehudah regains kingship. Until this occurs, the provisional protagonist of Amalek are the children of Rachel.

What is the concept expressed by the royal ring that was lent to the children of Rachel? It is their interim power, their status of viceroy as opposed to that of king. Rachel's children do not assume ultimate authority. They act only as the king's independent representatives. This is seen clearly in the case of Yosef, whose power originates with Pharaoh. This is also the position of Shaul, whose monarchy is predestined to be only temporary in order to make way for Dovid and his eternal monarchy. This is also the position of Mordechai, whose power derives from Achashverosh.

This is why a parallel exists between Yosef and Mordechai. In fact, it is striking to note their similarity. Yosef was treated by Pharaoh as follows:

וילבש אתו בגדי־שש וישם רבד הזהב על־צוארו וירכב אתו במרכבת המשנה אשר־לו: (בראשית מ"ב:מ"ב-מ"ג)

And he dressed him in garments of fine linen and placed a golden chain on his neck and seated him in the chariot second to him. (Bereishis 42:42–43)

Mordechai was treated by Achashverosh as follows:

ומרדכי יצא מלפני המלך בלבוש מלכות וכו'. (אסתר ח:ט"ו)

And Mordechai went out from before the King in royal gar-
ments... (Esther 8:15)

It is worthy of note that when the ultimate destruction of Eisav will
occur, it will be due to Yosef. Yaakov realizes this immediately upon Yosef's
birth.

כאשר ילדה רחל את יוסף. משנולד שטנו של עשו שנאמר והיה בית יעקב אש ובית
יוסף להבה ובית עשו לקש ודלקו בהם ואכלום (עובדיה פרק א':י"ח) וכו'.: (רש"י
בראשית ל':כ"ה)

"When Rachel gave birth to Yosef..." When the antagonist
of Eisav was born, as it is written (Ovadiah 1:18): "And the
House of Yaakov will be a fire, and the House of Yosef will be
a flame, and the House of Eisav will be straw—and they shall
burn them and consume them..." (Rashi, Bereishis 30:25)

Here, too, Yosef's power to consume Eisav stems from his mother Rachel.
The proof is that even the children of Bilhah, Rachel's handmaiden and,
later, mother surrogate, serve as antagonists of Eisav. In the famous encounter between Eisav and Yaakov's funeral procession ascending from Egypt, as
Eisav attempts to steal back the rights of burial in *Me'aras HaMachpelah,* it
is Naftali (son of Bilhah) who is given the task of running back to Egypt to
bring the documents proving that Yaakov had purchased from Eisav all rights
to the property. In addition, it is Chushim ben Dan (grandson of Bilhah) who
ultimately slays Eisav.

Returning to the idea set forth by the *Yaaros HaDevash* — that Rachel's act
of giving over the *simanim* to Leah is the power that ultimately defeats Amalek
— was Leah ever aware that Rachel gave her the *simanim*? It would seem that
the answer is a resounding no! If Leah would have known of her sister's great
sacrifice, could the harsh words that Leah spoke during the incident of the
duda'im ever have been uttered?

When Rachel asks Leah for some of the *duda'im* that Reuven found in the
field, Leah is taken aback and responds:

המעט קחתך את־אישי ולקחת גם את־דודאי בני: (בראשית ל':ט"ו)

Is it a small thing that you have taken my husband, and to take also the duda'im of my son? (Bereishis 30:15)

It is absolutely inconceivable that the righteous Leah would have accused her sister Rachel of taking "her" husband if she had known what Rachel had done with the *simanim*. Leah would have realized that the truth was the exact opposite: Rachel had given her husband to Leah!

Rachel, at this point, could have set the score straight and responded to her sister by revealing to her the horrible truth, but why would she have? It would have only made Leah feel worse. The whole reason she had given her sister the *simanim* in the first place was to save her embarrassment.

Thus, our holy mother Rachel accepted the hurtful event as a normal consequence of being the beloved second wife. Thereafter, she suffered the further pain of remaining childless as Leah had child five and six.

Who can even begin to fathom the esteem held for her in *Shamayim*, and the merits she has accrued for *K'lal Yisrael*?

6 Carrying the Burden of Others

כִּי נַשַּׁנִי אֱלֹקִים אֶת כָּל עֲמָלִי וְאֵת כָּל בֵּית אָבִי:

For G-d has caused me to forget all my toil and all my father's house. (Bereishis 41:51)

Rashi points out in *Parshas Vayeishev* that the story with Yosef and Potifar's wife is preceded by the words "and Yosef was beautiful of form and beautiful of appearance." This is because Yosef's involvement with taking care of himself and his looks was responsible for the incident—although not in the way we might think.

אמר הקדוש ברוך הוא, אביך מתאבל ואתה מסלסל בשערך, אני מגרה בך את הדב:
(רש"י בראשית ל"ט:ו').

*Said the Holy One Blessed be He: "Your father is mourning,
and you are curling your hair? I will incite the bear against
you." (Rashi, Bereishis 39:6)*

Yosef had to go through this entire cataclysmic episode with all the suffering that came in its wake because he was not *nosei be'ol im chavero* (See *Pirkei
Avos* 6:6). In other words, he did not have a proper sense of respect for the
feelings and the situation of his father.

In our *Parsha,* after Yosef becomes viceroy of Egypt and Pharaoh grants
him Osnas as a wife, Yosef gives his two children some interesting names. The
firstborn is named Menashe, "For G-d has caused me to forget all my toil and
all my father's house."

This name would seem most inappropriate. Was his forgetting about his
father not responsible for the punishment that befell him, as Rashi said in
Vayeishev?

Whereas when it comes to Efraim, Yosef chooses a name with a different
theme:

ואת שם השני קרא אפרים כי־הפרני אלקים בארץ עניי: (בראשית מ"א:נ"ב)

*And the name of the second one he called Efraim, for Hashem
has made me fruitful in the land of my suffering. (Bereishis 41:52)*

Here, Yosef emphasizes the land of "my" suffering. He refers to his own
suffering, which he now identifies with his father's suffering. Previously, he
emphasized the fact that he had forgotten his own suffering as well as that of
his father.

Perhaps this helps to explain why from its very inception, the tribe of Efraim
is greater than that of Menashe. The name of Efraim is completely appropriate
even though superficially it strikes a pessimistic and melancholy note. That is
the way it is supposed to be; Yosef is not supposed to forget the suffering of
his father.

Menashe, on the other hand, expresses the positive aspect of Yosef thanking

Hashem for all the goodness that he has received. On its own, this is very positive. However, it is lacking something: *nosei be'ol im chavero* [27a]. Perhaps that is why in the course of history, Efraim shows greater leadership abilities: He possesses the essential quality that no Jewish leader can be without: *nosei be'ol im chavero.*

7 The Ubiquitous Donkey

n our *Parsha,* there is a strange emphasis on donkeys. Why does the Torah keep reminding us that the brothers are carrying everything on donkeys, that they are riding on donkeys and that they are concerned over the fate of their donkeys?

For example:

וישאו את־שברם על־חמריהם וילכו משם: (בראשית מ"ב:כ"ו)

And they loaded their purchase upon their donkeys and they went from there. (Bereishis 42:26)

Why is the detail about the donkeys necessary? Then again in the next verse:

ויפתח האחד את־שקו לתת מספוא לחמרו במלון וכו'. (שם מ"ב:כ"ז)

And the one opened his sack to give fodder to his donkey at the lodging place... (ibid., v. 27)

As we go through the *Parsha,* we notice that the donkeys keep coming up again and again, seemingly without justification. If they had used camels or carried the sacks on their own backs, would it have changed the story?

Occasionally, the donkey seems to take on an almost ridiculously great significance.

27a   הראה לי בני הרב אברהם אליהו הי"ו דלפי מש"כ בבראשית רבה פרשה ע"ט פסקה ה' דאפשר לתרץ בענין זה.

...ולקחת אתנו לעבדים ואת־חמרינו: (שם מ"ג:י"ח)

...And to take us for slaves, and our donkeys. (ibid., 43:18)

If the brothers suspect that they are about to be abducted and made into slaves, ostensibly a fate worse than death for the noble sons of Yaakov, why in the same breath do they express concern over who makes use of their donkeys?

Why also is the word חמר, "donkey," written without a ו'?

There are so many other verses referring to donkeys in the *parshiyos* of *Vayeishev* and *Mikeitz*.[27b]

Perhaps this connects to a similar concern that *K'lal Yisrael* expressed when they heard the report of the *meraglim*.

ולמה הבאתם את־קהל ה' אל־המדבר הזה למות שם אנחנו ובעירנו: (במדבר כ':ד')

And why have you brought the congregation of Hashem to this wilderness to die there, we and our animals? (Bamidbar 20:4)

This issue requires further thought. *Tzarich iyun.*

---

8 Undue Delay

When the grain that the sons of Yaakov brought back from their first journey to Egypt runs out, they complain:

כי לולא התמהמהנו כי עתה שבנו זה פעמים: (בראשית מ"ג:י')

If we would not have delayed, we would have already come back twice. (Bereishis 43:10)

27b List of further *p'sukim* referring to חמורים in פ' מקץ-וישב:

ויתן־מים וירחצו רגליהם ויתן מספוא לחמריהם (שם מ"ג:כ"ד)

הבקר אור והאנשים שלחו המה וחמריהם (שם מ"ד:ג')

ויעמס איש על־חמרו וישבו העירה (שם מ"ד:י"ג)

ולאביו שלח כזאת עשרה חמרים נשאים וכו' ועשר אתנת נשאת בר ולחם ומזון (שם מ"ה:כ"ג)

Rashi explains their complaint. They were delayed by their father Yaakov; otherwise, they would have already come back with Shimon (who was being held in Egypt). Thus, we learn that the word להתמהמה, usually translated as "to delay," really means to be delayed by an external factor.

This raises a problem. How are we to understand the following verse?

אם־יתמהמה חכה־לו כי־בא יבא לא יאחר: (חבקוק ב:ג')

> *If it (the Ge'ulah) delays, wait for it. For it will surely come; it will not be late. (Chavakuk 2:3)*

How could the *Ge'ulah* be delayed by an external factor?

Perhaps it refers to the fact that we, *K'lal Yisrael,* are causing the delay through our own actions. That would explain the Malbim's comments on this verse. He explains that "being late" implies passing a specific time that is set. Thus, he explains that even if *K'lal Yisrael* does not have merits and therefore the *Ge'ulah* delays, we should still await it. The verse is telling us that the *Ge'ulah* will not pass the final, distant date that is set for it. It will surely come.

9   Wordy Episodes

The Torah goes on and on as it recounts Eliezer's mission to go to Charan and find a wife for Yitzchok. To explain this lengthiness, *Chazal* say:

א"ר אחא יפה שיחתן של עבדי בתי אבות מתורתן של בנים פרשתו של אליעזר שנים וג' דפים הוא אומרה ושונה ושרץ מגופי תורה ואין דמו מטמא כבשרו אלא מריבוי
המקרא: (מדרש בראשית רבה פרשה ס' פסקה ח' הובא ברש"י בראשית כ"ד:מ"ב)

> *Said Rabbi Acha: The conversation of the servants of the households of the Avos is preferable to the Torah of the children. The passage of Eliezer takes two or three sheets. The Torah says it and repeats it. But the laws of the sheretz are a main part of the Torah, and the fact that its blood does not impart impurity as its flesh does is derived only from a Scriptural allusion.*
>
> *(Bereishis Rabba 60:8, cited by Rashi, Bereishis 24:42)*

This brings us to the question: Why does our *Parsha* have to recount to us what Pharaoh dreamed, then repeat it as Pharaoh tells it to Yosef and then inform us what Yosef said about Pharaoh's dream? Why is all this necessary? The Torah could have just said that Pharaoh had a dream, motivating him to take Yosef out of the dungeon in order to interpret it, and then tell us what the dream was. Alternatively, the Torah could have told us what the dream of Pharaoh was, and then say that he took Yosef out of the dungeon in order to repeat it to Yosef for the sake of its interpretation. Then, Yosef would tell him what the dream means. Yet, the Torah repeats the entire dream. Why?

When we get to *Parshas Vayigash*, we will see another example of a repeated story. Yosef tells his brothers that when they come to Pharaoh, if Pharaoh asks them what they do for a living, they should tell him that they are shepherds (*Bereishis* 46:33).

Indeed, Pharaoh wants to meet Yosef's family members, and, at that time, they tell him what Yosef said to tell him. The Torah recounts exactly how they explain to Pharaoh about their profession as shepherds (ibid., 47:3). Why do we need all of this repetition? What seems important to know is that Yosef tells his brothers what to say, they do as instructed and are thus sent to Goshen, which is a good place for shepherds. The message of this constant repetition is unclear.

This issue requires further thought. *Tzarich iyun.*

10 Chanukah

One of the questions most commonly addressed is the connection between Chanukah and *Parshas Mikeitz*. There seems to be no overt link, although there are some allusions to Chanukah in *Parshas Mikeitz*. Rabbi Shlomo Goldstein of Baltimore, Maryland, pointed out to me that there is an allusion mentioned by the Vilna Gaon at the end of the *Parsha*: The number of words in the *Parsha* totals 2,025. The *gematria* of *ner* is 250. Thus, we multiply 250 by 8, for the 8 lamps of the Menorah. Then we add 25, for the 25th of Kislev. This equals the number of words in the *Parsha*.

Rabbi Goldstein also cited the *Chana Dovid* who finds an allusion to Chanukah in Pharaoh's dream. The healthy cows were consumed by the lean cows, and the hearty ears of grain were consumed by the thin ones. This is an allusion to the victory of the few over the many, i.e., the Hasmoneans over the Greeks. Yet, these are just allusions. There does not seem to be any overt relationship between the *Parsha* and Chanukah.

Why is this lack of connection problematic? Because the confluence of two significant events, both of which affect the Jewish people, can be no mere coincidence. This is certainly true of the yearly convergence of *Parshas Mikeitz* and the festival of Chanukah.

In order to resolve this enigma, we need to delve into the *haftarah* of Chanukah, and then return to the *Parsha*. The *haftarah* is from *Zechariyah* and ends with his prophecy of the Menorah.

Zechariyah (4:1-7) sees a golden Menorah with two olive trees on each side of it producing fruits. The olive oil is squeezed from them into a bowl (*Malbim*, loc cit. v. 11-12) that is positioned above the Menorah. The oil flows through seven pipettes to feed the lamps on each of the seven branches of the Menorah. What is the symbolism of this vision?

According to the Malbim (loc. cit.), the trees represent *K'lal Yisrael*, and the fruits of the tree represent their deeds, the mitzvos of *K'lal Yisrael*. These mitzvos produce the oil that is then brought back into the world, "recycled," providing the world with its spiritual sustenance. This vision illustrates how all of the goodness that exists in the world emanates from the mitzvos of *K'lal Yisrael*. There is a symbiotic relationship, a metaphysical ecosystem, such that all the goodness and light of the world depends on the mitzvos of *K'lal Yisrael*.

If we think deeper into the relationship of this *haftarah* to Chanukah, we realize that the mitzvos of *K'lal Yisrael* are not external and superficial acts. Rather, they emanate from the *ruchniyus* of the soul. If we examine the letters of נשמה, "soul," we discover that they spell שמן ה' , "the oil of Hashem." This internal energy source, this holy oil, is the fountain that flows from the *neshamah* of *K'lal Yisrael*. It is the *ruchniyus* that extends out into the world and illuminates it through *K'lal Yisrael*'s Torah and mitzvos. The "jug of oil" of the Chanukah miracle is thus represented by a Jew's body, and the seal of the holy *Kohen Gadol* that this jug bears is the seal of the Holy One Himself.

Every morning we say:

אלקי נשמה שנתת בי טהורה היא, אתה בראתה אתה יצרתה אתה נפחתה בי וכו'.

(ברכות השחר)

My L-rd, the soul that you have given me is pure. You created,
formed and blew it into me... (Daily morning blessings)

We have a daily obligation to remind ourselves of the holiness and purity
of the *neshamah* that is within us.

Thus, *K'lal Yisrael* is the great depository of holy oil, the ultimate *pach
hashemen*. This lesson from the *haftarah* will open our eyes to the true connection of our *Parsha* to Chanukah.

First, let us get straight bearings on Chanukah itself. Some say that Chanukah is the festival of *galus*.[28] This seems to be a strange statement. If anything, Chanukah is the festival of *Eretz Yisrael*. One of the reasons that we
recite Hallel on Chanukah and not on Purim is because Chanukah was a miracle that took place in *Eretz Yisrael* whereas Purim was a miracle that took
place in *chutz la'aretz*. Thus, Chanukah relates to *Eretz Yisrael* and not to
galus.

Yet, from the Ramban we see a totally different picture, one emphasizing
Chanukah's significance and importance in the *galus*.

אמר לו הקב"ה למשה וכו'. "ואני עושה בה לישראל על ידי בניך נסים ותשועה וחנכה
שקרויה על שמם, והיא חנכת בני חשמונאי" וכו'.

Said the Holy One Blessed be He to Moshe... "I will perform
for Israel, through your (Aaron's) children, miracles and sal-
vation and a dedication, a chanukah, that will be called after
their (the kohanim's) name. And it is the Chanukah of the sons
of Chashmonai..."

---

28 מנורת המאור אות קל"ג

שפת אמת בראשית-לחנוכה שנת תרל"א

שם משמואל תצוה שנת תרע"ה

שם משמואל מקץ שנת תרע"ז

וראיתי עוד וכו'. במדרש רבה (ט"ו:ו), אמר לו הקב"ה למשה, לך אמור אל אהרן אל
תתירא, לגדולה מזאת אתה מוכן, הקרבנות כל זמן שבית המקדש קיים הן נוהגין, אבל
הנרות לעולם אל מול פני המנורה יאירו וכו'.

*And I further saw in... Midrash Rabba (15:6) that the Holy
One Blessed be He said to Moshe: "Go, say to Aharon, 'Do not
be afraid. You are fitting for something greater than this. The
sacrifices are practiced as long as the Temple exists. But the
lights will always shine on the Menorah...'"*

והנה דבר ידוע שכשאין בית המקדש קיים והקרבנות בטלין מפני חורבנו אף הנרות
בטלות, אבל לא רמזו אלא לנרות חנכת חשמונאי שהיא נוהגת אף לאחר חורבן
בגלותנו וכו'. (רמב"ן במדבר ח':ב')

*It is well known that when the Temple does not exist and the
sacrifices are no more, due to its destruction, also the lights
[of the Temple's Menorah] are no more. Rather, [the meaning
of the above Midrash is that Chazal] alluded to **the lights of
the Chanukah of Chashmonai, which is practiced even
after the Destruction, in our exile**... (Ramban, Bamidbar 8:2)*

I would venture to say that there are two types of Chanukah. There is
the Chanukah of Hillel and the Chanukah of Shammai. We find a *machlokes*
between them over how to celebrate Chanukah. Bais Shammai says that each
night we should kindle one light less, corresponding to the number of days
remaining, whereas Bais Hillel says that each night we should kindle one light
more, corresponding to the number of days passed (*Shabbos* 21b). We will
discuss the issue underlying this disagreement.

I would humbly propose that the Chanukah of Shammai is the Chanukah of
Eretz Yisrael, whereas the Chanukah of Hillel is the Chanukah of *galus*. Sham-
mai himself was always in *Eretz Yisrael*. Shammai represented the tradition of
Toras Eretz Yisrael. On the other hand, we find Hillel described as follows:

אדם אחד יש שעלה מבבל, והלל הבבלי שמו: (פסחים ס"ו ע"א).

*There is a certain man who ascended from Bavel, and his name
is "Hillel the Bavli." (Pesachim 66a)*

Hillel came with his students to *Eretz Yisrael*. He brought with him the roots of the *Talmud Bavli*. This was the *Toras Bavel* that had been there for centuries, since King Yechoniah came to *Bavel* accompanied by a group of Torah scholars even before the destruction of the First Temple. The period when the schools of Hillel and Shammai held their great debates and controversies was a unique one for *K'lal Yisrael*. It was the era just before the great exile of the destruction of the Second Temple.

Chazal (quoted by *Arizal*) say that in future times, the halacha will follow Bais Shammai. There is a deep explanation to this (See *Pri Tzaddik, Chanukah*, ch. 8), but we shall attempt to explain this enigmatic teaching of *Chazal* in terms more familiar to us. We should ask ourselves: Why should the halacha change? If Bais Shammai is right, why shouldn't we follow their views nowadays, or at least strive to? Yet, *Chazal* criticize someone who takes upon himself the stringencies of Bais Shammai (See *Brachos* 10b).

This, perhaps, is the explanation: There is a *Toras Eretz Yisrael* and there is a *Toras hagalus*. In *Eretz Yisrael,* when the Temple stands, the halacha follows Bais Shammai. When we are to leave our land and go into *galus* then the *Toras hagalus* becomes the criterion by which we live; then the obligations and requirements change. We follow *Toras Bavel,* and the halacha is in accordance with the rulings of Bais Hillel. The *sifrei Kabbalah* express this idea when they say that Hillel represents Rachel, while Shammai reflects Leah (*Shaar HaGilgulim hakdama* 36, *Sefer HaLikutim Taytzei* ch. 23, et al.). Similarly, Temple times have the aspect of Leah, whereas the *galus* has the aspect of Rachel.

As we mentioned above, Bais Shammai says we should kindle eight lights on the first day and work our way down to one light on the eighth day. According to one opinion in *Shabbos* 21b, this is because Bais Shammai compares the Chanukah lights to the bulls offered in the *Musaf* sacrifice on Sukkos. There, the number decreases as every day passes. We see that Bais Shammai bases its view on the laws pertaining to the *Bais HaMikdash*. This is *Toras Eretz Yisrael*. The *Bais HaMikdash* is standing, so we follow the rules applying to *korbanos*.

What does Bais Hillel say? It says: "מעלין בקדש ואין מורידין". In matters of holiness, we never decrease. We only increase. These are the rules that apply while we are in *galus*, when we are required to be constantly climbing up the ladder toward the *Ge'ulah*. We are constantly ascending and propelling ourselves forward, gathering encouragement and strength to go from one to eight.

By understanding that the Chanukah we celebrate is the Chanukah of *galus*, we come to a more sublime and transcendent message. We realize that the "jug of oil" we constitute, and the holy oil that our *neshamah* comprises, must be carefully guarded from contamination and defilement from our surrounding environment. We must protect its purity — and this Chanukah message is actually the message of the Jew's survival in *galus*.

Where do we find the paradigm for this lesson? What was the first time that the nations of the world attempted to sully the purity of *K'lal Yisrael's* soul and tempt them away from Torah? It was in the story of Yosef. Yosef represents victory against all odds in the struggle to remain pure in enemy territory. Yosef protected his purity as a Jew even in Egypt, called by the Torah "*ervas ha'aretz*." He was the paradigm of the jug of oil that remained pure and untouched throughout Greek domination over our holy Temple. The brothers' search for Yosef represents searching for and finding the *pach shemen* bearing the seal of the *Kohen Gadol*. What did they find?

ומנותר קנקנים נעשה נס לשושנים: (מעוז צור)

And from the remnant of the flasks a miracle was performed for the roses. (Maoz Tzur ¶5)

פך אחד של שמן שהיה מונח בחותמו של כהן גדול: (שבת כ"א ע"ב)

The one flask of oil remaining with the seal of the High Priest (Shabbos 21b)

In this way, Yosef prepared the way for Yaakov and his sons to come to Egypt, which was the seat of all the tum'ah of that time.

The Torah warns us before entering *Eretz Yisrael*:

כמעשה ארץ־מצרים אשר ישבתם־בה לא תעשו: (ויקרא יח:ג')

You shall not do like the acts of the land of Egypt in which you dwelled. (Vayikra 18:3)

Rashi explains what we learn from this verse:

מגיד שמעשיהם של מצרים ושל כנענים מקלקלים מכל האמות: (רש"י שם)

This tells us that the deeds of the Egyptians and of the Canaanites were more corrupt than those of all the nations. (Rashi, ad loc.)

It was Yosef who set the example for how *K'lal Yisrael* may live as Jews in *galus*. He paved the way for the Chanukah of Bais Hillel, of living in *galus* in the way of "מעלין בקדש ואין מורידין". Therefore, it is most appropriate that Chanukah falls during the weeks in which the *parshiyos* teach us the story of Yosef in Egypt.

וִיגַּשׁ

VAYIGASH

1 Having It All

When it comes to *gashmiyus*, i.e., a person's material possessions and the fulfillment of his physical needs, a person needs to know that he has only what Hashem wants him to have. As a recipient of Hashem's beneficence, it is incumbent to understand this. We find this exemplified in *Parshas Vayishlach*. When Yaakov wants to grant Eisav gifts, Eisav initially declines by saying (*Bereishis* 33:9): "I have a great amount (*rav*)." Rashi (ibid., v. 11) compares this remark with Yaakov's, who says "I have everything" (ibid.).

Rashi brings out a world of difference between these statements. Yaakov expresses that he has all he needs, whereas Eisav arrogantly expresses that he has much more than he needs. In other words, Yaakov recognizes that he has only what Hashem wants him to have — no more and no less.

In other matters, this is not so. When it comes to a person's feelings of happiness, satisfaction, fulfillment, contentment, etc., a different set of rules apply. We see this in our *Parsha*. When *Yaakov Avinu* finds out that Yosef is alive, it is written:

ותחי רוח יעקב אביהם ויאמר ישראל רב, עוד יוסף בני חי: (בראשית מ"ה:כ"ז-כ"ח)

And the spirit of Yaakov their father was revived. And Israel said, "It is great (rav); my son Yosef still lives!" (Bereishis 45:27–28)

229

Here, *Yaakov Avinu* does not say as before, rather he employs the term *"rav."* A person must understand that when it comes to the pleasures of this world, nothing is merited. Nobody "owes" him anything. The blessings of this world that Hashem gives a person are not something deserved. Rather, a person should take the attitude of קטנתי מכל החסדים, that everything is *chesed*. When it comes to the experience of joy, it is all part of a special *brachah* from Above. That may be termed *"rav."* The joy that *Yaakov Avinu* experienced was actually beyond what he believed he needed or deserved; it was a special act of kindness from Hashem, and he had a special level of *hakaras hatov* to Hashem for it. Thus, he described it as *"rav."*

We find a similar thought in the Maharal (*Gevuros Hashem*, ch. 6). Commenting on the mitzvos that a person reaps benefits (*peiros*) from in this world (*Mishnah, Peah* 1:1), he explains that the satisfaction and sense of gratification that a person has from doing a mitzvah of the *bein adam lechavero* type is actually the benefit that accrues to him in this world. Examples of such mitzvos are doing *chesed,* honoring one's parents, Torah learning, etc. All of these are good for the world and its inhabitants. The benefit in this world emanates, says the Maharal, from Hashem's kindness. He gives us these opportunities that bear this satisfaction and sense of accomplishment. Still, this is not defined as actual reward for the mitzvah. It is not something that is "earned" or rightfully coming due to our having done the mitzvah.

Yet, our service of Hashem would be no different without this added benefit that we receive. Our responsibilities and requirements would be absolutely the same even if we did not have these extra advantages. It is merely a kindness on the part of Hashem that we receive them. It would certainly be a lot more difficult, from our perspective, to do what we must if we would never feel any fulfillment or receive any benefit from it. If we would not experience joy and satisfaction in anything we did, it would be a depressing situation. Hashem in His kindness did not wish it to be that way.

That is the *"rav"* that *Yaakov Avinu* was expressing when he heard that Yosef was alive.

We see this idea expressed also in *Parshas Shemos:*

וייטב אלקים למילדת וירב העם ויעצמו מאד. ויהי כי־יראו המילדת את־האלקים:

(שמות א':כ'-כ"א)

And G-d bestowed goodness upon the midwives, and the people increased and became very powerful. And it was that because the midwives feared G-d, that He made for them houses. (Shemos 1:20–21)

The above verse tells us that G-d bestowed goodness upon Miriam and Yocheved who saved the male babies from Pharaoh's harsh decree. Rashi explains:

וייטב אלקים למילדת. מהו הטובה ויעש להם בתים: (רש"י שם)

What was the goodness? "That He made for them houses." (Rashi, ad loc.)

Superficially, this comment of Rashi does not seem to sit so well with the verses it is coming to explain. There is a big gap in the verses between *"And G-d bestowed goodness"* and *"That He made for them houses."* After mentioning G-d's goodness to the midwives, the verse instead says, *"And the people increased and became very powerful."*

We could say that when the midwives saw their actions come to fulfillment ("the people increased") and thus knew that their efforts were not for naught, this itself was the goodness bestowed upon them. Accordingly, Rashi understood that the fulfillment and contentment of seeing the success of one's good deeds is not the actual reward, rather, it is merely the benefits reaped in this world. That is what brought Rashi to explain the actual reward of the midwives as the Houses of *Kehunah, Leviyah* and *Malchus* that they eventually received.

This could also explain why Hashem's trait of mercy, known as *rav chesed*, is not called simply *chesed* or *oseh chesed*. It is because Hashem's *chesed*, emanating from an infinite source without any basis in the merit or worthiness of the recipient, is described as *"rav."*

I subsequently found this concept expressed by the Malbim in his commentary on *Sefer Tehillim*:

כי מתנאי החסד שלא יתום לעולם, כי הרחמים ושאר כל המדות הם תלוים לפי המרוחם או המחונן, לפי עניננו או לפי מעשיו, ולא כן החסד שהוא מצד האל ולא לפי המקבל, שעז"א בחסד עולם רחמתיך וכו'. (מלבי"ם תהילים פ"ה:ח')

It is among the qualities of chesed that it never is finished. For rachamim and all the other midos are dependent on the recipient of the rachamim or the chaninah. It is according to his state or according to his deeds. But it is not this way with chesed; it comes from G-d's side and is not according to the recipient. About this was said (Yeshaya 54:8): "With eternal chesed, I have shown compassion for you..." (Malbim, Tehillim 85:8)

כי חסד יאמר על מה שעושה מבלי חיוב ומבלי הבטחה קודמת ואף שאין המקבל החסד ראוי לזה עפ"י מעשיו, וגם חסד אצל ה' במובנו המדויק בא על הנס למעלה מדרך הטבע וכו'. (מלבי"ם תהילים ק"ז:א)

Chesed is the name given to what is done without obligation and without a prior promise, even if the recipient of the chesed is not worthy of it according to his deeds. And also chesed attributed to Hashem, in its proper meaning, refers to a miracle that is above the ways of nature. (ibid., 107:1)

2   Critical Timing

מַהֲרוּ וַעֲלוּ אֶל אָבִי וַאֲמַרְתֶּם אֵלָיו כֹּה אָמַר בִּנְךָ יוֹסֵף... רְדָה אֵלַי אַל תַּעֲמֹד:

Hurry and go up to my father and say to him: "So said your son Yosef: '...Come down to me, do not delay.'" (Bereishis 45:9)

We sense an urgency in Yosef's instructions, and his brothers and father seem to accept this request for haste.

We see from the Torah that *Yaakov Avinu*, who was living in Chevron, stopped at Beer Sheva when he began his journey down to Egypt to see Yosef.

ויסע ישראל וכל-אשר-לו ויבא בארה שבע ויזבח זבחים לאלקי אביו יצחק. ויאמר אלקים לישראל במראת הלילה:

(בראשית מ"ו:א'-ב')

And Israel, and all that he had, traveled. And he came to Beer
Sheva. And G-d said to Israel in the visions of the night... (Bere-
ishis 46:1–2)

The Ramban (*Bereishis* 42:9) informs us that it took six days to get to Egypt
from Chevron and, given the short distance, we can assume that it is less than
a day's journey from Chevron to Beer Sheva. Yet, here we find Yaakov having
to stop in Beer Sheva for the night.

We could make sense of their itinerary if we say that they set out on their
journey from Chevron in the middle of the day. When Yosef said, "Hurry... do
not delay," that meant to set out the very same day that the brothers arrived
with the message. Once Yaakov found out that Yosef was waiting for them, they
wasted no time, even though they would only be able to reach Beer Sheva that
day.

This actually enabled Yaakov to receive his nighttime prophecy in *Eretz
Yisrael,* which might never have happened if he would have waited for the next
day and traveled straight to Egypt.

3   The Wealthy Eisav

Whenever we think we have finally plumbed the sullied personality of
Eisav, another facet arises to prove us wrong. Eisav was an extraor-
dinarily wealthy individual and he knew it. When Eisav comes to
Yaakov he says to him: "I have plenty (*rav*)," meaning, "I have much more than
I need" (See explanation of this in the section above titled *Having It All*).

Eisav tried to turn down the gifts that Yaakov wanted to give him. It was not
until Yaakov urged him that he agreed to accept the gifts that he claimed he had
no use for. Now, according to his own calculations, he had more than *"rav."* Yet,
he had an unquenchable desire for superabundance. There was nothing that
was too much for him. He personified the teaching of Shlomo HaMelech:

אֹהֵב כֶּסֶף לֹא־יִשְׂבַּע כֶּסֶף: (קהלת ה':ט')

He who loves money will not be satiated with money (Koheles 5:9)

This is seen from the fact that Eisav only agreed to sell Yaakov his portion in *Me'aras HaMachpelah* for an extraordinary amount of money, a truly exorbitant sum. When we talk about Efron the Hittite, we talk about the paradigm of "he says a lot and does a little." It was Efron who promised *Avraham Avinu* the plot of *Me'aras HaMachpelah* for free and then took from him "four hundred silver shekalim, in tradable currency." What did Avraham get for that ridiculously overpriced sum? Six graves. How many graves was Eisav now selling Yaakov? One — and at what a price!

The Torah states (*Bereishis* 46:6) that Yaakov came down to Egypt with the wealth that he acquired in the land of Canaan. What happened to all the wealth that he had acquired in Charan?

Rashi (ad loc.) points out that everything Yaakov brought from the House of Lavan he no longer owned. Eisav took it all in payment for his single grave in *Me'aras HaMachpelah*. Rashi describes how Yaakov piled up gold and silver as if it were heaps of grain, and gave it all to Eisav. This was after Eisav's initial protests that he didn't need anything and that he had much more than he needed. Ultimately, not only did Eisav accept the initial gifts that Yaakov offered, but he ended up with every last bit of material possession that Yaakov owned upon his return to *Eretz Yisrael*!

4　Crowns of Greatness

וְאֶת יְהוּדָה שָׁלַח לְפָנָיו אֶל יוֹסֵף לְהוֹרֹת לְפָנָיו גֹּשְׁנָה וכו'.

And he sent Yehudah in front of him, to Yosef, to instruct (lehoros) before him, to Goshen... (Bereishis 46:28)

The word *lehoros* is mentioned four times in *Chumash,* in various contexts. Perhaps this alludes to the four crowns mentioned in *Pirkei Avos*:

רבי שמעון אומר, שלשה כתרים הם, כתר תורה, כתר כהונה, כתר מלכות, וכתר שם טוב עולה על גביהם: (אבות ד':י"ג)

Rabbi Shimon says: There are three crowns. The crown of Torah, the crown of Kehunah, the crown of Kingship. And the crown of a good name ascends upon them. (Pirkei Avos 4:13)

The *lehoros* of Yehudah in our verse is the crown of Kingship, as Dovid is from Yehudah.

The *lehoros* of Aharon is the crown of *Kehunah* as it is written:

וידבר ה' אל אהרן לאמר: יין ושכר אל־תשת וכו' ולהורת את בני ישראל את כל החקים
אשר דבר ה' אליהם ביד משה: (ויקרא י':ח',ט',י"א)

And Hashem spoke to Aharon, saying: Do not drink wine and strong drink... to instruct the Children of Israel all the laws... (Vayikra 10:8–9, 11)

The crown of Torah is expressed in the verse:

זאת התורה, לכל־נגע הצרעת ולנתק וכו' להורת ביום הטמא וביום הטהר זאת תורת
הצרעת: (ויקרא י"ד:נ"ד,נ"ז)

This is the Torah for any affliction of tzara'as... to instruct on the day of the impure and on the day of the pure. This is the Torah... (Vayikra 14:54, 57)

The crown of a good name belongs to Betzalel and Oholiav, who built the *Mishkan*:

ויאמר משה אל בני ישראל ראו קרא ה' בשם בצלאל בן אורי בן חור למטה יהודה וכו'
ולהורת נתן בלבו הוא ואהליאב בן־אחיסמך למטה־דן: (שמות ל"ה:ל',ל"ד)

And Moshe said to the Children of Israel: See, Hashem has called Betzalel by name... to instruct, He placed in his heart—he and Oholiav... (Shemos 35:30, 34)

Visible Kedushah

וַיֹּאמֶר יוֹסֵף אֶל אֶחָיו גְּשׁוּ נָא אֵלַי...

And Yosef said to his brothers, "Please approach me..."
(Bereishis 45:4)

———

Rashi explains our verse: Yosef called over his brothers because he wanted to appease them in their moment of shame by showing them that he, too, was circumcised.[29]

Ostensibly, *bris milah* was a sign of brotherhood. It was the sign that set the sons of Yaakov apart from the rest of humanity. Yet, if we keep in mind the recent events in Egypt, we will see that this was not exactly true. About Yosef, Pharaoh had told his people:

אשר יאמר לכם תעשו: (בראשית מ"א:נ"ה)

What he tells you, you shall do. (Bereishis 41:55)

Rashi explains why Pharaoh had to give them a special admonition:

לפי שהי' יוסף אומר להם שימולו וכשבאו אצל פרעה ואומרים כך הוא אומר לנו
א"ל למה לא צברתם בר והלא הכריז לכם ששני הרעב באים אמרו לו אספנו הרבה
והרקיבה אמר להם א"כ כל אשר יאמר לכם תעשו הרי גזר על התבואה והרקיבה מה
אם יגזור עלינו ונמות: (רש"י שם)

It was because Yosef was telling them to circumcise themselves. And when they came to Pharaoh and said, "This is what he is telling us," he said to them, "Why did you not store up produce? He declared to you that the years of famine are coming." They said to him, "We collected a lot but it rotted." He said to them, "If so, all that he tells you, you shall do. He decreed that the grain would rot. What if he decrees that we should die?" (Rashi, ad loc.)

---

29   In truth, Yosef was actually born circumcised (*Avos D'Rav Nassan* 2:5)

Thus, we see that circumcision had become a national trait in Egypt. If so, what did Yosef prove by showing his brothers that he was circumcised when every other male in Egypt was also?

We can answer this question based on the following true story.

A few decades ago, a fine yeshiva man who was engaged to be married went to the Steipler, HaGaon HaRav Yaakov Yisrael Kanievsky, *zatzal.* He waited his turn outside the cramped Bnei Brak apartment and eventually was called in. He asked the Steipler for a *brachah,* a perfectly normal and even standard thing to do in those days. The Steipler seemed not to notice his request and started to ask him his name, where he learned, the name of his rosh yeshiva, etc., and then the young man's turn ended without him actually receiving any *brachah* for his upcoming wedding.

When the young man exited, the Steipler requested that an urgent message be sent to the young man's rosh yeshiva, asking to speak to him. When the rosh yeshiva came in to the Steipler he was presented with a bewildering question: Why was the rosh yeshiva allowing a non-Jew to learn in his yeshiva and marry a Jewish girl? Needless to say, the rosh yeshiva did not understand what the Steipler was talking about — the rosh yeshiva knew the young man and his family personally. They were fine Jews in every way.

Nevertheless, the Steipler was insistent, and the rosh yeshiva agreed to look into the matter. It turned out that the mother's mother had undergone a non-Orthodox conversion to Judaism. Halachah dictated that the young man was a non-Jew.

A proper conversion was quickly arranged for this young man who sincerely wished to be a Jew and continue his dedication to Torah study. The wedding was held on time, he gave the ring to his bride *kedas Moshe veYisrael,* and the joy was great.

How did the Steipler know?

That is what the rosh yeshiva asked the Steipler, to which the Steipler humbly replied that there was nothing out of the ordinary involved with it, no *ruach hakodesh* or anything like that. It was very simple: "When the young man entered the room," the Steipler said, "I could not see his *neshamah.*" So he realized that he was not Jewish. To the Steipler, seeing someone's *neshamah* was a normal and expected thing.

This story took place in the latter half of the 20th century. If so, how much more so were Yosef's brothers capable of seeing *neshamos*! Why did they not realize who Yosef was? Why did they not sense the *neshamah* of the towering tzaddik who was standing right in front of them and speaking to them?

It is clear that Hashem prevented them from using their eyes in the normal fashion. It was Heaven's will that they not have any way of recognizing him as their brother. In fact, they were convinced that he was *not* their brother Yosef, as they obviously would have recognized a Jew by his *neshamah*. Yosef appeared to them as the young man in the above story appeared to the Steipler.

Realizing this, Yosef had to prove to his brothers who he was. He did not show them that he had undergone the surgical procedure known as circumcision, as the Egyptians had. Rather, he showed them that he possessed a *bris milah* — he had an *os bris kodesh*.

Hashem opened their eyes, and the brothers perceived that the man standing in front of them was imbued with a special sanctity, the sanctity of *bris milah,* something specially associated with the trait of Yosef. This sanctity expressed who Yosef really was. This special quality was something that no surgical procedure could bestow on an Egyptian; they knew beyond any doubt that it was their brother Yosef.

6   Which Way is Up?

It is a quite obvious and seemingly unexceptional fact that *Eretz Yisrael* is north of Egypt.

ויעל אברם ממצרים הוא ואשתו וכל אשר לו ולוט עמו הנגבה: (בראשית פרק י"ג:א')

And Avram went up from Egypt, he and his wife and all he had, and Lot with him, to the south[ern part of the land of Canaan]. (Bereishis 13:1)

As Rashi (ad loc.) explains, when you travel from Egypt to *Eretz Yisrael* you are moving north. Thus we should be able to assume that every time the Torah says "and he went up" from Egypt to *Eretz Yisrael,* it means a movement from south to north. Similarly, "and he went down" from *Eretz Yisrael* to Egypt would mean traveling from north to south.

Yet in our *Parsha*, we find Yosef in Egypt telling his brothers:

מהרו ועלו אל־אבי ואמרתם אליו וכו'. (בראשית מ"ה:ט')

Hurry and go up to my father and say to him... " (Bereishis 45:9)

Here, Rashi (ad loc.) explains "and go up" by saying that *Eretz Yisrael* is higher than all the lands. Why did he not say simply that *Eretz Yisrael* is to the north as he did on the earlier verse that we cited?

The first approach to going up and down is also reflected in *Parshas Mattos*, where the Torah describes the borders of *Eretz Yisrael*.

וירד הגבול וכו'. (במדבר ל"ד:י"א)

And the border goes down... (Bamidbar 34:11)

Here, Rashi (ad loc.) says that as the border goes from north to south, it goes down. *Devarim* 3:1, also speaking of traveling in *Eretz Yisrael,* uses the term "going up," which Rashi again explains as going north.

Both of these cases, though, are speaking of *Eretz Yisrael* proper; the former its boundaries and the latter the movement of *K'lal Yisrael* on the other side of the Jordan. The problem is as follows: Once we define northward movement as going "up," where is there any proof from our *Parsha* that *Eretz Yisrael* is higher than all the lands?

In reality, the source for the concept that *Eretz Yisrael* is higher than all the lands is derived in *Massechet Kiddushin* 69b as coming from the following verse:

לכן הנה ימים באים נאם ה' לא יאמר עוד חי ה' אשר העלה את בני ישראל מארץ מצרים כי אם חי ה' אשר העלה ואשר הביא את בני ישראל מארץ צפון ומכל הארצות אשר הדחתים שם: (ירמיה כ"ג:ז'-ח')

Therefore behold, days are coming, says Hashem. It will no longer be said, "Hashem lives, for He brought up the Children of Israel from the land of Egypt." Rather, "Hashem lives, for He brought up and transported the Children of Israel from the land of the north and from all the lands to which He dispersed them there." (Yirmeyahu 23:7–8)

The Gemara does not bring a proof from *Chumash* at all! It has to search for a proof in *Nevi'im*. This verse from Yirmeyahu is a convincing proof since traveling even from the land of the north to *Eretz Yisrael* is described as "up." If the verse was speaking in terms of north-south, it should have called it "down."

The source for Rashi's explanation here in *Parshas Vayigash* seems to be the *Sifri* (*Devarim*, ch. 23, 37). It brings proofs from the passage of the *meraglim* and from our topic here in *Parshas Vayigash*, albeit from a later verse, that *Eretz Yisrael* is higher than all the lands.

It is puzzling that the Sifri completely disregards the verse we mentioned first, dealing with *Avraham Avinu*'s travels. Furthermore, it disregards many other places that could have proved just as well that going to *Eretz Yisrael* from Egypt is "up."

It is worth mentioning one place I found where the meaning of "up" is quite enigmatic:

ויאמר יוסף אל אחיו ואל בית אביו אעלה ואגידה לפרעה ואמרה אליו אחי ובית אבי אשר בארץ כנען באו אלי: (בראשית מ"ו :ל"א)

And Yosef said to his brothers and to his father's house, "I will go up and tell Pharaoh and will say to him, 'My brothers and my father's house in the land of Canaan have come to me.'" (Bereishis 46:31)

Why is going to Pharaoh called "up?"

This issue requires further thought. *Tzarich iyun*.[30]

---

30   There are a few other places not mentioned in the above sources where the Torah speaks of going up and down. The meaning of the terms in these places needs to be resolved since they could be understood both ways. For instance, when Hashem speaks to Yaakov before his descent to Egypt:

אנכי ארד עמך מצרימה ואנכי אעלך גם עלה ויוסף ישית ידו על עיניך: (בראשית פרק מו:ד')

*I will **descend** with you and I will surely bring you **up**. And Yosef will place his hand on your eyes.* (Bereishis 46:4)

Another place is when *K'lal Yisrael*, who are in the *Midbar*, wish to enter *Eretz Yisrael* and ask Edom for permission to pass through their borders:

ויאמרו אליו בני ישראל במסלה נעלה ואם מימיך נשתה אני ומקני ונתתי מכרם רק אין דבר ברגלי אעברה: (במדבר פרק כ:י"ט)

*And the Israelites said to him, "We shall go **up** on the main way. And if we drink from your water, I or my flock, I will give their price. Indeed, there is nothing wrong. I will pass through on foot.* (Bamidbar 20:19)

Here, the direction of travel is from south to north, and would fit with that approach. Yet, it could also be referring to the fact that *Eretz Yisrael* is higher than all the lands.

7 Everything is Fine?

After Yosef spends twenty-two years in Egypt and after all the harrowing episodes of his brothers coming to him twice, Yosef says:

מהרו ועלו אל־אבי ואמרתם אליו ככה אמר בנך יוסף שמני אלקים לאדון לכל־מצרים רדה אלי אל־תעמד: (בראשית מ"ה:ט')

Go up to my father and tell him, "So says your son Yosef: 'G-d made me a master over all Egypt. Come down to me, do not tarry.'" (Bereishis 45:9)

Just tell him everything is fine; he is invited to come down for a visit. Now, suddenly, everything is fine? Will Yaakov have amnesia? He won't want to understand why Yosef put his brothers through all the anguish and torment of the preceding events? He won't want to understand why Yosef put his own father through the ordeal of such prolonged bereavement?

The Ramban (ibid., 42:9) explains why Yosef did not reveal himself the first time they came, and instead insisted that they bring him Binyamin. It was because he understood it to be Hashem's will that his first dream should be fulfilled, which required that all his brothers would bow down to him together. Thus, he sought to bring about the fulfillment of the dream. The second time they came, he hid the goblet in Binyamin's sack in order to take Binyamin lest they attack him, as he was not yet sure that they loved him. In fact, as the Ramban explains, everything that Yosef did was in order to bring about the fulfillment of his dreams.

The Ramban further states (ibid., 45:27) that all his life Yaakov never found out that his sons threw Yosef in the pit and sold him to Egypt. No one told him. He thought that Yosef simply lost his way in the field and was kidnapped and brought to Egypt as a slave.

While the Ramban masterfully explains Yosef's mindset, it still remains puzzling why Yosef did what he did until the point that he revealed himself and how Yaakov was to understand this otherwise strange behavior.

After Yosef finally revealed himself to his brothers, he sat and spoke to them. Yet, his message to them seems to be incomplete.

ועתה אל-תעצבו ואל-יחר בעיניכם כי-מכרתם אתי הנה כי למחיה שלחני אלקים
לפניכם: (בראשית מ"ה:ה')

And now, do not be sad and do not be upset that you sold me to here. Because it was for sustenance that G-d sent me before you. (ibid., 45:5)

This message explains why Yosef was in Egypt and why he did not bear any hard feelings. However, it does not explain why he treated them as he did. Yosef just explained the end result of their actions. After these brief and very incomplete remarks, he told them in so many words, "Just bring my father."

What is even more astonishing is that Yosef, seemingly begged the question by comparing them to Binyamin in order to calm them from their initial embarrassment and fear.

והנה עיניכם ראות ועיני אחי בנימין כי-פי המדבר אליכם: (שם י"ב)

And behold, your eyes see, as do the eyes of my brother Binyamin, that my mouth is speaking to you. (ibid., v. 12)

Rashi explains this comparison as follows:

ועיני אחי בנימין. השוה את כלם יחד, לומר שכשם שאין לי שנאה על בנימין אחי,
שהרי לא היה במכירתי, כך אין בלבי שנאה עליכם: (רש"י שם י"ב)

Just as I have no hatred toward Binyamin my brother, since he was not involved in my sale, so I have no hatred in my heart toward you. (Rashi, ibid.)

That's it? Didn't Yosef want to explain what took place, or at least touch on some of the burning issues that must have been on their minds? However, that is the end of the discussion. Yosef said tersely that he had no hard feelings, and the subject seemed to go away and not resurface until after *Yaakov Avinu* passed away.

Further, we need to understand the following: The brothers overcame their embarrassment and began speaking with Yosef after they saw him weep and show that his heart was whole with them, as Rashi explains on verse 15. This is fascinating! Although Yosef demonstrated empathy and compassion for his brothers, how did that take their shame away? One would think it would have made the shame twice as great. When they realized that his heart was whole with them after all they had done to him, this should have magnified their embarrassment to an unbearable degree.

How are we to understand these events?

This issue requires further thought. *Tzarich iyun.*

8 Seventy People for Six Days

The *Ramban* says (*Bereishis* 42:9) that it was a six-day trip from Egypt to *Eretz Yisrael*. The Torah tells us that there were seventy souls that went down to Egypt, which does not include all the wives and children, so perhaps it was closer to 150 people or more. The Torah describes Yosef's preparations for this journey:

ולאביו שלח כזאת עשרה חמרים נשאים מטוב מצרים ועשר אתנת נשאת בר ולחם
ומזון לאביו לדרך: (בראשית מ"ה:כ"ג)

And to his father he sent this: ten donkeys bearing the best of Egypt, and ten mules bearing grain and bread and food, for his father for the way. (ibid., 45:23)

Obviously, Yosef was not sending Yaakov food that he would not need, since there was plenty of food waiting for him in Egypt when he came down. Thus, we may assume that the brothers brought up to *Eretz Yisrael* only the supplies that Yaakov would need in order to come down to Egypt, a journey of six days. That took ten donkeys and ten mules? If they needed twenty animals laden with supplies just for their entourage to travel six days there and six days back, imagine how many donkeys the brothers originally must have brought with them down to Egypt. It must have been a tremendous number in order to bring back food for even one month.

When the food that they had brought back on the first trip ran out, Yehudah remarked that they could have gone back and forth twice (ibid. 43:10). That is twenty-four days. So from the time they returned from the first trip, it would appear that they had enough food for at least four times the amount mentioned in our *Parsha,* which was carried by twenty animals. Thus, we could calculate that the ten brothers came down the first time with at least forty donkeys and forty mules, and that was the food they needed for just twenty-four days. If this calculation is anywhere near accurate, we may conclude that it would have required a tremendous amount of traveling back and forth to Egypt to get through a year of famine. The numbers involved seem incredible.

This leads to our question: What did the brothers expect when they initially came down to Egypt? How many donkeys were actually brought down? Did the food actually run out in twenty-four days, or perhaps it was much more than twenty-four days until this happened and they returned to Egypt with Binyamin?

This issue requires further thought. *Tzarich iyun.*

9   They're Coming

Yosef says he will tell Pharaoh that his family has come (*Bereishis* 46:31), then he actually tells Pharaoh that his family has come (ibid. 47:1) and then Pharaoh says back to Yosef that his family has come (ibid. v. 5). Why all the repetition? What is involved here?

The Ramban on this last verse explains that Pharaoh was commenting to Yosef that the family had come because they heard of Yosef's eminent position, and had placed their hopes on him. Thus, he should take care of them according to his abilities.

Still, the first two verses remain unexplained, and the constant repetition of the same idea indicates that there is another level of meaning here.

The *Ha'amek Davar* already noticed this repetition. He resolved the difficulty in his way, and further explanation is found in *Ohr HaChayim, Sifsei Kohen* and other commentaries.

Nevertheless, this issue still requires further thought. *Tzarich iyun.* (See *Wordy Episodes* in *Parshas Mikeitz.*)

ויחי

VAYECHI

1 Yaakov Avinu Lives On

Our *Parsha* describes *Yaakov Avinu*'s last words, the embalming of his body, his cross-country funeral procession and subsequent burial in *Eretz Yisrael*. The only problem is that he never died.

הכי אמר רבי יוחנן: יעקב אבינו לא מת. — אמר ליה: וכי בכדי ספדו ספדניא וחנטו חנטייא וקברו קברייא? — אמר ליה: מקרא אני דורש, שנאמר (ירמיהו ל') ואתה אל תירא עבדי יעקב נאם ה' ואל תחת ישראל כי הנני מושיעך מרחוק ואת זרעך מארץ שבים, מקיש הוא לזרעו, מה זרעו בחיים — אף הוא בחיים: (תענית ה' ע"ב)

So said Rabbi Yochanan: Yaakov Avinu did not die. He said to him: Was it for naught that he was eulogized, embalmed and buried? He said back to him: I derive it from a verse. It says (Yirmeyahu 30:10), "'And you, my servant Yaakov, do not fear,' says Hashem. 'And Yisrael, do not be afraid. For behold, I am saving you from afar, and your descendants from the land of their captivity.'" The verse compares Yaakov to his descendants. Just as his descendants are alive, so is he alive. (Taanis 5b)

Yaakov Avinu never died, as the Gemara proves from a verse in *Tanach*. This is alluded to also in our *Parsha* in a verse describing the death of *Yaakov Avinu*:

ויכל יעקב לצות את־בניו ויאסף רגליו אל־המטה ויגוע ויאסף אל־עמיו: (בראשית מ"ט:ל"ג)

And Yaakov finished commanding his sons, and he brought his legs into the bed, and he expired, and was gathered to his people. (Bereishis 49:33)

Rashi notes that the verse never says, "and he died," which is the usual expression, and then Rashi cites the above teaching of *Chazal* that Yaakov, in fact, never died. Another allusion is to be found at the very beginning of the *Parsha*.

ויחי יעקב בארץ מצרים שבע עשרה שנה ויהי ימי־יעקב שני חייו שבע שנים וארבעים
ומאת שנה: (בראשית מ"ז:כ"ח)

And Yaakov lived in the land of Egypt seventeen years. And the days of Yaakov, the years of his life, were one hundred and forty-seven years. (ibid., 47:28)

This information is quite strangely placed. Normally, the years of a person's life are counted after his death is mentioned. First, it says "and he expired, and he died," and then it says how long he lived. Yet, at the point of *Yaakov Avinu*'s demise, we are not informed how long he really lived. The Torah tells us at the beginning of *Parshas Vayechi*, at a relatively random point, that Yaakov was one hundred and forty-seven years old—and then, strangely enough, it goes on to say (ibid., v. 29) that his days to die are approaching.

Thus, according to the information we are given, *Yaakov Avinu* could have died at one hundred and forty-eight or at one hundred and fifty-seven. It is also possible that his days to die merely approached, but his death never actually took place. The Torah is never clear about the age of *Yaakov Avinu* at his death.

Another proof that the age given by the Torah for Yaakov was not his age at the time of death is from the end of the *Parsha*.

ויחי יוסף מאה ועשר שנים וכו' וימת יוסף בן־מאה ועשר שנים: (בראשית נ':כ"ב, כ"ו)

And Yosef lived one hundred and ten years... and Yosef died at the age of one hundred and ten years. (ibid., 50:22, 26)

Here, we see the repetition of Yosef's age when he dies. That repetition would not be necessary if, originally, *"and Yosef lived"* referred to the years until the date of his death. The very fact that the Torah finds it necessary to repeat his years at his death shows that living for "x" number of years and dying after "x" number of years are two different things. So when our *Parsha* starts out by saying, *"And Yaakov lived... one hundred and forty-seven years,"* there is no reason to assume that he died after said number of years.

Now we may ask: Does this also apply to *Dovid HaMelech*? We find about *Dovid HaMelech* that it says:

ויקרבו ימי־דוד למות: (מלכים א' ב':י')

And the days of Dovid approached to die. (Melachim I, 2:1)

Again, we do not find a mention of Dovid's age. The verse just says (ibid., v. 10) that Dovid lied down with his fathers and was buried. It never says, "and he died." After the *Tanach* mentions his "lying down" and his burial, it counts (ibid., v. 11) the years of his reign. We are told that Dovid ruled forty years: seven in Chevron and thirty-three in Yerushalayim. However, we are never told how old he was when he died. We are led to believe that he must have been seventy, since the verse says that he became king at the age of thirty and that he ruled for forty years.

Obviously, when Shlomo became king, perforce Dovid was not king any longer. Yet, who says Dovid died? Before we get up and exclaim *Dovid melech Yisrael chai vekayyam* too literally, let us consider the following verse that appears much later in *Tanach*:

ודויד בן־ישי מלך על־כל־ישראל וכו'. וימת בשיבה טובה שבע ימים וכו'.

(דברי הימים א' כ"ט:כ"ו-כ"ח)

And Dovid the son of Yishai ruled over all Israel... And he died in good old age, satiated of days... (Divrei Hayamim I, 29:26, 28)

Here, we see clearly that Dovid died. In fact, *Chazal* describe the circumstances of his death and how the *malach hamaves* managed to gain power over him by distracting him from his learning for a moment.

אמר דוד לפני הקדוש ברוך הוא: רבונו של עולם, הודיעני ה' קיצי וכו'. כל יומא דשבתא הוה יתיב וגריס כולי יומא,וכו'. הוה סליק בדרגא, איפחית דרגא מתותיה, אישתיק ונח נפשיה: (שבת ל' ע"א-ב')

All the day of Shabbos, he (Dovid) would sit and learn the whole day... the step collapsed under him, he was silent, and his soul passed away. (Shabbos 30a–b)

Here, too, we see that Dovid did in fact die. The *malach hamaves* did get a hold of him in the end. What remains unresolved is why *Sefer Shmuel*, which describes at great length Dovid's life and deeds, fails to say this expressly. What is the meaning of the mysterious absence of the mention of Dovid's death?

This issue requires further thought. *Tzarich iyun.*

2   Telling Secrets

T he beginning of *Parshas Vayechi* is hard to find in the *Sefer Torah*. This is because there is not the usual space before it. It is a *Parsha stumah,* a "closed up" *Parsha*. Rashi on the first verse of our *Parsha* offers two reasons for this. The second reason is that *Yaakov Avinu* wished to reveal the secrets of the end of time, but he was barred by Heaven from doing so. It was "closed up from him." (We will discuss the first reason shortly.)

The question we should ask is: Why did Yaakov wish to reveal the secrets now? Why was this point in Jewish history preferable to all others? Avraham did not attempt to do this with Yitzchok, or Yitzchok with Yaakov, so why should Yaakov wish to reveal the end of time to his children? Was this a more significant juncture in the saga of Egyptian subjugation than that of when Yaakov originally came down to Egypt, or the time when Yitzchok was born—the point from which the four hundred years of the sojourn in Egypt are counted?

Conventional wisdom says that since *K'lal Yisrael* was now entering a new level of the subjugation to Egypt in which they would become slaves, they needed to be encouraged that they would eventually be redeemed.

This approach is based on the first reason offered by Rashi for our *Parsha's* being "closed up." Rashi says that when *Yaakov Avinu* passed away, the eyes and hearts of the people of Israel "were closed up" because of the trouble of the subjugation, since the Egyptians then began to subjugate them. Since the first *galus* was about to climax in its full oppressive force, Yaakov felt it necessary to tell his children when the last *galus* would end.

However, as we know, the Final Redemption was not something that was going to happen in a year or two. The events leading up to the end of time were going to take three-and-a-half thousand years to play themselves out. Let us imagine that *Yaakov Avinu* actually reveals the end of time to them. He tells them: "Don't worry. It will be very harsh. You will be brutally enslaved by Pharaoh. There are several more exiles to come after this one, each one bearing unimaginable suffering, degradation and persecution, but in three-and-a-half thousand years everything will be all right. The *Mashiach* will come and save us all."

What does it help them to know this? How does it help them deal with the immediate onslaught of tyranny? If anything, it should have made them dejected. The knowledge that waves of trouble are about to break over their heads and the end is nowhere in sight would not make most people feel happy and confident. Is it encouraging to know that one will never live to see any benefit from one's efforts?

Furthermore, we have an important principle of faith that states: "And although he (the *Mashiach*) may tarry, I will wait every day for him to come." If the end of time would have been revealed to them, it would have precluded any possibility of "I will wait for him." It would create a situation in which they could not expect any real redemption for thousands of years. In light of all the above, for them to know the end of time would seem to lack any rationale.

I found that the *Shem MiShmuel* asks this question. He discusses the fact that there are actually two "ends of time." There is the end that comes in its fixed time, and the end that Hashem hurries. For it is written: בְּעִתָּהּ אֲחִישֶׁנָּה, *"In its time, I will hurry it,"* [31] implying that it can either come at the fixed time or be hurried. [32] The *Shem MiShmuel* writes:

מה שיעק"א ביקש לגלות להם את הקץ, בודאי הפירוש שיזדרזו לעשות מעש"ט המביאים את הגאולה כאמרם ז"ל זכו אחישנה, דאת הקץ בעתו מה תועלת להם בהוודעם?

That which Yaakov Avinu wished to reveal to them (his sons) the end [of time], certainly the explanation is that it was so they would be zealous in doing good deeds that bring the redemption. For Chazal say: "If they are worthy, 'I will hurry it.'" Whereas regarding the end that comes in its fixed time, what would they gain by finding out about it?

אדרבה דבאשר הוא לאורך ימים רבים כמו שאנו רואין שעדיין לא בא, יש מקום לחשוש על רפיון ידים וחשש יאוש ר"ל, ויותר טובה ההעלמה שכל דור ודור יצפה לישועה בימיו:

---

31   *Yeshayahu* 60:22

32   *Sanhedrin* 98a

On the contrary, since it is many days away, as we see that it has not yet come, there would be a concern about weakening their spirits and causing them to despair. It would be better for it to be hidden, so that every generation would hope for salvation in their days.

אלא ודאי שבא לגלות את הקץ של אחישנה, ובזה אין שייך הודעה, כי בכל יום ויום
זמנו אם בקולו תשמעו, אלא הודעת המעשים המביאים את הגאולה:

Rather, [Yaakov Avinu] surely wished to reveal to them the end of "I will hurry it." However, this is not something that one can be informed of. For every single day is its time. It will be "today—if you will obey His voice."[33] Rather, Yaakov wished to inform them of the deeds that bring the redemption.

וא"כ למה נקרא זה מסתורין של מלך כאילו הדבר צריך להיות בסוד? ולמה? ועוד כי
מעש"ט המביאים את הגאולה הם בודאי מצוותי' של תורה וקירוב ודביקות לשמים,
והרי הכתוב מכריז ואומר לכל העולם (ישעי' מ"ה) פנו אלי והושעו כל אפסי ארץ:

But if this is the case, why is it called the mysteries of the King, as if the matter must be kept secret? What is the reason for this? Furthermore, the good deeds that bring the redemption are surely the mitzvos of the Torah and being close to Hashem and cleaving to Him. And Scripture declares to the whole world, saying: "Turn to Me and be saved, all the ends of the earth!"[34]

This matter is surely perplexing, as the *Shem Mishmuel* stated so eloquently. If Yaakov wished to reveal the secret of the fixed time, it would be counterproductive to do so. If he wished to reveal the time of "I will hurry it," there is no "time" to tell of because it can be any day. If he wished to reveal to them the deeds that hasten the Final Redemption, what is the secret? Just obey Hashem and keep His mitzvos!

The *Shem MiShmuel* offers a certain answer in the name of the Kotzker Rebbe. Nevertheless, this dilemma requires further thought. *Tzarich iyun.*

---

33 *Tehillim* 95:7, see *Sanhedrin* 98a

34 *Yeshayahu* 45:22

3 Adding a Wrinkle to the Original Plans

וַיְהִי אַחֲרֵי הַדְּבָרִים הָאֵלֶּה וַיֹּאמֶר לְיוֹסֵף הִנֵּה אָבִיךָ חֹלֶה וכו'.

"And it was after these matters that he said to Yosef, 'Behold, your father is ill...'" (Bereishis 48:1)

In our *Parsha* we find Yosef being told that his father Yaakov is ill. This announcement is introduced by the word *hinei*, "behold," which indicates surprise. Indeed, this announcement was unusually surprising, as *Yaakov Avinu* was the first person to fall sick before he died, as is explained in *Chazal* (See *Bava Metzia* 87a; *Pirkei D'Rabbi Eliezer*, ch. 51).[35]

Before *Avraham Avinu's* time, people did not look elderly no matter how old they were. Father and son would appear to be the same age. Thus, Avraham prayed that the appearance of old age should come into existence. Yaakov later prayed that people should become ill before they die. Why did *Avraham Avinu* want the elderly to look aged? So people would give proper respect to them. Why did *Yaakov Avinu* want them to fall ill? So a person could be forewarned of his impending demise and properly instruct his children of his desires.

To take this literally would mean that no one ever showed signs of age or had an illness before death. This would require us to believe that the entire nature of the world changed suddenly in one moment. This presents numerous questions. First of all, we find no mention in *Chazal* of the impact this had on the inhabitants of the world. When other cataclysmic events took place, for instance, when the sun stopped, we find Midrashim replete with stories of the impressions this made on people. But here, nothing.

---

35 עד אברהם לא היה זקנה, מאן דהוה בעי למשתעי בהדי אברהם משתעי בהדי יצחק, בהדי יצחק משתעי בהדי אברהם. אתא
אברהם, בעא רחמי והוה זקנה, שנאמר (בראשית כד) ואברהם זקן בא בימים. עד יעקב לא הוה חולשא, אתא יעקב בעא רחמי
והוה חולשא, שנאמר ויאמר ליוסף הנה אביך חלה: (בבא מציעא פ"ז ע"א)

Second of all, we find the following in Rashi:

שהיה למך סומא ותובל קין מושכו: (רש"י בראשית ד':כ"ג)

For Lemech was blind and his son Tuval Kayin would lead him. (Rashi, Bereishis 4:23)

Obviously, Lemech was infirm.

We also find the following in Rashi:

ולמה הִקְדים הכתוב מיתתו של תרח ליציאתו של אברם, שלא יהא הדבר מפרסם לכל, ויאמרו לא קים אברם את כבוד אביו שהניחו זקן והלך, לפיכך קראו הכתוב מת: (שם י"א:ל"ב)

And why did Scripture place the death of Terach before the exit of Avram [from Charan]? So that the matter would not be publicized to all, since people would say: "Avram did not fulfill the honor of his father. For he left him elderly and went on his own way." Therefore, Scripture called him (Terach) dead. (ibid., 11:32)

Obviously, Terach was visibly old.

Furthermore, if there was no visible aging process until Avraham, why was it so miraculous that Sarah had a child at ninety?

Thus it is difficult to say that old age and illness did not exist at all. Rather, I would humbly propose that it was a phenomenon that did not normally affect the tzaddikim.

Moshe Rabbeinu said at the end of his life:

לא אוכל עוד לצאת ולבוא: (דברים ל"א:ב')

I can no longer go out and come in. (Devarim 31:2)

Rashi explains what *Moshe Rabbeinu* meant by this:

יכול שתשש כחו, תלמוד לומר לא כהתה עינו ולא נס לחה (להלן לד:ז), אלא מהו "לא אוכל", איני רשאי: (רש"י שם)

Perhaps his strength became weakened? Therefore, the Torah says, His eye did not dim and his freshness did not depart (Devarim 34:7). Rather, what is the meaning of "I can no longer?" I no longer have permission. (Rashi, ibid.)

Although Moshe was as strong at one hundred and twenty as he was at forty, he did not have permission from Hashem to continue on. The verse cited by Rashi clearly states that his strength had not waned even on the day of his death.

We find that the bodies of the tzaddikim do not deteriorate after death, and certainly their bodies should not deteriorate whatsoever while they are alive. The Gemara tells us (*Shabbos* 152b) that the bodies of the tzaddikim will turn to dust only a moment before *techiyas HaMeisim*. (See also *Rashbam, Bava Basra* 58a, s.v. *Bishnei akeivav*.)

Thus, we must realize that human bodies deteriorate only because a person deserves to have some sort of punishment; he needs to undergo a *kapparah*. We could explain it as follows: Hashem is patient and forgiving when people are young. He gives youngsters plenty of time to do *teshuvah*. However, as time begins to catch up with them, so, too, the *aveiros* of a lifetime begin to catch up with them. Thus, people undergo some sort of a deterioration as they grow older. The deterioration of a person's body while he is alive is a *kapparah*, just as is the deterioration of the body after he passes away. Nonetheless, great tzaddikim should not need to go through such an experience.

According to this approach, it appears that until *Avraham Avinu* prayed for the change, people in general did look old but tzaddikim did not. There was no reason for their bodies to deteriorate to the extent that they would begin to show their age. *Avraham Avinu* therefore prayed that there should be some sort of a change in the character of humanity—even that of a tzaddik— so that there would necessarily be a sign of old age. However, this was not a *kapparah*, nor a punishment. It is the same idea with *Yaakov Avinu*. There was no drastic change in the natural order when *Yaakov Avinu* prayed for illness to come because most people would fall sick anyway. Rather, *Yaakov Avinu* prayed that even tzaddikim who are not deserving of punishment or in need of such a *kapparah* would begin to feel some sort of a waning of their strength. Thus, they would be aware of their impending death and would be able to set their house in order. This was for a blessing, not for a curse or *kapparah*.

Even after these changes took place, there were still exceptions to the rule in certain cases (such as with *Moshe Rabbeinu*), but our goal in this section is not to explain the exceptions, but rather the rule. Thus, after *Yaakov Avinu* came along, falling ill in old age no longer implied that the person was experiencing punishment. Rather, the weakness of old age became a positive phenomenon.

Now we can understand more fully the significance of what the Torah writes: *"**Behold**, your father is ill."* The word *hinei,* "behold," means not just something surprising but also joyous, as Rashi says clearly on *Bamidbar* 18:8. Indeed, the illness came as a blessing.

4   True Chesed

חסד שעושין עם המתים הוא חסד של אמת, שאינו מצפה לתשלום גמול:

(רש"י בראשית מ"ז:כ"ט)

What is true *chesed*? Let us consider the following statement of Rashi on our *Parsha:*

Chesed that one does for the deceased is true chesed. For one does not look forward to compensation. (Rashi, Bereishis 47:29)

Simply speaking, a dead person cannot return the favor. Ostensibly, Rashi is telling us that true *chesed* is when there is no compensation. What does Rashi mean by this? It is obvious that the *chesed* of burying someone—in this case, Yosef burying Yaakov — does not mean doing it without any expectation whatsoever of compensation for one's deed. There are a number of reasons why Rashi cannot mean this.

First of all, anyone who does a mitzvah, even if he does it *lishmah,* knows that Hashem gives *s'char* for mitzvos. The person does not do the mitzvah in order to receive the *s'char,* but he surely expects it to come. After all, reward for mitzvos is a basic principle of faith. The *chesed* of helping the deceased is not something that one expects to be returned. Yet, it seems no different than any other act of *chesed* that is done *lishmah.* In what way is burying the deceased a truer *chesed* than any other?

Furthermore, anyone who is aware of the reality of the *olam haneshamos* knows that it is possible for the *neshamah* of the deceased to plead on his behalf in Heaven. In this way, there is a potential of great compensation — it is a service that no money can buy!

In addition, it is quite evident as the story of our *Parsha* unfolds that there is significant compensation involved, and in this world. When Yaakov requests from Yosef to care for his burial after his demise, he promises Yosef:

וַאֲנִי נָתַתִּי לְךָ שְׁכֶם אַחַד עַל־אַחֶיךָ: (בראשית מ"ח:כ"ב)

And as for me, I have given you Shechem, one [portion] more than your brothers. (Bereishis 48:22)

Rashi (ad loc.) states that the city of Shechem was given to Yosef as a burial plot in return for troubling himself to take care of Yaakov's burial. So why is Yosef's act of burying Yaakov the Torah's ultimate example of true *chesed*?

If we take another look at the Rashi we quoted at the beginning of this section, we will see that Rashi never said that a true *chesed* is one that has no compensation. Rather, Rashi is stressing that the person who does the *chesed* does not *look forward* to the compensation.

This is because the appropriate compensation for caring for those who passed away is to be cared about after one passes away oneself. As such, it is not the type of compensation that people are looking forward to experiencing in the near future. Rashi's definition of true *chesed* is quite clear: It is *chesed* for which one does not desire nor wish to anticipate quick compensation.

5 Paternal Request

וַיִּקְרְבוּ יְמֵי יִשְׂרָאֵל לָמוּת וַיִּקְרָא לִבְנוֹ לְיוֹסֵף וכו'.

And the days of Yisrael drew near to die, and he called for his son, for Yosef... (Bereishis 47:29)

It is noteworthy that when Yaakov calls for Yosef, the verse emphasizes that he calls for *his son* Yosef. We know why Yaakov called for Yosef and not any of his other sons. As Rashi explains (ad loc.), Yaakov had a difficult request to make—he wanted to be buried in *Eretz Yisrael*. So he called for someone who had the authority and the ability to get the job done. However, this does not explain why the verse emphasizes Yosef as his son.

It is both perplexing and amazing that even though Yaakov is making his last request to his close and loyal son, a loyalty extending back over the past seventeen years and even further back to their life together in Beer Sheva, he still is asking for it as a kindness, a favor.

‫...ועשית עמדי חסד ואמת אל נא תקברני במצרים: (שם)‬

...And you will do for me a true kindness: do not bury me in Egypt. (ibid.)

Yaakov does not give Yosef orders. He does not say to him, "This is what I want you to do, and I fully expect that you will take care of it." Rather, he says, "...*If, please, I have found favor in your eyes...*" (ibid.). This is amazing. Yaakov is surely aware that Yosef will do anything he asks him to, but still he says it in an imploring type of way.

What is even more remarkable is that, at this point, Yaakov does not choose to explain why he buried Rachel, Yosef's mother, by the wayside near *Bais Lechem* instead of bringing her into the city for a more respectable burial. He awaits a later opportunity for this. Here, he comes not in the way of a father to a son, but in the way of a total stranger asking for a simple favor: "...*If, please, I have found favor in your eyes...,*" then do me this one *chesed* and bury me in *Eretz Yisrael*.

This issue requires further thought. *Tzarich iyun.*

6 Spiritual DNA

אֶפְרַיִם וּמְנַשֶּׁה כִּרְאוּבֵן וְשִׁמְעוֹן יִהְיוּ לִי:

Efraim and Menashe, like Reuven and Shimon will they be for me. (Bereishis 48:5)

Each of Yaakov's children was special in his own way, but only Yosef merited becoming two *shevatim*, two individual tribes. He was not the firstborn, yet, in this way, he received the double portion. There surely are many complex reasons for the special blessing that was bestowed upon him. Among them we may assume is that Yosef was deserving of becoming two *shevatim* due to a special quality that he alone possessed, not shared by any of his brothers and sisters.

Yosef lived in Egypt and still developed into a towering tzaddik. Only he is known as "the tzaddik." We do not speak of Reuven "the tzaddik" or Yehudah "the tzaddik" or even Levi "the tzaddik" — only *Yosef HaTzaddik.* The other brothers developed while they were with their father Yaakov in *Eretz Yisrael,* in a holy place. Yosef, however, demonstrated that even in the *galus,* when one is surrounded by the most morally corrupt of societies and is experiencing difficulties and the most terrible persecutions and difficulties — and no one can say he has greater *nisyonos* than those of Yosef — a Jew can come out looking as he should. Even as a slave incarcerated in prison, a Jew can retain his *kedushah* and remain a tzaddik like Yosef.

Even in times of dizzying prosperity, when Jews are on top of the world and are powerful and rich, they can still retain their *kedushah* to the utmost degree and remain tzaddikim like Yosef. This is a quality of *gevurah,* of overpowering spiritual strength, that worked itself into the "spiritual DNA" of Yosef's soul and, ultimately, into that of the Jewish people as a whole.

However, why can't the other brothers argue that Yosef's spiritual success was merely a matter of circumstance? Yosef happened to be in Egypt and that is why he turned out as he did. If any of the others had been in Egypt, who says the same thing would not have happened with them? Why is it only Yosef who receives the blessing of two *shevatim,* as if he is inherently more deserving?

The answer is that the other brothers would not have achieved the same status, even given the same opportunity. They would not have prevailed against the *nisyonos* of Egypt like Yosef did. How do we know this?

A person is not allowed to put himself into danger, physically or spiritually. Hashem gives a person only the *nisyonos* he can overcome. As people say, everyone has his own *"pekel,"* his "own baggage," to carry. Yosef was sent to Egypt not because of his own decision. It was not an adversity of his own making; he was sold into slavery against his will, as an act of G-d. This is the experience that the *Ribono Shel Olam* had in store specifically for him.

Let us imagine that one of the other brothers would have chosen voluntarily to take a trip down to Egypt and live there. What would have happened? Undoubtedly, he would have been completely swallowed up. He would have ended up a total loss, spiritually speaking. Why? Because this was not his challenge. This was not the *nisayon* that Hashem had in store for him. Therefore, he would not have had the *siyata dishmaya* needed to survive in Egypt as a Jew.

A person survives the *nisyonos* and faces the life challenges that Hashem puts him into, but the hardships that he chooses for himself do not bear any guarantee of success. A person can never know if he has what it takes to overcome self-created challenges. On the other hand, Heaven-sent challenges emanate from a source that ensures a person's ability to overcome them. The ability to succeed in the most challenging circumstances and situations comes from the fact that Hashem would not put a person in a place where he will have to fail.

Therefore, Yosef's greatness was not because he just so happened to have succeeded in a place where everyone else would have succeeded as well. Of course, Yosef's successful passage of his *nisyonos* was a matter of his *bechirah.* He didn't "have to" succeed; rather he made a free choice to. However, we cannot deny that Yosef inherently contained the ability for that success. That blessed spiritual strength of Yosef was what he transmitted to his children Efraim and Menashe.

That is why it was necessary to have two of the *shevatim* come from Yosef. It was not Yosef's reward for what he had accomplished. Instead, it was a natural outcome of what Yosef inherently was.

Explanations

וַאֲנִי בְּבֹאִי מִפַּדָּן מֵתָה עָלַי רָחֵל בְּאֶרֶץ כְּנַעַן בַּדֶּרֶךְ וכו'.

And I, when I came from Padan, Rachel died upon me in the land of Canaan, on the way... (Bereishis 48:7)

It is commonly explained, based in Rashi (loc cit.), that the reason that *Yaakov Avinu* brought up the sensitive subject of Rachel's burial at this specific occasion is because he was now requesting of Yosef to go through the great difficulty of burying him in *Me'aras HaMachpelah*. Thus, Yaakov needed to explain to Yosef why he did not accord Yosef's mother a proper burial. Why, in fact, did Yaakov not bring her to *Me'aras HaMachpelah*?

However, if this is really the reason why Yaakov had to bring up the subject now, then this entire incident seems not to be located in the right place in the Torah because it was in the earlier part of our *Parsha* that Yaakov actually asked Yosef to bury him in *Eretz Yisrael*. When that entire story happened, absolutely no explanation was asked for or given. Yet, now, suddenly, at this point in time, Yaakov digresses and explains why he buried Rachel in Bais Lechem. This all seems misplaced.

After Yaakov requested burial in *Eretz Yisrael*, it is written:

ויהי אחרי הדברים האלה ויאמר ליוסף הנה אביך חלה: (בראשית מ"ח:א')

And it was after these matters that it was said to Yosef: "Behold, your father is sick." (Bereishis 48:1)

We do not know when the earlier incident took place, but it clearly was not at the same time. Only now, in this second incident when Yaakov is already sick, does he digress and explain why he buried Rachel in Bais Lechem. This calls for an explanation.

An answer to this enigma is indicated by the order of how the events actually occurred. Yaakov recounts to Yosef events that took place back in *Parshas Vayishlach*.

וַיֹּאמֶר יַעֲקֹב אֶל־יוֹסֵף קֵל שַׁקַּי נִרְאָה־אֵלַי בְּלוּז בְּאֶרֶץ כְּנַעַן וְכוּ'. וַיֹּאמֶר אֵלַי הִנְנִי מַפְרְךָ וְהִרְבִּיתִךָ וּנְתַתִּיךָ לִקְהַל עַמִּים וְכוּ': (שם:מ"ג-ד')

And Yaakov said to Yosef, "Kel Shakkai appeared to me in Luz, in the land of Canaan... and He said to Me: 'Behold, I will make you to a congregation of nations...'" (ibid., vv. 3–4)

As Rashi explains (ibid.), Yaakov was promised that he would have "a congregation of nations," i.e., at least two more children who would become heads of tribes. Yet, these children were not born to Yaakov subsequent to this Divine promise. Thus, Yaakov explains that he is bestowing this gift upon Yosef — by making his two children into heads of tribes, as if they were Yaakov's own children. This is how Efraim and Menashe became tribes in their own right, just like Reuven and Shimon, and this is what Hashem meant when He promised Yaakov "a congregation of nations."

It was immediately following this Divine promise that Rachel died. Therefore, it makes perfect sense that at this juncture, Yaakov now recounts the events connected with Rachel's death and burial. Since this is their proper place, chronologically speaking, this seems the most appropriate point for Yaakov to bring up Rachel's burial. It would seem that this is the reason why Yaakov chose this moment to explain to Yosef the fateful decisions of that time.

8   Kivras Eretz

...מֵתָה עָלַי רָחֵל בְּאֶרֶץ כְּנַעַן בַּדֶּרֶךְ בְּעוֹד כִּבְרַת אֶרֶץ לָבֹא אֶפְרָתָה וכו'.

...Rachel died upon me in the land of Canaan on the road, while there was still kivras eretz to come to Efras... (ibid.)

The burial of *Rachel Imeinu* in the place known today as Kever Rachel, located in Bais Lechem just south of Jerusalem, seems shrouded in mystery. In the above verse, the phrase *kivras eretz* was left in the original Hebrew because of the wide range of possibilities regarding what it could mean. In *Parshas Vayishlach* (35:16), we find Rashi offering various possible explanations of this phrase, attempting to explain where — or why — Rachel was buried where she was buried.

Kivras eretz could mean: 1) a long way, or 2) the land was light and airy due to the time of year, and thus was easily travelable, or 3) a certain measurement of land, i.e., a *parsah* (equal to 4 *mil* or 8,000 *ammos*) or more.

Rashi comments that the second possibility, which is based on a Midrash, is not the *peshat*. Thus, he rejects it in favor of the third.

Now we come to our *Parsha*. Here, Rashi again attempts to define *kivras eretz,* and although he still maintains that it is a measurement of land, he, unhesitatingly, brings the Midrash without commenting that it is not the *peshat*. Here, Rashi does not see any contradiction between the definition he gives for *kivras eretz* and what the Midrash says. Rather, he feels that they are complementing one another. How can Rashi now adopt the same explanation he summarily rejected in *Parshas Vayishlach*?

Amazingly enough, Rashi here in our *Parsha* offers as his first explanation one that he did not offer at all in *Parshas Vayishlach*. He says in the name of Rabbi Moshe HaDarshan that *kivras eretz* is a measurement identical to that of the *techum Shabbos*, i.e., 2,000 *ammos*.

How do we resolve all of these difficulties?

The answer is that it all depends on the purpose of the phrase *kivras eretz* in the story. In *Vayishlach* it was simply telling us that when Yaakov was coming to Bais Lechem, it was still *kivras eretz* to come to Efras. This had nothing really to do with the death of Rachel, which was mentioned only later. Accordingly, Rashi understood that it was not so important for the Torah to tell us exactly how far Yaakov was traveling. Similarly, knowing the time of the year was not so important. These factors had no direct bearing on what preceded, how Yaakov traveled from Bais El to Bais Lechem, or on what followed, that Rachel had a hard labor. For this reason, Rashi understands the Torah was merely informing us that Yaakov traveled a certain distance, like a *parsah* or more.

Here in *Parshas Vayechi,* as Yaakov is repeating this whole story to Yosef, he is recounting to Yosef, specifically, the story of his mother's death.

ואני בבאי מפדן מתה עלי רחל בארץ כנען בדרך בעוד כברת־ארץ לבא אפרתה
ואקברה שם בדרך אפרת הוא בית לחם: (בראשית מ"ח:ז')

And I, when I came from Padan, Rachel died upon me in the land of Canaan, on the way, while there was still kivras eretz to come to Efras. And I buried her there, in the way of Efras which is Bais Lechem. (Bereishis 48:7)

In this instance, Yaakov was speaking about what occurred after Rachel had already died and was emphasizing where she died and was buried. Here, the key point was not where Yaakov was coming from or where he was going, but rather what happened with Rachel in the end. In telling Yosef this information, he says that she was buried *"while there was still kivras eretz to come to Efras."*

What is Yaakov trying to tell Yosef with this particular detail? It seems to be an unnecessary piece of information. What does it add to the point of *"and I buried her there?"*

Rashi gives us two explanations. The first is that *kivras eretz* is the distance of Rachel's burial place from the town of Bais Lechem, telling us that it was outside of the *techum Shabbos*. This detail has great significance. As some of the Commentators explain, if Rachel would have died within the *techum Shabbos*, it would have been necessary to take her to the town. Normally, a deceased person, having the status of *mais mitzva*, acquires the place where he or she passed away, and must be buried there. However, if the death took place within the *techum Shabbos* of a town, even in such a case there is an obligation to take the deceased into the town itself to be buried there.[36] Accordingly, Yaakov was explaining to Yosef why his mother was not brought into the city for a more respectable place of *kevurah*: She passed away outside of the *techum*.

The second reason Rashi gives is that the land was quite fit for traveling at that time of year and Rachel was not buried outside of town, by the wayside, due to the unfortunate circumstance of impassable road conditions. Rather, Yaakov is saying to Yosef that he buried her there *al pi hadibbur*, because Hashem wanted her buried there for reasons known to Him. In other words, it was not dependent on Yaakov's decision at all.

That is why in our *Parsha*, the explanation of the Midrash (light and airy) fits well with the *peshat*, whereas the very same explanation does not fit at all in *Parshas Vayishlach*.

9 Parallel Lives

וַיִּשְׁלַח יִשְׂרָאֵל אֶת יְמִינוֹ וַיָּשֶׁת עַל רֹאשׁ אֶפְרַיִם... שִׂכֵּל אֶת יָדָיו כִּי מְנַשֶּׁה
הַבְּכוֹר:

And Yisrael reached out his right hand and placed it on the head of Efraim... he maneuvered his hands, for Menashe was the firstborn. (Bereishis 48:14)

Yaakov switched his hands for the *brachah* of Efraim and Menashe. As the verse emphasizes, Efraim would now precede Menashe.

Throughout the episode, Yosef expresses concern over the relative

---

36   עיין ירושלמי נזיר פ"ז ה"א ועיין תורה שלמה בראשית פרק מ"ח אות נ"ג בהערות

positioning of Efraim and Menashe, and even worries that his father has made an error. Yosef's attitude is perplexing, considering the fact that the precedent had already been set.

ועתה שני בניך הנולדים לך בארץ מצרים עד באי אליך מצרימה לי הם אפרים ומנשה כראובן ושמעון יהיו לי: (שם:ה')

And now, your two sons who were born to you in the land of Egypt, before my coming to you to Egypt, shall be mine. Efraim and Menashe—like Reuven and Shimon shall they be to me. (ibid., v. 5)

Thus, we see that on Yosef's earlier visit to his father, Efraim was already mentioned before Menashe and placed in front of him regarding the inheritance of *Eretz Yisrael,* which was not a small matter. At that point, there is no concern, no question, no emphasis, not by the Torah nor by Yosef. It just passes by as if without notice. Why did Yosef accept it the first time and protest it only the second time?

The answer is that when Yaakov promised that Efraim and Menashe would be "like Reuven and Shimon," the emphasis was not on the relative order of Efraim and Menashe. Rather, the emphasis was on Efraim and Menashe becoming *shevatim* in their own right, and furthermore, that they are compared to Reuven and Shimon. Yaakov was expressing a parallel: Efraim would be like Reuven, and Menashe, like Shimon. Thus, the order in which they were mentioned was dependent on the order of Reuven and Shimon alone.

We find this parallel in many different ways, and it expresses itself historically.

Reuven — the *bechor* who was born with the greatest potential, the innate ability to be king and kohen — let his potential slip away and lost what was naturally his. We find a parallel with Efraim. From him came Yerovam ben Nevat, the first king over the Ten Tribes. Yerovam ben Nevat had enormous potential when he ascended the throne of the Northern Kingdom, later known as Samaria. He was promised that he would be second only to *Dovid HaMelech.* Yet, he forfeited his spiritual kingship, and instead is listed amongst those kings who lost their share in the World to Come (See *Sanhedrin* 90a).

Yerovam ben Nevat will be remembered for all eternity as a sinner who led the people astray. He set up the idolatrous calves in Samaria and prevented the Jews he ruled over from going up to Jerusalem for the *shalosh regalim*. Momentous potential gone sour!

Menashe had descendants who paralleled those of Shimon. As we will discuss later, Shimon was the ancestor of Zimri ben Salu. Zimri is identified by *Chazal* (ibid., 82b) as being the same person as Shaul ben HaKena'anis (*Bereishis* 46:10) and Shlumiel ben Tzurishaddai, head of *shevet Shimon* (*Bamidbar* 1:6).

Zimri inherited Shimon's propensity for *kana'us*, a trait usually translated as "zealousness." *Kana'us* means taking the law into your own hands. Seeing something that you know to be wrong, in a situation where the law allows, and selflessly do battle for what you know, beyond a shadow of doubt, is right. You act in a supra-legal fashion. Shimon did just this when he saved his sister Dinah from Shechem.

Zimri believed he was doing the same when he saw the members of his *shevet* threatened with execution. Moshe had instructed that all those involved in the sin of *ba'al pe'or* and the Midianite women be put to death. Although Zimri was extremely old at that point and had no desires for procreation, he took Kozbi bas Tzur the Midianite princess because he chose to stand up and take the law into his own hands. He attempted to stop Moshe from executing his brethren in the fashion described at the end of *Parshas Balak* (*Bamidbar* 25:1–9).

We know Zimri's advanced age from the fact that, as we mentioned earlier, he was actually Shaul ben HaKena'anis of a much earlier generation. This individual was the son of Dinah and Shechem, and was born before Yaakov went down to Egypt. Thus, Zimri must have been at least 210 + 40 = 250 years old. As the Gemara explains (*Sanhedrin* 82b), and his entire intent in taking Kozbi bas Tzur was to save his tribe from execution, who had come to him pleading for help.

However, this *kana'us* was totally and completely misplaced. It led to disaster, both for himself and for his *shevet* at that time, and perhaps for all time.

(Paradoxically, the *kana'us* of Pinchas of the tribe of Levi, which was a *kana'us* for a proper cause, became the key to Levi's greatness. This is explained in the *Yalkut Shimoni* that I will cite in a later section. This, too, was taking the law into his own hands, but for the sake of the *Ribono Shel Olam*.)

So we see that Shimon's descendant expressed misplaced *kana'us*, and this is paralleled by Menashe's descendant. We are referring to King Yehu ben

Yehoshafat ben Nimshi, who was granted the monarchy over Samaria by the Prophet Elisha himself (*Melachim* II, 9:1–6). This merit came to Yehu because he stood up against the evil Achav and Izevel, and fulfilled Hashem's will to wipe them and their descendants out completely (*Melachim* II, 10:11).

What gave Yehu the right to execute the entire family of Achav without a ruling from the Sanhedrin, without a decision of a *Bais Din*? It was an act of *kana'us*, taking the law into his own hands. However, here it was lacking a significant condition of proper *kana'us*: Namely, you yourself have to be free of the evil you are eradicating in others. You have to be pure, and your intention has to be pure. If Yehu was going to obliterate the House of Achav for their involvement of idolatry, he had to be free of that sin himself, and, unfortunately, he was not. In fact, he never cleansed his kingdom of the idolatrous calves remaining from Yerovam ben Nevat (*Melachim* II, 10:31). Since he was not completely free of the sin himself because he allowed the *avodah zarah* of Yerovam ben Nevat to remain, his act of *kana'us* made him liable for his own ultimate destruction and the loss of his kingship. (See Hoshea 1:4, Rashi, ad loc.)

We can see a clear parallel between Efraim and Reuven, and Menashe and Shimon. This is why the order in which *Yaakov Avinu* put Efraim and Menashe was not problematic the first time. Yaakov Avinu had an order of Reuven and Shimon — and that was a correct order. He was saying that Efraim was like Reuven, and Menashe is like Shimon. There was no question about the order. Later, when Yaakov spoke to Efraim and Menashe independently and still placed Efraim before Menashe, he was showing Efraim's greatness over Menashe. Thus, Yosef protested at that point.

10 Looking Out for Number One

Interestingly enough, this episode of Efraim superseding Menashe highlights an intriguing phenomenon in *Sefer Bereishis*. What we would predict as the normal development of children is totally non-existent here. Let us consider the following:

In a normal population, the firstborns of any given family have greater chances of demonstrable success in life. This is borne out by testing. It is for good reason: The firstborn spends the initial months or years of his or her life as the exclusive emphasis and focus of his or her parents. They throw all of their efforts into that child. If the child has average or above average capabilities, he will have experienced tremendous amounts of learning opportunities from both father and mother. Usually, whatever dreams and hopes the parents might have for their children are thrown upon their firstborn. Psychological studies have proven this to be true.

K. Lorenz, advice editor for at CareerBuilder.com, writes the following: In his book *The Pecking Order: Which Siblings Succeed and Why*,[37] Dalton Conley demonstrates that 75% of the income inequality between individuals in the United States occurs between siblings in the same families. Research shows that firstborns (as well as only children) lead the pack in terms of educational attainment, occupational prestige, income and net worth. On the other hand, middle children in large families tend to manage the worst. "A child's position in the family impacts his personality, his behavior, his learning and ultimately his earning power," states Michael Grose, author of *Why First-Borns Rule the World and Last-Borns Want to Change It*.[38] "Most people have an intuitive knowledge that birth order somehow has an impact on development, but they underestimate how far-reaching and just how significant that impact really is."

So say the researchers in the field. Yet, if we take a look at the events in *Sefer Bereishis*, we immediately see right away that this expectation does not pan out.

Let's cite a few examples: Adam had three sons — Kayin, Hevel and Sheis. The successful son was Sheis. Noach had three sons — Shem, Cham and Yefes. Although Shem is mentioned first, Yefes was actually the oldest, while Cham was the youngest and Shem was the middle child. However, Shem was the ancestor of *K'lal Yisrael* and the preeminent son.

Terach had three sons — the oldest being Haran, the second, Avraham, and the third, Nachor. The success of the middle child in this family speaks for

---

37   *Pantheon; 1ST edition (March 2, 2004)*

38   *Random House Australia (February 6, 2003)*

itself. Avraham had two children — the older Yishmael, and the younger Yitz-chok. Who was preeminent and who was ejected? Yitzchok had two children — Eisav and Yaakov. Who took the birthright? Yaakov had twelve children — the oldest being Reuven. Reuven lost all of his advantages: The kingship went to Yehudah, the *kehunah* went to Levi and the rights of the firstborn went to Yosef.

Levi had three sons — Gershon, Kehas and Merari. The preeminent son was Kehas. Yehudah had Er, Onan, Sheilah, Peretz and Zerach. Peretz was the preeminent son. Yosef had two sons — Menashe and Efraim. As we know, Efraim was placed before Menashe.

Throughout *Sefer Bereishis*, we see that the firstborn, even if he was male—which in ancient times surely bestowed very significant advantages—fell far short of expectations. The shortfall is in fact extreme, as borne out by the above examples. What statistics say should be the predominant majority turns out not even to be a minority: It is a zero!

This is true even as we move into *Sefer Shemos*, where we find that Amram had three children — Miriam, Aharon and Moshe. As great as they all were, we know that Moshe was the preeminent child. There was only one firstborn up to this point, who actually fulfilled our expectations of the position. Kehas had four sons — Amram, Yitzhar, Chevron and Uziel. Amram was the oldest of the four and the primary child.

What can we learn from this resounding failure of statistics? That when it comes to spiritual achievement, there are no built-in advantages or disadvantages. Each person's efforts will decide what he or she will attain. There is complete free choice, and the only rule is *lefum tza'ara agra*, "The reward is according to the effort" (*Avos* 5:23). Every individual can reach the apex of spiritual achievement, based on his or her own efforts. The facts prove it.

11 The Council of Infamy

בְּסֹדָם אַל תָּבֹא נַפְשִׁי וכו'.

In their council, may my soul not enter... (Bereishis 49:6)

Yaakov Avinu was particular not to be connected with the "council" of Shimon. Rashi (ad loc.) explains that Yaakov wished to disassociate himself from the affront that Zimri made to *Moshe Rabbeinu*. Zimri was one of the leaders of the *shevet* of Shimon and he challenged Moshe over the issue of the Midianite women, as recorded at the end of *Parshas Balak*. Yaakov did not want his name mentioned there. His request was granted, and in that Torah passage, Zimri's lineage is delineated only back to Shimon, stopping one generation before Yaakov.

What is surprising is that Rashi emphasizes Zimri's initial challenge of Moshe[39] and does not mention the more heinous sin that Zimri went on to do — taking Kozbi bas Tzur, an act that brought about a plague causing the death of twenty-four thousand Jews from *shevet Shimon.*

In truth, Rashi is explaining a verse that says, *"In their **council**, may my soul not enter."* Accordingly, Rashi speaks of the planning that preceded the actual sin, in other words, the "council." Thus, we learn that even for this relatively minor infraction, *Yaakov Avinu* was opposed to the Torah mentioning his name.

This would all make perfect sense if not for the fact that Zimri's initial confrontation with *Moshe Rabbeinu* does not appear expressly in any of the Torah's verses. How, then, would the name of Yaakov ever be attached to this event, which is mentioned only in the Midrash?

Let us take a deeper look at the sin of Zimri. It would seem that Rashi's

---

39 בסדם אל תבא נפשי. זה מעשה זמרי, כשנתקבצו שבטו של שמעון להביא את המדינית לפני משה,ואמרו לו, זו אסורה או מותרת, אם תאמר אסורה, בת יתרו מי התירה לך (סנהדרין פ"ב ע"א), אל יזכר שמי בדבר, וכו': (רש"י בראשית מ"ט:ו')

point is not just that *Yaakov Avinu* did not wish his name attached to an act of wickedness. There were, unfortunately, many wicked people in the history of *K'lal Yisrael*, yet, Yaakov restricted his concern to two specific episodes: that of Zimri and of Korach. What is unique about these episodes?

In these two episodes, the Torah itself was used to perpetuate the lie. Both Zimri and Korach posed a "halachic" question and then mocked the answer. Yaakov represented the Torah of truth: *Titen emes leyaakov* (*Michah* 7:20). Thus, *Yaakov Avinu* could not bear that his name be associated with an attempt to distort the halacha. Any falsification of Torah was the most profound contradiction to his very being.

12 Shouldering the Burden

וַיַּרְא מְנֻחָה כִּי טוֹב וְאֶת הָאָרֶץ כִּי נָעֵמָה וַיֵּט שִׁכְמוֹ לִסְבֹּל וכו'.

He saw rest that it was good, and the land that it was pleasant, and he bent his shoulder to bear... (Bereishis 49:15)

I t was said about Yissachar, *"he bent his shoulder."* The words are not too hard and the meaning seems clear enough. Yet, Rashi (ad loc.) compares this expression to Scriptural expressions in which the heavens are "bent," or people "bend" their ears. Why the need for all this amplification?[40]

Rashi's point is that *"he bent his shoulder"* is not to be taken literally. It is a figurative expression just as "bending" the heavens does not mean that Hashem actually bent the heavens. If someone thinks that He did, then "bending" one's ears to hear proves that the expression is only figurative.

It comes out that Yissachar bends and lowers his shoulders in order to take upon himself the spiritual load of fulfilling the will of Hashem.

---

40   ויט שכמו. השפיל שכמו, כמו "ויט שמים" (שמואל ב' כב:י), "הטו אזנכם" (תהלים עח:א). (רש"י שם)

13 Independent Fathers

בִּרְכֹת אָבִיךָ גָּבְרוּ עַל בִּרְכֹת הוֹרַי וכו'.

The blessings of your father were greater than the blessings of those who conceived me... (Bereishis 49:26)

~~~~~~

Rashi here says that ברכת הורי means the blessings of "those who conceived me." Yaakov is saying to his sons that the *brachos* given to him by Hashem were greater than those He gave to those who conceived him, Avraham and Yitzchok. (Rashi, loc cit.) While this is one way of looking at the word הורי, it is possible that it also derives from the word הוראה — those who taught me.

How did Rashi know that הורי comes from הריון, "conception," and not from הוראה, "to lead and instruct one on a path?"

The answer is to be found in the definition of the term *"Avos."* Once we understand why the *Avos* are *Avos,* we will understand Rashi's comment as well. Avraham, Yitzchok and Yaakov have the unique status they do because each one independently found his path. Each one of the *Avos* stood alone and created his own universe, independent of his ancestors.

Let us start with *Avraham Avinu,* the pillar of *chesed.* It is quite clear that he did not receive *chinuch* in how to serve Hashem from his father *Terach,* but we might think that Yitzchok and Yaakov were made and molded by their righteous fathers, that they were extensions of their fathers. The truth is otherwise. That is not what an *Av* is. An *Av* is a spiritual entity that is independent. As the name indicates, an *Av* is a primary source. It is the wellspring from which all else originates. When we refer to *arba avos nezikin*[41] or *avos melachos*[42] or *avos hatumah,*[43] we are speaking of concepts that stand on their own and are

---

41 *Bava Kamma 2a*

42 *Shabbos 73a*

43 *Kaylim 1:1*

self-defining. Likewise with Yitzchok and Yaakov, they stood as *Avos* on their own.

That being the case, although in other contexts we could understand the word הורי in the sense of הוראה, when it comes to the *Avos* we cannot. In the context of our *pasuk* where *Yaakov Avinu* speaks of himself, Avraham and Yitzchok, it cannot have that meaning. Thus, Rashi explains that הורי has the sense of הריון, "conception." Yaakov's parents indeed conceived him, but they did not instruct him on his way as an *Av*. Yaakov's way was unique to him. In spite of how much Torah and *yiras shamayim* Yaakov imbibed from Avraham and Yitzchok, his path in the service of Hashem was his own doing.

---

14   Maternal Honor

שָׁמָּה קָבְרוּ אֶת אַבְרָהָם וְאֵת שָׂרָה אִשְׁתּוֹ שָׁמָּה קָבְרוּ אֶת יִצְחָק וְאֵת רִבְקָה
אִשְׁתּוֹ וְשָׁמָּה קָבַרְתִּי אֶת לֵאָה:

There they buried Avraham and Sarah his wife. There they buried Yitzchok and Rivkah his wife. And there I buried Leah.
(*Bereishis 49:31*)

I n our verse, Yaakov tells Yosef about who is buried in *Me'aras HaMach-pelah*. The verse obviously does not reflect the exact order of the burials, as we know that Avraham buried Sarah. Nonetheless, Avraham was buried there and arranged the future burials. The order of the verse is easy enough to understand—the generations are listed chronologically, with the man before the wife.

However, the end of the verse has a perplexing switch to it. Yaakov says *"I buried Leah,"* whereas before he did not say *"We buried Yitzchok."* This is problematic because Yaakov participated in Yitzchok's burial just as he participated in Leah's. The Ramban on our verse notes this incongruity and explains that if Yaakov would have said *"We"* regarding Yitzchok, he would be bringing Eisav into the picture, which he did not wish to do at this point.

Yet, this answer is difficult. Yaakov could have easily left Eisav out of the picture by saying "*I buried Yitzchok.*" This would still be correct; Yaakov indeed participated actively in the burial. Why does he not say it this way? Besides, doesn't saying "*they buried Yitzchok and Rivkah his wife*" also include Eisav?

The Ramban offers a second reason: If the verse would say "*We,*" an extra phrase would then have to be added for the burial of Rivkah, since Yaakov did not participate in her burial. For this reason, Yaakov skipped mentioning his participation in the burial of Yitzchok so he would not have to speak at length. So explains the Ramban.

Another answer emerges from what we explained in *Parshas Vayishlach* in the section titled "*Rivka Cries for her Children.*" If Yaakov would mention that he participated personally in Yitzchok's burial, he would draw attention to the fact that Rivkah was buried without any proper attendance at all. This would cause a lack of *kavod* for his mother, who died like a *mes mitzvah* with no one to take care of her funeral except for the local *b'nei Cheis*, the local Hittites. So in order to protect the *kavod* of Rivkah, the verse just says, "*There they buried Yitzchok and Rivkah his wife.*"

15 What is a Blessing for One...

When it was said about Yosef (*Bereishis* 37:33) that he was *tarof toraf,* "torn apart" by a wild animal, this was considered to be something negative. Yet, the same expression is used as a blessing for Yehudah and Binyamin. About Yehudah it is said:

מטרף בני עלית: (בראשית מ"ט:ט')

From the prey (teref), my son, you elevated yourself. (ibid., 49:9)

About Binyamin is said:

בנימין זאב יטרף: (שם:כ"ז)

Binyamin is a wolf who tears. (ibid., v. 27)

On the latter verse, Rashi explains that it is referring to the victorious battles of King Shaul, who came from the tribe of Binyamin.

In fact, when Yosef seemed to have been torn, it was actually the initiation of the entire process that brought *K'lal Yisrael* to Egypt and out, a process essential to the creation of the Jewish people. Thus, also Yosef's "tearing" was a blessing in disguise. It likewise took a prominent place in the development of the tribes who come from Rachel, Yosef and Binyamin, and affected the institution of kingship in the Jewish people as a whole, as Shaul of Binyamin was the first king of Israel. While Yehudah represents the kingship of the House of Dovid, the *teref* of Binyamin represents the kingship of Shaul.

In closing, it is worth mentioning that the term *teref* also brings to mind the olive leaf that the dove brought to Noach in the *Teivah*:

והנה עלה־זית טרף בפיה וכו'. (בראשית ח:י"א)

טרף. חטף (רש"י שם)

And behold, an olive leaf that was plucked (taraf) was in its mouth. (ibid., 8:11, Rashi, loc. cit.)

The true significance of *teref* requires further thought. *Tzarich iyun.*

16   Least Likely to Succeed?

Three personalities stand out as most responsible for having sold Yosef to Egypt. After perusing the whole story, we would have expected that those most responsible for this grievous sin would be the ones least likely to succeed in any sort of future endeavor in *K'lal Yisrael*. Who are the three? Shimon, Levi and Yehudah.

Although we have mentioned many times that it was the Divine plan that Yosef should go down to Egypt, we cannot escape the fact that his brothers sinned by selling him there. The proof is that they did *vidui* and *teshuvah* for their deed, and were embarrassed by it. They said, *"Indeed, we are guilty..."* (*Bereishis* 42:21).

Among the four older brothers, only Reuven actually tried to save Yosef. The Torah clearly says that Shimon and Levi initiated the entire process. When it says, *"And a man said to his brother... go and we will kill him"* (Bereishis 37:19–20), this refers to Shimon and Levi, as Rashi tells us (ibid., 49:5). Shimon and Levi would have actually killed Yosef if they would have been able to carry out their plans undeterred.

How do we know that Yehudah was also implicated in the crime? Because his prestige among the brothers subsequently fell, as it is written, *"And Yehudah went down from his brothers"* (ibid., 38:1). As Rashi (ad loc.) tells us, they all blamed Yehudah for the sale that took place since he failed to speak up and stop it.

Yet, when we finally get to the end of *Sefer Bereishis,* in our *Parsha,* we see quite clearly that Levi and Yehudah, at least, are far from being at the bottom of the bunch. They take the key leadership roles of kingship and priesthood.

Let us not think that *shevet Levi* somehow pulled themselves out of the hole many generations later in the days of *Moshe Rabbeinu,* when they acted in a laudatory fashion by staying loyal to Hashem and desisting from the worship of the *Egel HaZahav.* No, they did not redeem their ancestor at that point and suddenly shoot into an unexpected position of prominence. Rather, Levi already had a position of prominence in Egypt. Amram was the leader of *K'lal Yisrael* in Egypt. *Shevet Levi* was not subject to slave labor in Egypt. They were free men and the educators and leaders of *K'lal Yisrael* in Egypt.

It goes even further back. Before his death, Yaakov clearly delineated where each *shevet* would be positioned in carrying his casket to *Eretz Yisrael* for kevurah. Levi was not included in the group of carriers; he was set apart from the others due to his elevated status. As Rashi explains (*Bamidbar* 1:49), Levi was the exclusive legion of the King, even then.

How are we to understand Levi's continuous prominence despite his leading role in the fateful sin of selling Yosef to Egypt?

The answer lies in the power of *teshuvah.* This tremendous power that a human being possesses is capable of taking him from the lowest depths to the highest heights. This is clearly reflected by the story of Yehudah.

Yehudah finds himself in the position of *"And Yehudah went down from his brothers,"* as we explained above. Yehudah did not fulfill the role that was appropriate to him, he did not act properly regarding Yosef and he lost his leadership position entirely. Nevertheless, what goes down does not have to stay down. There are certain defining events that take place in an individual's life. Hashem gives a person certain challenges. They are not properly called *nisyonos,* but rather circumstances that constitute a special opportunity. Whether the person passes or fails them can sometimes mold that person's very essence. Even if he fails at a certain point, he might be given a new opportunity later on by which he can redeem himself from the lowered position that was his own making.

This power of self-redemption, given by Hashem to *K'lal Yisrael,* is expressed quite poignantly in Yehudah and Levi. Through considering the downs and ups of their lives, we come to realize the potential censure and condemnation that awaits a person who gives up hope of a second chance and complete renewal.

The cataclysmic event in the life of Yehudah was *"And Yehudah approached him"* (ibid., 44:18). Here, Yehudah faced Yosef once again, but this time to beg to save Binyamin. By standing up to the challenge that this situation presented, he went from the failure of *"And Yehudah (va'yered) went down from his brothers"* to the success of *"And Yehudah (va'yigash) approached him."* In this second situation, Yehudah induced Yosef to reveal his identity to his brothers and thus bring the great saga to its glorious ending. Due to this success, we find *Yaakov Avinu* saying to Yehudah:

מטרף בני עלית: (בראשית מ"ט:ט')

From the prey, my son, you elevated yourself. (ibid., 49:9)

As Rashi explains on this verse, Yehudah elevated himself from the depths of having preyed upon Yosef to the heights of success expressed in the continuation of this verse, prophesizing the victorious tranquility of the days of King Shlomo (descendant of Yehudah):

כרע רבץ כאריה וכלביא מי יקימנו: (שם)

He crouches; he lies down like a lion. And like a young lion, who can rouse him? (ibid.)

The same is also true of Levi. He was able to reconstruct himself from the depths of:

שמעון ולוי אחים כלי חמס מכרתיהם: (שם:ה')

Shimon and Levi are brothers; their weaponry is a stolen craft.
(ibid., v. 5)

As Rashi explains on this verse, Shimon and Levi had adopted the way of the sword, which rightly belongs to Eisav. Now, Levi is no longer like Eisav. Instead, amazingly enough, he becomes the paradigm of *"the voice is the voice of Yaakov"* (ibid., 27:22). For Levi is described as:

כי שפתי כהן ישמרו דעת ותורה יבקשו מפיהו כי מלאך ה'־צבקות הוא: (מלאכי ב':ז')

For the lips of the kohen shall guard knowledge, and they will seek Torah from his mouth. For he is an angel of Hashem of Hosts. (Malachi 2:7)

Levi is elevated to become the representative of *K'lal Yisrael* through *shevet Levi* serving in the Temple on their behalf. He is further elevated to become the representative of Hashem through the service of the Kohanim. That is what Levi was able to transform himself into. (See additional comments on this topic in *Parshas Vayeishev, Musings on the Brothers.*)

Subsequently, I discovered the following Midrash contrasting Shimon with Levi along these lines:

וללוי אמר למה נאמר, לפי ששמעון ולוי שתו בכוס אחד וכו'. משל לשנים שלוו מן המלך אחד פרע למלך ואחד לא די שלא פרע אלא חזר ולוה:

And about Levi, he (Moshe) said: 'Your Urim and Your Tumim" belong to Your pious one..."' (Devarim 33:8). Shimon and Levi drank from one cup (i.e., they performed the same act)... This may be compared to two people who borrowed from the king. One paid the king back. And the other, not only did he not pay back but he borrowed again.

כך שמעון ולוי שניהם לוו בשכם וכו'. לוי פרע מה שלוה במדבר שנאמר ויעמד משה בשער המחנה ויאמר מי לה'. וחזר והלוה את המקום בשטים שנאמר פינחס בן אלעזר בן אהרן הכהן:

Similarly, Shimon and Levi both borrowed in Shechem [when they sinned by slaughtering the people of the city].... Levi paid back in the Midbar what he borrowed. For it is written [that the Levites were faithful to Moshe and refrained from the sin of the Egel HaZahav]: "And Moshe stood in the gate of the camp, and said, 'Whoever is for Hashem—to me!' And all the Levites gathered to him." (Shemos 32:26). Then he went and "lent" to Hashem, in Shittim. For it is written [regarding the zealousness of Pinchas of the tribe of Levi]: "Pinchas the son of Elazar the son of Aharon haKohen turned aside My wrath..." (Bamidbar 25:11)

שמעון לא דיו שלא פרע אלא חזר ולוה שנאמר ושם איש ישראל המוכה: (ילקוט שמעוני

דברים ל"ג:תתקנ"ח)

Not only did Shimon not pay back, but he went and borrowed again, as it is written [regarding the above incident]: "And the name of the Israelite man who was struck, who was struck with the Midianite woman: Zimri son of Salu, leader of a father's house of the Shimonites." (ibid., v. 14) (Yalkut Shimoni, Devarim 33:958)

This leaves us with the question of Shimon: Why did he not rise to the challenge as Yehudah and Levi did? I have always been bothered by Rashi's comment at the end of *Parshas Vezos HaBrachah* on the fact that Moshe never expressly blessed Shimon. Moshe hinted a *brachah* to Shimon within the *brachah* of Yehudah. Similarly, Moshe scattered Shimon's portion in *Eretz Yisrael* among that of Yehudah. All of this was because of Shimon's sin with the Midianite women.

We see that Shimon receives his blessing in partnership with Yehudah. Similarly, in the beginning of *Sefer Shoftim* (1:3), we find a continued partnership that seems to actualize between Yehudah and Shimon. They are brothers and they work together. Yehudah calls Shimon to help him conquer *Eretz Yisrael* from the Canaanites, and Shimon joins him.

One would have thought from the partnership that developed in the beginning of *Sefer Shoftim* that the two brothers would be in concert for all time. Later on, throughout the entire first Temple era, we see that it is Yehudah and Binyamin, not Yehudah and Shimon, who continue on together, for the southern kingdom of Yehudah was actually composed of Yehudah and Binyamin, while the northern kingdom of Shomron was composed of the other ten *shevatim*. Yehudah's relationship with Binyamin appears to have developed from his standing up to protect Binyamin from being taken as a slave by Yosef who was posing as the wicked Egyptian viceroy, in the incident of *"And Yehudah approached him."* This relationship continues when Binyamin remains under the protection of Yehudah later on and does not leave to join the ten tribes in their secession. Even though Binyamin attempts to "usurp" the kingship from Yehudah during the reign of Shaul and Ish Boshes, nevertheless, Yehudah waits his turn until he becomes the king, and then safeguards Binyamin.

Where did Shimon disappear to? What happened to him? Throughout *Tanach*, there are very few references to *shevet Shimon*.[44]

Chazal say (*Megillah* 14b)[45] that in the days of King Yoshiyahu, the Prophet Yirmeyahu brought back the Ten Tribes who had been exiled by Sancheriv, and then there was a period when King Yoshiyahu ruled over all twelve *shevatim*. Consequently, the *Yovel* year was observed in that period, a mitzvah that requires all the people of Israel to be dwelling in their land.

It is clear that there were members of *shevet Shimon* among those who returned, and they continue to remain among *K'lal Yisrael*. So the question remains as to where, when and how, if at all, should we expect Shimon to regain his original, ancient prominence with his brothers?

This issue requires much further thought. *Tzarich iyun gadol.*

---

44 ומהם מן־בני שמעון הלכו להר שעיר אנשים חמש מאות ופלטיהו נעריה ורפיה ועזיאל בני ישעי בראשם: (דברי הימים א' ד':מ"ב)

ויקבץ את־כל־יהודה ובנימן והגרים עמהם מאפרים ומנשה ומשמעון כי־נפלו עליו מישראל לרב בראתם כי־ה' אלקיו עמו: (דברי הימים ב' ט"ו:ט)

45 ע"ע רש"י מלכים ב' כ"ב:י"ד, כ"ג:י"ט תוספות גיטין ל"ו ע"א בסוף ד"ה בזמן

אלה יעמדו על הברכה

אֵלֶּה יַעַמְדוּ עַל הַבְּרָכָה

לכבוד עקרת ביתנו

מרת רנה פיגא בת ר' חיים זאב
פרענקל

אֵלֶּה יַעַמְדוּ עַל הַבְּרָכָה

ברכתינו מעומקא דליבא
לכבוד הני נדיבי לב

יחיאל מיכל שלום וברינדל הינדא
פרענקל

יה"ר שיראו רוב נחת מכל
צאצאיהם שליט"א

אֵלֶּה יַעַמְדוּ עַל הַבְּרָכָה

לזכרון בהיכל ה'

לעילוי נשמות

ר' אברהם ראובן ב"ר דוד יהודה ז"ל

מרת חיה פייגא בת ר' יחיאל מיכל הלוי ע"ה

פרענקל

ר' אברהם חיים יהודה ב"ר מאיר הכהן ז"ל

מרת זיסא בתיה בת ר' ישראל משה ע"ה

תנצב"ה

אֵלֶּה יַעַמְדוּ עַל הַבְּרָכָה

ברכתינו מעומקא דליבא

Mrs. Sarah Lieberman

מרת שרה ליברמאן שתחי׳

אֵלֶּה יַעַמְדוּ עַל הַבְּרָכָה

לזכרון בהיכל ה׳

לעילוי נשמות

שמואל בן חיים ליברמאן ז״ל

משה דוד בן בנימין קאמינר ז״ל

אלה יעמדו על הברכה

לזכרון בהיכל ה'

לעילוי נשמות

משה יעקב בן יצחק מאיר הי"ד
פיגא טובא בת יחיאל אשר ע"ה
אסתר בת יחיאל אשר הי"ד
מרדכי בן משה יעקב הי"ד
יחיאל אשר בן משה יעקב הי"ד

רחל בת משה יעקב הי"ד
חיים בן אליעזר הי"ד
פיגא בת חיים הי"ד
פעשא בת חיים הי"ד

ברכה בת משה יעקב הי"ד
פיגא בת שמואל הי"ד

חיה זיסל בת משה יעקב הי"ד
גיטל בת משה יעקב הי"ד
באמשטיין-ראזענבלום

תנצב"ה

אֵלֶּה יַעַמְדוּ עַל הַבְּרָכָה

לזכרון בהיכל ה'

לעילוי נשמות

שמואל בן יוסף הי"ד
רֶנָה בת מרדכי הי"ד

חיים דוד בן שמואל ז"ל
שמעון בן שמואל הי"ד

בלימה בת מרדכי ובעלה חיים
בתם סאבינא ובנם שמואל סאנשיין הי"ד

משה נתן בן מרדכי ראזין הי"ד
חיים אשר בן מרדכי ראזין הי"ד
וישניצקי-ליכטנשטיין

תנצב"ה

אלה יעמדו על הברכה

הכרת הטוב

Dr. Stanley & Charnie Waintraub
שמואל אליהו בן יצחק אלעזר הלוי
טשארנא הינדא שינדל בת הרב שניאור יחזקאל
ומשפחתם

Drs. Fred & Betty Sugarman
אפרים בן נחום
ברכה זיסל בת ר' חיים זאב
ומשפחתם

Rabbi Benzion & Rochel Chait
הרב בן ציון משה בן הרב יוחנן
רחל גיטל בת ר' חיים זאב
ומשפחתם